ENGLISH BLUE AND WHITE PORCELAIN OF THE EIGHTEENTH CENTURY

The Faber Monographs on Pottery and Porcelain
Lately edited by W. B. HONEY and ARTHUR LANE

★

WORCESTER PORCELAIN *by* Franklin A. Barrett
NINETEENTH-CENTURY ENGLISH POTTERY AND PORCELAIN
by Geoffrey Bemrose
ANCIENT AMERICAN POTTERY *by* G. H. S. Bushnell *and* Adrian Digby
ROMAN POTTERY *by* R. J. Charleston
ENGLISH PORCELAIN OF THE EIGHTEENTH CENTURY *by* J. L. Dixon
ENGLISH DELFTWARE *by* F. H. Garner
ORIENTAL BLUE-AND-WHITE *by* Sir Harry Garner
CHINESE CELADON WARES *by* G. St. G. M. Gompertz
KOREAN CELADON AND OTHER WARES OF THE KORYO PERIOD
by G. St. G. M. Gompertz
COREAN POTTERY *by* W. B. Honey
FRENCH PORCELAIN OF THE EIGHTEENTH CENTURY *by* W. B. Honey
GERMAN PORCELAIN *by* W. B. Honey
WEDGWOOD WARE *by* W. B. Honey
LATER CHINESE PORCELAIN *by* Soame Jenyns
MING POTTERY AND PORCELAIN *by* Soame Jenyns
ENGLISH PORCELAIN FIGURES OF THE EIGHTEENTH CENTURY
by Arthur Lane
FRENCH FAÏENCE *by* Arthur Lane
GREEK POTTERY *by* Arthur Lane
EARLY ISLAMIC POTTERY *by* Arthur Lane
LATER ISLAMIC POTTERY *by* Arthur Lane
ITALIAN PORCELAIN *by* Arthur Lane
MEDIEVAL ENGLISH POTTERY *by* Bernard Rackham
EARLY STAFFORDSHIRE POTTERY *by* Bernard Rackham
ITALIAN MAIOLICA *by* Bernard Rackham
ARTIST POTTERS IN ENGLAND *by* Muriel Rose
ENGLISH CREAM-COLOURED EARTHENWARE *by* Donald Towner
ENGLISH BLUE AND WHITE PORCELAIN OF THE EIGHTEENTH CENTURY
by Bernard Watney
LONGTON HALL PORCELAIN *by* Bernard Watney

★

Other titles in preparation
SCANDINAVIAN FAÏENCE *by* R. J. Charleston
JAPANESE PORCELAIN *by* Soame Jenyns
JAPANESE POTTERY *by* Soame Jenyns
DELFT AND OTHER DUTCH PAINTED WARES *by* Oliver Van Oss

A. *Coffee pot, scratch 'R' mark, Bow, about 1750, ht.* $7\frac{7}{10}$ *in.*
Victoria and Albert Museum.
(See pages 20 and 23)

ENGLISH BLUE AND WHITE PORCELAIN OF THE EIGHTEENTH CENTURY

by

BERNARD WATNEY

FABER AND FABER

24 Russell Square

London

First published in mcmlxiii
by Faber and Faber Limited
24 Russell Square London W.C.1
Printed in Great Britain by
R. MacLehose and Company Limited
The University Press Glasgow

To
A. J. B. K.

CONTENTS

ix

ILLUSTRATIONS

ILLUSTRATIONS

ACKNOWLEDGEMENTS

I am fortunate in having as friends many of the outstanding collectors and connoisseurs of Blue and White, and offer this work hoping that they will feel that their instruction has not been wasted. I would like to mention particularly Aubrey Toppin, Norroy and Ulster King of Arms, and Dr. John Ainslie, who together know more about Bow than any other persons since the factory was in existence. On an equal plane are A. J. B. Kiddell and the late D. M. Hunting, who have placed on record their unrivalled understanding of Lowestoft. I am indebted to the staff of the many museums named in the plate captions, especially the excellent team in the Ceramic Department of the Victoria and Albert Museum, led by the late Arthur Lane, the distinguished editor of this series of monographs. Thanks are due to all those who have set aside pieces of particular interest for me to study, especially to Alan Green who also gave useful advice on the Derby chapter. Finally must be recorded my gratitude to Miss V. M. Hamblin, who typed the manuscript, and to David Bland of Faber and Faber for his wise counsel and great patience.

INTRODUCTION

English blue and white china, with few exceptions, was made for daily use. Being easier and cheaper to produce than coloured wares it was often the first marketable product of the early factories. When large-scale production became possible it had to compete not only with English salt glaze and delft, and later with cream and pearl ware, but also with a constant influx of blue and white 'East India' or Chinese export porcelain. Indeed, the original impetus came from the East where blue and white china had already been made and respected for more than four centuries.

There was secrecy and mystery surrounding the manufacture of porcelain, and the magical transformation of clay by fire into transparent porcelain inspired a widespread search for the necessary raw materials. In England attempts to imitate Chinese wares resulted at first in a complete failure to make hard paste, and instead three main kinds of soft-paste porcelain were invented. The fine translucency of Chinese porcelain and the luminosity of the cobalt blue were qualities that the English potters sought to emulate. It followed naturally that they should also attempt to copy the Chinese shapes and decorations for their own wares. In fact the influence of Chinese porcelain on the early development of English blue and white was far greater than that of any of the older-established European factories.

When Europeans first became widely acquainted with Chinese porcelain during the seventeenth century, as a result of the importing activities of the Dutch East India Company, it was the blue and white that predominated and set a fashion for imitative blue and white at Delft and other European potteries from about 1650 to 1700. For the Chinese themselves, blue and white was the 'classic' form of porcelain decoration until the beginning of the eighteenth century; the painting done in it was better than that done in enamels. However, from about 1683 onwards (when the Imperial kilns in China were re-organized) the Chinese improved the quality of their overglaze enamel-painted wares, and first the *famille verte* and its sub-varieties, and then, the *famille rose* gradually ousted blue and white from its pre-eminent position. Partly under Chinese influence polychrome decoration came back into fashion in Europe from about 1720, both on faïence and

1

delft ware, and on Meissen porcelain.[1] Thus, by the mid-eighteenth century, when the English porcelain factories were founded, enamel painting was more highly regarded than blue and white, both in Europe and China. Nevertheless, for a variety of reasons, England became and remained a stronghold of blue and white production. Its popularity may have partly stemmed from the growing English habit of drinking tea. By a happy coincidence the majority of English soft-paste wares looked well when decorated in underglaze blue and with a few exceptions were robust enough to stand up to daily use. Certainly blue and white was a good selling line, no doubt helping to finance the more costly and ambitious schemes for polychrome wares and also, in many cases, for figures.

The two leading English factories for the production of a satisfactory and durable porcelain were at Bow and Worcester. Bow made the important discovery that by using ox-bone ash a tough-textured, opalescent paste could be produced. Worcester took over and developed the secret formula of the Lund's Bristol factory using soapstone from the Lizard peninsula to make a steatitic paste of fine translucency with a widely famed ability to withstand boiling water. However, owing to a failure to fire dinner plates satisfactorily on a commercial scale, even at Worcester, most factories were forced to concentrate on tea wares and sauce boats, leaving Bow and to some extent Caughley alone with any success in that field.

The glassy pastes which were used at Chelsea, Longton Hall and Derby were generally too frail to withstand constant wear. The Chelsea factory wisely made less blue and white[2] (1) than any of the other English factories; while the Longton Hall concern failed in attempting a large-scale manufacture of it. At Derby blue and white was not produced until comparatively late, about 1756; there were frequent unsuccessful attempts to find a satisfactory glassy paste and the production consisted mainly of sauce boats and ornamental wares.

William Cookworthy's discovery of Cornish kaolin and china stone in about 1748 resulted in the production of hard-paste blue and white

[1] In spite of frequent early attempts, relatively little blue and white had been made at Meissen owing to their difficulty in getting a good blue colour.

[2] Three examples are shown here, but very few other patterns could have been produced. It is interesting to note that in spite of the great rarity of Chelsea blue and white, a waster of a tea bowl of the pattern illustrated, Plate 1B, was discovered on the factory site. This being an outstanding example of the observation that on eighteenth-century porcelain factory sites decorated wasters are nearly always blue and white, as the enamelled wares suffered far less kiln wastage due to the comparatively low temperatures of the enamel firing.

(1) *Plates* 1A, B, C,

INTRODUCTION

at Plymouth (1768–70), later to a lesser extent at Bristol (1770–81) and finally with the turn of the century at New Hall. At Plymouth it was found difficult to control the colour of the underglaze blue owing to the high firing temperature; furthermore kiln wastage, judging from the final products, was probably enormous. The best effects were obtained when designs were painted in fine lines and the decoration reduced to a minimum. The Bristol factory attempted unsuccessfully to cut down costs by the use of underglaze transfer prints. New Hall continued the use of transfers in an unpleasant smudgy dark blue, though occasionally attractive results were achieved. The colour tended to run in the glaze requiring the embellishment of gilding.

The finest English blue and white, partly by accident and partly by design, was no mere lifeless copy of the Chinese as the smooth lead glaze on soft paste gave to the cobalt a rich luminosity. The comparatively low temperatures required for firing soft paste enabled a good blue colour to be obtained with reasonable ease. Chinese designs were assimilated, and imbued with a sense of the rococo. Chinese porcelain prototypes were copied for tea ware and vases that could be thrown or turned, but contemporary English silver vessels provided easily available models from which sauce boats, cream jugs and tureens could be moulded. The resulting porcelain wares were decorated with Chinese fishing scenes, pagodas and peonies, and sometimes finished with complicated diaper borders. Such was the exuberance of this new vision that the scroll-work and moulding of the silver shapes were often disregarded and painted over with fanciful oriental designs.

Each factory developed its own mannerisms in potting and decoration, sometimes absorbing the local traditions through employment of skilled earthenware potters. However, the differentiation into factory groups by a study of these peculiarities is complicated by the fact that there was a large amount of inter-factory copying; although it is occasionally difficult, or even impossible, to tell whether the factories copied each other or used the same original Chinese or silver prototypes. Where factories copied each other, the influences of Bow, Lund's Bristol and Worcester predominated, even to some extent affecting the shapes and decoration of the Longton Hall and Derby glassy-paste wares, and the hard-paste wares of Plymouth and Bristol. Those factories using a body containing bone ash did not necessarily follow Bow as regards potting and painting their wares, nor did those factories making a soapstone body always show soft-paste Bristol or Worcester characteristics. At Liverpool, for example, the stylistic influences of Bow, Lund's Bristol and Worcester seem to have been adopted almost irrespective of the type of paste used by the

B

different factories. Lowestoft, a factory which stemmed directly from Bow as regards its type of paste, showed remarkably little influence of its mother factory in other respects. Instead, it developed its own naïve chinoiserie, painted in a cobalt which was often the colour of schoolboy's ink. Moreover, Lowestoft was one of the few factories to decorate its porcelain with local English scenes. Caughley, often a rather dull shadow of Worcester, at times deserving to be called fake Worcester, managed for a short while to launch out into making exceedingly clever replicas of Chantilly blue and white.

Each factory passed through phases of development with technical and stylistic changes. These often resulted in remarkable alterations in the appearance and physical properties of the glaze and body and even in the colour of the underglaze cobalt blue. It is extremely important to appreciate the extent of these possible variations when attempting to separate family groups. At Bow, for example, the early porcelain was quite glassy in appearance through being somewhat over-fired, but later the china body was under-fired and very opaque, almost resembling earthenware. At Worcester, on the other hand, the appearance of the porcelain body and glaze remained practically unchanged throughout the whole of the so-called Dr. Wall period, 1751–83. Some factories, such as Lund's Bristol, were soon able to produce fine, well potted wares, others like Longton Hall were at the start involved in a desperate struggle with an intractable paste in an attempt to improve their first primitive wares and make them salable.

It is frequently impossible to judge correctly the constituents of a given piece of porcelain without chemical analysis. Both a phosphatic and a steatitic paste may be highly translucent or very opaque and have a translucency varying from whitish green to dark green, cream or even brown. They can be physically quite hard or very soft. In particular it was found necessary to perform a number of qualitative, spectrographic analyses in order to discover the ingredients of the different porcelain bodies made by the Liverpool factories. However, scientific investigations by themselves can be misleading and should always be treated with caution when the subject is English eighteenth-century porcelain, the making of which depended so much upon trial and error.

It is still comparatively easy to form a collection of English blue and white porcelain. Nonetheless it remains a most difficult class of wares to study. The output of each factory should be seen in relation to its enamelled wares and even its figures. In this way factory mannerisms and characteristics are discovered and the appearances of different pastes and glazes are recognized. For instance, whether the china body is press-moulded, thrown and turned, or slip-cast. The appearance of a thick mass of soft-paste porcelain such as a large tiered Worcester shell centre-piece can deceive the inexperienced into thinking it to be hard paste. It is of prime importance to be able to distinguish hard paste from soft paste, no matter what the thickness of the potting. With experience it is possible to appreciate the different degrees of body hardness that are grouped together as soft paste. We also come to learn that, although to a lesser extent than in hard-paste wares, some soft-paste bodies fuse with their lead glazes at the paste-glaze interface, lead glazes do not always form a well demarcated layer of glass. The boundary between glaze and paste is generally least obvious in Chinese hard-paste porcelain where the unfired, but decorated, 'green' body was covered with glaze before firing. From its completely fused appearance some English hard-paste porcelain may also have had only a single firing.[1] The use of a file in differentiating hard paste from soft is to be strongly discouraged as being both disfiguring and unrewarding. It is far better and more certain in its results to train the senses to observe the differences by frequent handling of representative examples.

No amount of reading can replace constant first-hand experience. The written word cannot adequately convey what the trained senses discern, sometimes in a flash without the mind being fully conscious of all the criteria involved. Books cannot describe, for example, the special effects of reflected light on glazed surfaces in combination with the various tints of underglaze blue.

Begin collecting modestly with a few cups including a typical Chinese blue and white example. Learn all you can from broken pieces, observing the granular appearance of soft paste, somewhat like the broken end of a stick of Edinburgh rock, or the conchoidal shining appearance of a chipped piece of hard paste like the surface of a piece of brittle slab toffee that has been broken by a hammer. Do not specialize in one factory too early but try to develop a feeling for the types of ware each factory produced. Eventually learn to arrange each factory's products chronologically by reference to dated pieces, both polychrome and blue and white, in museums and private collections. A weekly visit to the sale rooms where it is possible to handle pieces and study them intelligently is more valuable than a whole library of books on ceramics. However, nothing can replace the knowledge gained by forming, cataloguing and living with a really representative collection.

[1] George Harrison, *Memoir of William Cookworthy*, 1854, Appendix V. Cookworthy declared, 'I know this can be done, for I have done it'.

1

COBALT

Cobalt is the essential colouring material in the manufacture of all blue and white china, not only for underglaze painting, but also for tinting bodies and glazes to imitate the appearance of imported Chinese wares as nearly as possible.[1] The method for obtaining a satisfactory blue pigment from cobalt to withstand the temperatures required for making glass and ceramics has been known for at least four thousand years.[2] Cobalt has in fact been found in blue glass excavated at Eridu near Ur which can be dated about two thousand B.C.[3] In early times Persia was the source of supply. The technique of using cobalt spread from the near East to Europe, for example it is found as a colouring agent in Byzantine mosaics, in Roman glass such as the Portland vase and in Celtic enamels. It was not, however, an easy pigment to use for obtaining precise patterns, and as early as the thirteenth century potters at Kashan in Persia had difficulty in controlling the fluxing properties of cobalt with glaze.[4] From the beginning of the fourteenth century Persian cobalt was exported to China for decorating porcelain, although subsequently a certain amount of native Chinese ore appears to have been used.[5] In the eighteenth century cobalt was exported from Europe to China in quantity.[6]

In Europe the subject of cobalt was a confused one owing to inaccurate nomenclature, lack of proper methods of assay and the mistaken belief that lapis lazuli and even artificial ultramarine could be readily used to decorate porcelain. The first accurate description of the

[1] The colour of Chinese porcelain was produced by iron impurities fired in a reducing atmosphere.

[2] Sir Harry Garner, 'The Use of Imported and Native Cobalt in Chinese Blue and White,' *Oriental Art*, 1956, vol. 2, no. 2, pp. 8–10.

[3] R. A. Mostyn, 'Spectographic Analysis of Eridu Blue Glass,' *Min. of Supply Chem. Inspectorate Technical paper*, 1956, no. 7.

[4] Arthur Lane, *Early Islamic Pottery*, London, 1947, p. 45.

[5] Sir Henry Garner, *op. cit.*, and *Oriental Blue and White*, London, 1954.

[6] Royal Soc. of Arts, A Register of the Premiums and Bounties given by the Society, 1778, p. 15; and Joseph Lygo's letters to William Duesbury, Derby Public Library, 1795, stating that it was then difficult to get smalts in the pure state as the East India Company was exporting them to China.

mining, preparation and use of cobalt in Europe was written in the seventeenth century and is to be found amongst Dr. Robert Hooke's papers.[1] It describes how cobalt ore was mined at Schneeberg in Saxony and zaffre prepared locally for export to Holland and other countries for decorating pottery. The Duke of Saxony forbade the export of natural cobalt to maintain a monopoly in the two manufactured products, zaffre and smalt.[2] The pigment, because of its intensity, needs a high degree of dilution and it was prepared by fritting calcined cobalt ore with sand to produce zaffre. Smalt was made by fusing zaffre with potassium carbonate to form a dark blue glass. The molten glass, made friable by pouring it into water, was then pulverized and finally levigated in water to be graded and sold according to particle size. The coarse variety, known as strewing smalt, had rough angular fragments up to a sixth of an inch in diameter;[3] it was used for the blue ground-work of the old-fashioned blue and gold sign boards. Smalt in a fine powdered form called powder blue was bought in considerable quantities for whitening linen.[4] Apparently both finely powdered zaffre and smalts were used in England for decorating porcelain in underglaze blue. According to Dossie zaffre was required for darker tints, it being fluxed with borax and a little calcined flint or Venetian glass to 'take off the soluble quality of the borax'.[5]

In the transactions of the Royal Society of Arts there is a record over a period of seven years giving the amount of smalt imported into England; this rose from 179,564 pounds weight in 1747 to 286,739 pounds weight in 1754. No zaffre or cobalt ore was imported during that time.[6] The Royal Society of Arts was anxious to discover a profitable supply of cobalt in England as Saxon smalt was a very expensive commodity and import dues were heavy. In 1754, the year of the inception of the Society, a premium of £30 was offered for the best sample of English cobalt.

As early as James the First's reign, 1603–25, a man named Abraham Baker had been granted a patent for the manufacture of smalt in England.[7] Then in 1744 some inferior smalt was produced

[1] Royal Society Classified M.S. Papers, vol. 20, no. 95. Wrongly catalogued by Sir Arthur Church as being by Martin Lister. Robert Hooke, 1635–1703, was an experimental philosopher and a friend of the potter John Dwight (Mavis Bimson, 'John Dwight', Trans. E.C.C., vol. 5, part 2, 1961, p. 99).

[2] Robert Hooke, loc. cit.

[3] 'Cobalt,' Enc. Brit., 9th ed., 1877.

[4] Parke's Chemical Catechisms, 2nd ed., 1807, p. 420.

[5] R. Dossie, Handmaid of the Arts, 1758, 1st ed., vol. I, p. 253 and vol. II, p. 359.

[6] Royal Soc. of Arts, Transactions by Dr. Templeman, 1754–8, M.S., vol. 2.

[7] Trans. E.C.C., vol. I, no. 4, p. 45.

from Cornish cobalt;[1] however, among three tons of this cobalt, four to five hundredweight was reported as being extremely good. The scientist and Fellow of the Royal Society, Emanuel Mendez da Costa, a Portugese Jew, visited Cornwall in 1749 and saw some cobalt ore in a mine at St. Columb, and a large quantity of good cobalt at the Trugoo mine near Truro. In 1755 Francis Beauchamp was awarded the premium of the Society of Arts for obtaining rich deposits of cobalt ore from Pengreep, another mine near Truro. His find was confirmed by the learned Dr. J. Albert Schloffer, F.R.S., of Amsterdam.[2] Considerable difficulty was experienced in the manufacture of zaffre and smalt from English cobalt ore due to lack of technical knowledge. The Saxon monopoly had resulted in cobalt being 'a mineral we have been little aquainted with'. Consequently, in 1755 the Royal Society of Arts offered a further premium of £30, this time for the manufacture of zaffre and smalt from native cobalt ore. Eventually in 1764 the versatile Nicholas Crisp, one of the founder members of the Society, was awarded a prize for making zaffre and smalt.[3]

William Cookworthy, who was trained as a chemist, appears to have had some interest in cobalt production.[4] He is said to have instructed Roger Kinnaston in the art of preparing zaffre and smalt. About 1772 Kinnaston set up a cobalt-smelting works at Cobridge. Early in the nineteenth century, about 1807, a rich vein of cobalt was discovered in a disused mine at Wheal Sparnon near Redruth.[5] Ore from this re-opened mine was refined at the British Cobalt Smelting Company at Hanley, and claimed to be superior in strength and genuine brilliancy to any yet imported from Saxony or Sweden. A certificate dated 4th April, 1817, from Josiah Wedgwood II testifies to the superiority of this blue pigment. The certificate was also signed by other Staffordshire potters, including George and Charles Mason and John Yates.[6] However, judging from the harsh indigo blue of a documentary Spode pottery plate in my own collection[7] the enthusiasm of the Staffordshire potters must have been based on other considerations than aesthetic ones. The reasonable conclusion is that during the

[1] Royal Soc. of Arts, *Transactions by Dr. Templeman*, 1754–8, M.S., vol. 2, p. 26.

[2] William Borlase, *The Natural History of Cornwall*, 1758, p. 131, and the *Gents. Mag.*, May 1755, p. 234, also p. 539.

[3] Royal Society of Arts, A Register of the Premiums and Bounties.

[4] Simeon Shaw, *History of the Staffordshire Potteries*, 1829, p. 211. Ll. Jewitt, *A Life of Josiah Wedgwood*, 1865, p. 232, states that Cookworthy was the first to succeed in this country in manufacturing cobalt blue direct from the ore.

[5] Royal Soc. of Arts, Letters D7/199 and D2/64–5.

[6] Royal Soc. of Arts, Letters D2/97–9.

[7] Inscribed 'This blue-ware is printed from the calx of British cobalt, produced from Wheal Sparnon mine in the county of Cornwall, Aug. 1816'.

eighteenth century at least, England was dependant on Saxony for the supply of good quality smalt.

Perhaps the most technically successful blue and white came from Worcester, and an eye witness in the early nineteenth century noted that their blue colour was 'burnt before it is glazed'.[1] Cyril Shingler[2] tells me that this is the present practice. 'It consists,' he says, 'of letting the applied decoration dry out then spraying over it just a whiff of glaze and firing it at 820° C, after which it is ready for glazing. The essential function of the hardening-on is to get rid of the oils which were the medium for the colour and which would affect the glaze if allowed to remain. By devoting a special type of kiln for this purpose and by applying a slight covering of glaze we ensure a dependable standard of quality, but the colour itself contains a proportion of glaze material which, fired at a rather higher temperature, as for instance, in the glost kiln, would serve to fix it to the biscuit and it seems more likely than not that in the early days the cooler parts of the glost kiln would have been used and no preliminary glazing applied.'

[1] 'Extracts from the Diary of Hon. Anne Rushout, daughter of the 1st Lord Northwick,' 21st September, 1802. *Apollo*, vol. LXIII, no. 375, May 1956, p. 163.
[2] Curator of the Worcester Royal Porcelain Company Works Museum.

2

BOW

Pointing away from London in a north-easterly direction, the Bow road crosses the river Lea at Bow bridge and then becomes Stratford High Street; as it does so the road leaves Middlesex and enters the county of Essex. In Middlesex before coming to the bridge the Bow road separates the parish of St. Mary Stratford le Bow on the north side from the parish of St. Leonard's, Bromley, on the south. After crossing the Lea the road, now Stratford High Street (formerly Queen Matilda's Causeway) runs through the parish of West Ham. Until the end of the last century a small row of wooden-fronted cottages known as China Row stood on the north side of Stratford High Street about 250 yards from Bow bridge. At the far end of China Row was an inn called New Canton.[1] These cottages were the small tenements mentioned in 1790 by Thomas Craft[2] in his description of the Bow china works where he had been employed as a painter. The site of the Bow china factory was adjacent to these buildings; it was there between 1921 and 1922 that Mr. Toppin found large quantities of factory wasters, including some of the earliest blue and white, moulds and kiln furniture,[3] and actual kiln foundations were discovered a few years later. There is no contemporary map marking the factory site; however the following evidence substantiates its whereabouts. Thomas Craft stated that in 1790 the factory had become a turpentine works. Marryat, in 1868, added the information that Mr. MacMurdo, the calico printer, had a chemical works there after the Bow factory closed down.[4] Contemporary directories and entries in Court books

[1] Mr. Toppin mentioned this in his unpublished paper on Bow read to the English Ceramic Circle in May 1959.

[2] In a note written on the lid of the box containing the Craft Bowl in the British Museum. See *Bow Exhibition Catalogue*, British Museum 1959, p. 43.

[3] Prior to this in 1867 (see *Art Journal*, 1869, or Ll. Jewitt, *The Ceramic Art of Great Britain*, London, 1878, vol. 1, pp. 203–6) large quantities of wasters, moulds and kiln furniture were discovered on the opposite side of Stratford High Street, a find considered to be of such importance that it was mentioned in Parliament by Mr. Charles Schreiber, M.P. See also A. J. Toppin, *Burlington Magazine*, vol. XL, 1922, p. 224. Some fragments from the 1867 excavations are now in the Victoria and Albert Museum.

[4] Joseph Marryat, *Pottery and Porcelain*, 3rd edition, London, 1868 p. 407.

discovered by Dr. Ainslie show that Edward L. MacMurdo owned turpentine works amongst a number of other industrial premises in Middlesex and Essex from 1790 well into the nineteenth century. Furthermore an indexed map of 1821 shows that the firm of MacMurdo and Company were then occupying the Bow factory site.[1]

The Bow factory was called New Canton. This name is inscribed on three blue and white ink pots, two dated 1750 and the third dated 1751. It was also used in the works accounts for biscuit ware in 1754,[2] and in an advertisement of 1756:[3] 'any person that has any stacks of oak top wood to dispose of may send their proposals to the china work at New Canton near Bow bridge, or the Bow china warehouse in Cornhill.'[4] Thomas Craft stated that 'the model of the building was taken from that of Canton in China' and that 300 persons were employed there.

The first Bow patent of 6th December, 1744, was limited by a previous act of Parliament to not more than five shareholders. It was granted to Edward Heylyn of the parish of Bow in the County of Middlesex, merchant, and Thomas Frye of the parish of West Ham in the County of Essex, painter. Edward Heylyn was born at West-minster in 1695 and died in the Isle of Man in 1765. He was the son of John Heylyn of Wrexham, a master of the Saddlers' Company, and his wife Susanna Sherman. He was admitted to the Freedom of the City of London as a saddler in October 1718. He had early connections as a merchant with Bristol possibly in partnership with an elder brother Henry, a copper merchant who became joint master of the Saddlers' Company with Frederick, Prince of Wales in 1737. Edward Heylyn was gazetted a bankrupt at Bristol with Robert Rogers in August 1737 and on a number of other occasions, for example in December 1757 when a proprietor of the Bow factory.

The other patentee, Thomas Frye (1710–62) came to England from Ireland about 1734. The eldest of his five children was baptized at St. Olave's, Old Jewry on 10th October, 1735.[5] Thomas Frye is likely to have met Edward Heylyn at the Saddlers' Company some years before they became proprietors of the Bow china factory. About the end of 1736 the Saddlers' Company had commissioned Frye to paint a very

[1] Hugh Tait, 'Some consequences of the Bow Porcelain Special Exhibition,' *Apollo*, April 1960, vol. LXXI, no. 422, p. 93.

[2] British Museum, Add. M.S.S. 45905.

[3] *General Evening Post*, 12th August, 1756, No. 3527. Discovered by G. Wills (*Apollo*, vol. LXIV, Sept. 1956, p. 87).

[4] 'Top wood' was still used at the Wattisfield pottery, Suffolk, to obtain a brisk heat for glazing pottery up till about fifty years ago.

[5] Thomas, later a china painter at Bow. Frye had two daughters, Sarah, born 26th Feb., 1736, and Mary, born 3rd May, 1743, who were also china painters at Bow.

large portrait of Frederick, Prince of Wales and he also painted a companion picture of Princess Augusta, the Prince's consort. Frye's portrait of the Prince was eventually presented to the Saddlers' Company on 25th July, 1741, by Thomas Sherman,[1] Edward Heylyn's uncle, who had been Master of the Saddlers on two occasions. Thomas Sherman was one of the witnesses to the specification of the first Bow patent.

The obituary notice of Thomas Frye in the *Gentleman's Magazine*[2] describes him as 'the inventor and first manufacturer of porcelain in England to bring which to perfection he spent 15 years amongst the furnaces till his constitution was near destroyed'. It is puzzling why this successful painter and mezzotint engraver became deeply involved in such a risky venture as the manufacture of porcelain. However, he may possibly have moved to West Ham to engrave original designs for calico printers[3] who had large and important factories there, the industry having been founded by William Sherwin, an engraver, in 1676. William Pether, whose name appears on the base of a Bow cream jug dated 1754 (1), was awarded a prize in 1756 by the Society of Arts for 'the most ingenious and best fancy designs composed of flowers, fruit, foliage and birds, proper for weavers, embroiderers or calico printers by boys under 17'. Later Pether and Frye entered into partnership as mezzotint engravers. A mezzotint of John Ellis,[4] Master of the Scriveners' Company and friend of Dr. Johnson, shows Ellis holding a parchment deed which reads 'Frye and Pether, 21st April, 1761, co-partnership'. The engraving is signed 'Thomas Frye Pinxit An:Dom : 1761 W. Pether Olim Discipulus Ejus Sculpsit 1781'.[5]

Another proprietor of the Bow factory in its early days was George Arnold.[6] Dr. Ainslie made the important discovery that George Arnold

---

[1] From the Minutes of the Saddlers' Company destroyed during the Second World War but copied by Mr. Toppin.

[2] Vol. XXXIV, 1764, p. 638.

[3] Robert Hancock is said to have engraved the first copper plate for printing on calico (A. Rendal Ballantyne, *Robert Hancock and his Works*, London, 1885, p. 46).

[4] Ellis was a witness to Thomas Frye's will and the executor of Mrs. Frye's will proved 21st June, 1774 (in Somerset House, P.C.C. 227 Bargrove). In his own will he left his portrait by the 'ingenious Mr. Frye' to the Scriveners' Company.

[5] In 1777 William Pether exhibited his self portrait at the Society of Artists signed with his name in reverse: Don Mailliw Rehtep.

[6] A wealthy Alderman and Master of the Haberdashers' Company who was reported as being 'one of the principal proprietors of the Porcelain Manufactory at Bow' in his obituary in the *London Daily Advertiser*, no. 98, Tuesday, 25th June, 1751, discovered by Alexander Lewis. Will proved 1st July, 1751 (in Somerset House, P.C.C. Busby 197).

(1) *Plate* 8A.

and Edward Heylyn acquired property in Bow, Middlesex in the latter part of 1744[1] and another property there in or before 1750.[2] It is possible that the early experiments of the Bow china concern were carried out at Bow in Middlesex between 1744 and 1749, before the permanent factory was built in Essex. This would seem to be confirmed by the earliest-known contemporary account of the china factory, in Samuel Richardson's 1748 edition of Defoe's *A Tour of Great Britain*. Here the factory is definitely described as being lately set up in the village of Bow before the traveller crosses Bow bridge into Essex. By that time the manufactory had 'already made large quantities of tea-cups, saucers, etc. . . . .'.[3]

The overseer's account books for the parish of West Ham[4] have entries from Lady Day 1749 to Lady Day 1750 in which the Bow factory is referred to as 'Alderman Arnold and Company'. However, from Lady Day 1750 the entry refers to 'Messrs. Porcelain and Company' and later from Michaelmas Day 1750 to 'Frye and Company'. Whatever the early title of the Bow factory in these account books it is clear that Frye and Heylyn were the actual makers of the porcelain and that Arnold merely gave them his financial backing. Arnold played no part in porcelain production. Dr. Ainslie discovered in the Court Books that apart from the permanent Essex site and the earlier Middlesex property, the Bow proprietors also acquired some land in St. Leonard's, Bromley, Middlesex in 1752 under the name 'Edward Heylyn and Company', the name being changed to 'The Porcelain Company' in 1753; but there are no further entries after that date. This property seems to have been a short-lived addition to the factory's premises. The land-tax returns and the poor-rate books for the parish of St. Leonard's, Bromley have similar entries to the Court Books for 1752 and 1753,[5] but again there are no further entries for the property in connection with porcelain making.

The specification of the first Bow patent enrolled on 5th April, 1745, claims the invention and perfection of 'a new method of manufacturing a certain material whereby a ware might be made of the same nature or kind and equal to, if not exceeding in goodness and beauty, china or porcelain ware imported from abroad'. It describes a recipe

---

[1] Court Book 1744, Record Office, County Hall, London.

[2] Both these properties were taken over by John Crowther about 1757, probably as the result of Heylyn's bankruptcy. Crowther had another property in Bow, Middlesex, from 1752 and also a property in St. Leonard's, Bromley from 1754.

[3] 4th edition, vol. 1, p. 2.

[4] Discovered by Mr. Saintsbury, Borough Librarian of West Ham, as a result of the Bow Exhibition at the British Museum, 1959. H. Tait, *Apollo*, vol. LXXI, no. 420, Feb. 1960, p. 40.

[5] Discovered by Mr. Hellicar in the Poplar Borough Library.

for blue and white using china clay called *unaker* imported from North America.[1] This kaolinic clay was intended to be used both in the glassy body and in the lead-free glaze. It is practically certain that as described this *unaker* formula was unworkable, indeed it may have been patented merely as an attempt to monopolize the use of *unaker* while experiments were being made to discover the secrets of Chinese hard-paste porcelain as had already been done at Meissen. The only customs record of a material likely to be *unaker* imported into London from Carolina was '20 tons, value £5', in 1743/4 classed as 'earth, unrated'.[2] However, the possibility of *unaker* clay being actually used at Bow for a short period is strengthened by an important discovery made by Mr. Toppin. He found that a man named John Campbell reported to Arthur Dobbs[3] about 24th June, 1749, on some land in North Carolina stating, 'I send you in a small box a sample of white clay and the ore intermixed with the vein which has been traced above a mile in Edgecombe county. The clay resembles what I saw at Bow for their china ware which I believe is only a bubble with the undertakers. This clay is near water carriage and if worth anything enough might be had. The land is vacant and it is communicated to me as a secret by some persons who pretend to be judges of these fossils but desire your opinion.'[4]

It is possible that the first Bow patent was an attempt to stop the American potter Andrew Duché[5] (1710–88) obtaining the exclusive patent rights which he had been seeking for making his own wares in America, the necessity for a Bow patent having become especially urgent owing to Duché's arrival in England.[6] The popular alternative suggestion is that Duché encouraged the Bow proprietors to obtain

[1] Ll. Jewitt, *The Ceramic Art of Great Britain*, vol. 1, London, 1878, pp. 112–113. 'The material is an earth, the produce of the Chirokee nation in America, called by the natives unaker. . . .' The wares were 'to be painted blue, with lapis lazuli, lapis armenis, or zapher . . .'.

[2] *Registers of Inspector-General of Imports & Exports.* Entry discovered by Mr. Toppin.

[3] Arthur Dobbs of Carrickfergus in Ireland was appointed Governor of North Carolina in 1754. Clay was exported from Carrickfergus to the Liverpool potteries.

[4] *Castle Dobbs M.S.*, Public Record Office, Belfast. A man named John Campbell L.L.D., a prolific writer and authority on industry and trade and on the European settlements in America, was made agent for Georgia in 1765.

[5] A potter from Savannah in Georgia who claimed to have been the first person to have found the true material and manner of making porcelain in Europe, Africa or America. He was seeking patent rights from 1738/9 for his method of manufacture in all parts of His Majesty's Dominions. 1st Earl of Egmont, *Journal of the Georgia Trustees*, London, 1886, p. 78.

[6] The phrase in the specification 'A New Method of Manufacturing a certain material whereby a ware might be made,' suggests this urgency, as if only preliminary experiments had been made with the material for making porcelain.

their patent so that he could sell them *unaker*.[1] Duché had been very secretive about his porcelain-making activities and had refused to send to the Trustees of Georgia in England any of his clay, alleging that it was a nostrum of his own.[2] Furthermore, he was evasive when asked to send samples of his own china to justify his claims for a patent. In October 1738 the Earl of Egmont notes a report from General Oglethorpe that 'earth is found which Duché the potter has baked into china ware'.[3] In May 1741 Colonel Stephens, the Secretary to the Trustees in Georgia, reported that Duché 'was reputed to make china ware as cups and basins transparent, but too much given to political schemes to form colonies'.[4] Later in the same year Stephens describes Duché's wares as 'differing very little (if anything) from some of our finest earthenware made in England'. Duché arrived in England on 26th May, 1743,[5] about eighteen months before the first Bow patent, but there is no evidence of his association with Bow and no record of his having brought any *unaker* to England or of his resumption of china making in America.[6]

In May 1745 the Quaker chemist William Cookworthy wrote to a friend that 'I had lately with me, the person who discovered the china earth. He had with him several samples of the china ware, which I think were equal to the Asiatic. It was found on the back of Virginia, where he had been in quest of mines; and having read Du Halde, he discovered both the petunze and kaolin. It is this latter earth, which he says is essential to the success of the manufacture. He is gone for a cargo of it; having bought from the Indians, the whole country where it rises. They can import it for £13 per ton; and by that means afford

[1] See F. Severne Mackenna, *Cookworthy's Plymouth and Bristol Porcelain*, Leigh-on-Sea, 1946, pp. 21–6, for an exposition of R. P. Hommel's investigations into the circumstantial evidence of Duché's connection with Bow.

[2] *Journal of the Georgia Trustees*, London, 1886, p. 77, March 1738/9.

[3] *Ibid*, October 1738, p. 26.

[4] *Ibid*, p. 343.

[5] Public Record Office, M.S. *Journal of the Trustees* CO5 687, 1737–45, 23rd September, 1743, pp. 261–3.

[6] Duché's memorial to the Trustees of 9th September, 1743, read *in absentia*, states that he applied for a grant to visit England in July 1741, presumably to obtain his patent. This was refused and he decided to defray the expenses himself. He set sail with 'several casks of his earthenware' but was arrested on a warrant as he was said to have owed the Trustees £400. He eventually came to England via Virginia. He set out his grievances in the form of questions which he asked the Trustees to answer. From these it appears that his pottery had not been a profitable concern and he had decided to leave the colony; he had, however, not been allowed to sell his property in Savannah. Colonel Stephens in his Journal for 15th September, 1741, reports a conversation with Duché about the proposed voyage to England: '. . . . neither did it appear to us, that what he now proposed to carry with him for that purpose, could merit the name of china-ware,' (A. D. Candler, *The Colonial Records of Georgia*, Atalanta, 1908, Supplement to vol. IV, p. 242.)

their china as cheap as common stone ware; but they intend only to go about 30 per cent under the company. The man is a Quaker by profession, but seems to be as thorough a Deist as I ever met with. He knows a good deal of mineral affairs, but not *funditus.*'[1] A careful reading of Cookworthy's account suggests that the china ware this un-named man had with him was actually made in England from the imported clay and at that date there is no place more likely than Bow. This assumption is strengthened by Dossie's statement that the proprietors of a china work near London had sent their agent to Carolina for kaolin.[2] However, there is no direct proof that Cookworthy is referring to Andrew Duché, in spite of the fact that Duché is described in the Earl of Egmont's diary in similar terms as 'a worse believer even than a Deist'.[3] Duché was a Huguenot and not a Quaker. Like his father he was a potter and as far as we know he had not 'been in quest of mines'. There are, on the other hand, a number of important merchant prospectors who should be considered by future ceramic historians.[4]

The second Bow patent was enrolled on 17th December, 1749, and again limited to five proprietors. In it Thomas Frye claimed to be able to make 'a certain ware which is not inferior in beauty and fineness and is rather superior in strength than the earthenware that is brought from the East Indies and is commonly known by the name of China, Japan or porcelain ware'. The patent, unlike the first one, extended to the colonies and the plantations of America. The specification was enrolled on 17th March, 1749/50. It again describes the making of a blue and white ware; there is thus no evidence that any enamelled wares were produced at Bow before 1749/50. As in the first patent, part of the formula is somewhat misleading. 'Virgin earth'[5] and pipe-clay were used in the recipe for a body which was

[1] John Prideaux, *Relics of William Cookworthy*, London, 1853. 'The company' probably refers to the East India Company. Duché seems to have been in Norfolk, Virginia in 1754 and he was still in Virginia in 1761. See Ruth M. Gilmer, 'Andrew Duché and his China', *Apollo*, vol. XLV, May 1947, pp. 128–30.

[2] Dossie states that kaolin was discovered 'in some mountains on the back of Carolina in great abundance; whither the proprietors of a work near London sent an agent to procure it for them: but he neglecting it for other persuits, I believe no quantity has hitherto been brought from thence . . .' (*The Handmaid of the Arts*, 1758, vol. 11, p. 338).

[3] *Diary of the first Earl of Egmont*, vol. 3, p. 230, 15th November, 1741.

[4] Amongst these were associates of the influential Quaker Joshua Gee, the friend of Silvanus Bevan to whom Cookworthy had been apprenticed; they had active interests and property in Carolina and thereabouts. Desmond Clarke, *Arthur Dobbs Esquire 1689–1765*, London, 1958, p. 35. Also Ernest Cripps, *Plough Court*, London, 1927, p. 213.

[5] 'Virgin earth' in this context probably included both bone ash and gypsum, see Wedgwood's Bow formula below. The specification describes 'virgin earth' as the

painted with smalt or zaffre according to the depth of blue colour required. The vessels were dipped in a lead glaze. A more straight-forward formula is given in Josiah Wedgwood's Experiment Book;[1] it agrees fairly well with the second Bow patent except that ball clay is mentioned and not pipe clay. The entry is as follows—'4 parts bone ash; 4 parts Lynn sand; a $\frac{1}{4}$ part of gypsum[2] plaster or alabaster; a $\frac{1}{4}$ part of blue ball clay. This is the composition of Bow china but I am not certain of the proportions. In the early period of the manufactory they used to frit the bone ashes, sand and gypsum mixed up together and made into bricks, but have for sometime past omitted that process and used them crude'.

Chelsea porcelain was 'calculated rather for ornament than for use'.[3] By contrast Bow porcelain was eminently usable though nonetheless attractive in appearance. A contemporary account of the Bow factory describes the porcelain as being stronger than that made at Chelsea or Dresden, and 'cheaper than any other china'. There was a great demand for it.[4] Production at Bow was enormous, as early as 1753 a warehouse had been opened in Cornhill, and for the same year the sale of porcelain was nearly £10,150 rising to over £12,120 by 1755.[5] Bow made more satisfactory flat wares than any other contemporary

fixed indissoluble matter produced by calcination of animal and vegetable sub-stances and calcarious minerals such as chalk or limestone. For the original word-ing see Ll. Jewitt, *The Ceramic Art of Great Britain*, vol. 1, p. 113. Herman Boerhaave, *Elements of Chemistry*, translated from the original Latin by Timothy Dallowe, London, vol. 1, 1735, p. 364–5, gives the following description: 'If a person catches pure rain-water and distills it carefully, he will find some Faeces left at the bottom. . . . If the faeculent matter thus collected is perfectly dried, and then thoroughly burnt, it will yield some ashes, which being very accurately freed from all the salt that is in them, produce a fine pure earth, which goes by the name of Virgin Earth.' This description was discovered by Dr. Ainslie. See also p. 117.

[1] 13th February, 1759, no. 9, p. 10, in the Wedgwood Museum at Barlaston.

[2] Possibly from the large works at Newark, Notts. There is a reference to 'the blue Newark pattern, on Bow china in the Bowcock papers in the British Museum. John Bowcock seems to have been part clerk, part outside representative and part general sales manager to the Bow factory. He married Ann Wilkinson. The Bow-cock papers were once owned by Lady Charlotte Schreiber and excerpts were printed from them in the *Art Journal*, 1869. A pencilled note written in 1866 on the papers by Thomas Bailey states that it was 'One hundred years since John Bowcocke died, Tuesday, Feb. 26th 1765 at 6 o'clock in the evening of lock jaw. He was brother to William Bowcocke of Chester, painter, my mother's father'. See also p. 25 footnote.

[3] *Gentleman's Magazine*, vol. XXXIII, 1763, p. 191.

[4] Defoe's *Tour of Great Britain*, edited by Samuel Richardson, 6th ed., 1762. Entry discovered by Bernard and Therle Hughes (*English Porcelain and Bone China*, London, 1955, p. 73). Hugh Tait drew attention to the different wording in the 4th ed., 1748 (and 5th ed. 1753), see *Apollo*, vol. LXXI, no. 424, June 1960, p. 181

[5] The *Bow Account Book*, British Museum. Add. M.S. 45905.

English china concern and excelled in making immense octagonal
dishes imitating and competing with those imported from China.
Their finest examples include octagonal platters of 16 inches in length
with designs such as the so-called 'image' pattern (1). Mr. Toppin
owns a magnificent circular platter of 12 inches diameter, an early
piece[1] showing a Chinese fishing scene in a well balanced design which
fits the circular shape to perfection. The remarkable toughness of the
Bow paste made possible the production of large quantities of satisfactory knife and fork handles and these were mentioned in some contemporary advertisements and in the Bowcock papers.[2] Powder-blue
decorated plates, tankards and tea wares with scenic and ornamental
designs in reserves were a special feature (2) from about 1759, which
at their best were unexcelled in depth of colour, the evenness of its
application, and control in the glost firing. One amusing pattern on
octagonal plates shows two extremely puzzled Chinese confronted with
a vase inscribed 'Bow' round the foot.[3]

It is convenient to divide the blue and white output of the Bow
factory into three consecutive periods to correspond approximately with
the changes in potting styles and appearance of the wares. First the
early period from the time of the second patent 1749/50 to 1754.
Then the middle period from 1755 to 1763, the date of John Crowther's
bankruptcy; finally the late period from 1764 till the closure of the
factory in the mid 1770's. Dated wares, although not always typical,
can be used as nucleii around which to group other contemporary
examples. The known dated pieces are as follows:

Early Period (1749/50—1754)

An ink pot inscribed 'Made at New Canton 1750' marked with a
capital 'B' on the base (Colchester Museum) (3)

A bowl inscribed 'William and Elizabeth Martin November 20
1750' (Dr. Ainslie's collection) (4)

An ink pot inscribed 'Eward Bermingham 1752' (British Museum)

An ink pot inscribed 'Edward Vernon Esqr. July 1752' (Brighton
Museum) (5)

A cream jug inscribed 'W. Pether May 10, 1754' (Dr. Watney's
collection) (6)

---

[1] E.C.C. *Commemorative Catalogue 1927–48*, London, 1949, no. 152.
[2] 21st May, 1760, 16 knife and fork handles at 6d.——8/-.
[3] *Trans. E.P.C.*, no. IV, Plate XXX.

---

(1) *Plate* 10c (1); (2) *Plate* 12; (3) *Plate* 2A; (4) *Plate* 2c;
(5) *Plate* 3D; (6) *Plate* 8A.

Middle Period (1755—1763)

A mug inscribed 'E.P.   with a heart-shaped handle terminal
         E.C.   (British Museum)
        1757',

The powder-blue decorated bowl inscribed 'John and Ann Bowcock 1759' (British Museum) (1)

A ribbed mug with a heart-shaped handle terminal inscribed 'Mrs. Ann Ambler 1762' (National Museum of Wales) (2)

A cup with a grooved handle inscribed 'I:C 1763' (Dr. Ainslie's collection). Possibly from a tea-set made for John Crowther, who became bankrupt in the same year (3)[1]

Late Period (1764—about 1776)

Two octagonal plates with countersunk bases inscribed 'Mr. Robert Crowther, Stockport, Cheshire, January 1770' (Fitzwilliam Museum and British Museum)

A mug with a heart-shaped handle terminal inscribed 'Joseph and Margret Pennyfeather April 1770' (Victoria & Albert Museum)

Mr. Toppin's circular dish which has been mentioned above shows the typical features of early blue and white Bow. It is heavy in weight, thickly potted and painted in a fine pale luminous royal blue colour. The glaze forms a thick layer and is tinted with cobalt so that where it has pooled on the flat under-surface the glaze is blue-green. Early wares of this type usually have thousands of minute bubbles trapped in their glaze giving an opalescent quality which softens the effect of the underglaze blue patterns (4). The bubbles are most numerous where the glaze has run into blobs or formed shallow pools at foot-rings; as if a fine froth of bubbles had been caught in the glaze drips, at the same time imprisoning an undue amount of glaze colour. This gives a scummy effect, as the reflected light from these minute bubbles suggests to the naked eye that a finely divided substance has come out of solution and is suspended in the glaze. Sometimes it looks as if there has been a double glazing with both a clear and a scummy glaze. Where bubbles have burst on the surface the glaze is finely pitted giving what potters call an egg-shell appearance. Bubbly glazes are due to lack of proper maturation resulting from an inadequate glost-firing. It may have been a deliberate policy at Bow to under-fire

[1] 19th Nov. 1763, creditor 'George Harrison of Tottenham' who was previously a creditor of Edward Heylyn, 16th Dec. 1757, when Harrison is described as a 'glassmaker', (Public Record Office, B4, 22648 and 22650).

(1) *Plate* 12B; (2) *Plate* 14D; (3) *Plate* 16B; (4) *Plate* 6A.

the glaze in an attempt to stop the underglaze blue designs from running badly. This possibility is strengthened by the observation that these very bubbly glazes are extremely rare on enamelled wares.

However, some early wares, possibly the earliest, have a glaze that is fully matured, usually when the glaze has been thinly applied and the body fairly thinly potted. In these examples the blue designs have often run badly, sometimes almost completely obliterating the original patterns (1). This properly matured lead glaze has an attractive softness with a smooth brilliant appearance that enhances the fine underglaze blue colour.

Wares with a capital 'R' or a single line scratched in the paste on the under-surface usually have this type of smooth glaze (2). The 'scratch R' group includes a number of somewhat atypical shapes with enamelled or plain gilt designs or with applied flower sprigs. Blue and white designs with this mark are sometimes embellished with overglaze *rouge de fer* and gilding. The underglaze blue sometimes shows flecks of white, and the glaze over it tends to crawl, as with tin glazes, leaving little areas uncovered. By artificial light nearly all examples have a dirty white opalescent translucency like sodden snow. They have some definite connections with the attractive early enamelled wares having a 'drab-tinted' glaze,[1] for example, the same grotesque mask is sometimes used for the lower handle terminal.

In general the Chinese blue and white patterns on early Bow were painted with characteristic boldness well suited to the heavily potted wares and often showing signs of having been painted very rapidly. There were a number of stock designs which appear to have been used up to about 1754, but in some cases they were continued well after that date. One of the earliest designs in vivid blue includes a peony, a stylized rock formation and a pine tree, often bordered with a complicated flower-head and trellis pattern. The border is to be seen on the superb coffee pot which is marked with a 'scratch R' (3). It is also found together with the peony and rock pattern on a bellied mug in the Norwich Museum whose shape exactly corresponds with that of an early enamelled example, having a 'drab-tinted' glaze. A small mug in Mr. Toppin's collection with a spreading base and a widely grooved handle is another example with this pattern and has the same distinctive border (4). It has a fairly broad shallow unglazed footring sloping steeply on the inner side to a glazed base, marked underglaze

[1] Probably due to an opacifier in the glaze. See F. Hurlbutt, *Bow Porcelain*, London, 1926, Plate 16b, p. 95.

---

(1) *Plate* 2c; (2) *Plates* 3a, b, 4a, b, c;
(3) *Frontispiece*; (4) *Plate* 3b.

with an incised nick mark. A large 'scratch R' marked tureen at Temple Newsham also bears this blue and white pattern in a badly blurred state. It has, however, a well-moulded crabstock handle on the cover and on the body two large double arched rope-like handles with a woman's head moulded under each terminal. All these examples are painted with a vivid cobalt blue and the glaze is smooth and brilliant.

Another interesting pattern includes a peony at the end of a fence over the centre of which appear three daisy-like flowers (1). Above this there is sometimes a border of paired leaves and on the inner sides of the vessels is a flower head and leaf border, the leaves often being widely cross-striated. Besides the examples with tall pedestal feet two types of three-footed sauce boats bear this pattern. One type as illustrated by Fisher[1] has a heavy lion mask without a mane, the other type has a more flattened mask surrounded by a mane rather like a judge's wig. The sauce boat handles have complicated shapes, some being a double scroll and others having a moulded human face on them. Sometimes these sauce boats are marked with a script 'G' in underglaze blue (2).

The script 'G' mark occurs on other early wares including large rock and shell centre-pieces clustered with seaweed, coral and smaller shells, the latter often moulded directly from real shells.[2] The script 'G' is also found on a coffee can painted with islands, a crudely drawn pagoda and pavilion and fir trees looking rather like battle-ship turrets.[3] This pattern occurs on the ink pot inscribed 'Made at New Canton 1750' (3), which has a capital 'B' mark underneath. A coffee cup in Mr. Toppin's collection[4] has the same pattern as well as a capital 'B' mark. Wasters of this pattern were discovered on the factory site. A variant of this island and fir tree design was more common on early Bow (4).

Other standard patterns included a seated cross-legged Chinaman (5); stylized banana trees, with or without a standing stork (6);

[1] Stanley Fisher, *English Blue and White Porcelain of the 18th Century*, London, 1947, Plate 8, p. 31.

[2] In the 1867 excavations actual seashells were found from which mouldings could have been taken.

[3] Stanley Fisher, *English Blue and White Porcelain of the 18th Century*, Plate 7, p. 26.

[4] *Bow Exhibition Catalogue*, British Museum, 1959, No. 22. Toppin (personal communication) has suggested the possibility that the script 'G' painter was John Gazeley (Bow Parish Registers 1749–60), and that the 'B' painter was Lewis Barber, an apprentice of Heylyn, who later went to Worcester.

(1) *Plate* 3c; (2) *Plate* 3c; (3) *Plate* 2a; (4) *Plate* 6c;
(5) *Plate* 5b; (6) *Plates* 5a, c;

a charming scene of a stag being followed by a doe; a design of a house on an island surrounded by rocks and trees like telegraph poles (1) and various rock, trellis and peony patterns such as that on the Pether cream jug (2). Another pattern of four Chinese emblems is found on bowls with very thick footrings, sometimes marked with a 'J' or an 'I' in underglaze blue (3). A most unusual design is a charming mixture of Chinese and English tastes (4). A woman in eighteenth-century European dress and a Chinese boy stretch out their arms from a fanciful, canopied barge towards a strange figure standing on the shore, carrying in her left hand a half-closed parasol and with her right hand raised in greeting.

The early Bow designs are often blurred as if a little out of focus, especially on straight-sided vessels such as coffee cans and mugs. This blurring is caused by a slight fluxing effect of the cobalt with the glaze. The blue pigment varies in depth of colour from a thinly applied pale wash to a most vivid royal blue.[1] It often has a granular appearance due to spots of darker pigment, but this granularity becomes even more obvious in the middle period. The designs are usually painted in two tones, sometimes in marked contrast, as in the middle period when a darker less luminous blue was used. Some of the earliest blue and white has overglaze iron-red decoration in the oriental manner. This matt-surfaced pigment, 'foul red' as Dossie describes it, was inexpensive and easy to prepare and fire compared with the true enamels, consequently it appears to have been the first overglaze colour to be used at Bow. Its dull effect was relieved by gilding; the overglaze embellishments helping to disguise the blurred outlines of the underglaze blue patterns.

The wares of the early period do not stain brown on unglazed bases and along the margins of cracks as readily as the later porcelain, possibly because the early body was fired to a higher temperature. The glaze is occasionally crazed. Even the thickly potted wares are fairly translucent, usually showing an opalescent pale straw colour with a tinge of green by artificial light. Some of the more thinly potted wares have a 'colder' translucency. All Bow porcelain as we know it contains bone ash and no porcelain has yet been found which can be ascribed to the period of the first patent.

The early Bow shapes for tea wares were generally practical and robust, copying Chinese examples, but English silver was imitated

[1] The second patent specification mentions the use of either zaffre or smalt for a deeper or paler blue colour as required, and the Bowcock papers for 1756 mention 'the bordered image, blue and pale as you please' and '12 dragon breakfast cups and saucers with good deep colour'.

(1) *Plate* 6D; (2) *Plates* 8A, B, C; (3) *Plate* 6A. (4) *Plate* 3A.

for the more ornate types of sauce boat, salts, centre-pieces (1), baskets and tureens (2). Cup and coffee-can handles were usually either made from a simple roll of clay, partly flattened on the inner side, or else moulded as a stylized crabstock with a central interlocking knot (3). Early cups often taper downwards to very shallow footrings, surrounding slightly convex glazed bases, while cylindrical coffee cans have bases which are flat and unglazed. Most teapots are almost spherical (4), but a few have a more upright silver shape (5); their lids have spherical or stylized twig knobs. Teapot spouts are steeply arched, and the handles are often thick unflattened rolls which are somewhat thinner at the lower terminal. Cream jugs are rather stumpy and fat bellied with fairly wide spouts (6). Butter tubs are well designed and capacious (7). Plates and dishes either have flat unglazed bases, glazed countersunk bases or shallow footrings. The magnificent early coffee pots (8) are decidedly uncommon and early leaf-shaped pickle trays are perhaps rarer still (9). Practically all the known blue and white finger bowls and their stands are marked either with an incised line or a 'scratch R', sometimes together with a dagger mark in underglaze blue.

Various letters of the alphabet and marks in underglaze blue occur on early Bow besides those already mentioned, including 'W', 'C', a cross, an arrow, and three dots. There are also a few alchemical and other signs which are usually incised, such as an arrow and annulet, and the sign for Mercury. Numerals in underglaze blue are rare up till about 1754.

From the early days of the factory Bow china was advertised in the London[1] and provincial newspapers[2] and there was trade with Ireland,[3] America[4] and with the West Indies. It appears that the proprietors had a part ownership of the *Antelope*.[5] This ship, which

[1] John Sotro, Goldsmith and Toyman, 'Bow China not Inferior to Old Japan,' the *Daily Advertiser*, 9th January, 1750. Discovered by A. J. B. Kiddell. John Sotro's trade card also mentions Bow china, see Ambrose Heal, *The London Goldsmiths*, Cambridge, 1935, Plate LXVI, facing p. 246.
[2] In *Aris's Birmingham Gazette*, 5th March, 1753, and the *Derby Mercury*, 9th March, 1753. J. E. Nightingale, *Contributions*, 1881, pp. XLIV and XLV.
[3] Early advertisements for useful and ornamental Bow china appeared in *Faulkner's Journal*, Dublin.
[4] A Boston newspaper of November 1754 announces that Philip Breading of Fish Street had just imported a variety of Bow china, cups and saucers, bowls etc. Discovered by Alexander Lewis.
[5] Listed under ships belonging to the City of London 1732, the *Antelope* 40 tons, 6 men. Maitland, *The History of London*, 1739.

(1) *Plate* 9A; (2) *Plates* 7A, B; (3) *Plates* 5A, 6C. (4) *Plate* 5C;
(5) *Plate* 5D. (6) *Plate* 6B; (7) *Plate* 7C; (8) Frontispiece;
(9) *Plate* 2B.

carried cargoes to Montego Bay, is mentioned in the Bowcock papers. Some bankruptcy proceedings against the master of the *Antelope* dated 5th April, 1756,[1] reveal that John Crowther,[2] Edward Heylyn, John Weatherby[3] and Thomas Frye were then partners. Chaffers states in the *Art Journal* for 1869 that according to the Bow account books Messrs. Crowther and Weatherby were connected with the Bow factory from 1750. However, they probably did not become proprietors until some time after that date.

The middle period (1755–63) is notable for the number of stock Chinese patterns which tend to be more ambitious than those produced earlier. Most of the better quality examples were probably made before Frye's retirement in 1759. The china body appears to be more porous and less vitrified. The glaze, although not so attractive as previously, is better matured and the underglaze blue is generally darker in colour and flatter in appearance. The porcelain is fairly thinly potted, but the shapes are generally more routine and less interesting.

The 'dragon' pattern is well known (1)[4] and is instantly distinguishable from the usual Worcester and Lowestoft versions by, appropriately for Bow, an arrow sticking out of its mouth. Among the favourite patterns are the charming seated zither or 'koto player'(2); the rather

[1] Public Record Office, B1 31.

[2] Son of Ralph, a farmer of Butley, Cheshire. He was master of the Skinners' Company in 1759, a glass seller and a wholesale potter. In bankruptcy proceedings against him dated 22nd February, 1764 (B1 42, fol. 22), he is stated to have carried on a large trade as a potter, glass maker and chinaman with John Weatherby from 1725 until the latter's death on 14th October, 1762. The Skinners' Company minutes for 27th October, 1790, show that Crowther was then lately dead. Thomas Craft stated that the Bow manufactory was carried on for many years by Crowther and Weatherby. John Smith in *Nollekens and his Times*, 1828, records a conversation between Panton Betew a silversmith, and Nollekens, in which it is mentioned that Crowther was the proprietor of the Bow manufactory.

[3] His family came from Staffordshire. He is described in his will as a porcelain maker (in Somerset House, P.C.C. St. Eloi 441 Proved 15th October, 1762). With Crowther he opened a Bow warehouse in Cornhill in February 1753 (*General Evening Post*, 8th February, 1753, discovered by G. Wills); this was closed in May 1764 as a result of Crowther's bankruptcy. Weatherby is described with John Crowther as late of Cornhill, London, chinaman (21st February, 1764, Public Record Office, B1 42, Folio 52). Crowther and Weatherby are also mentioned in the *London Directories* from 1744 as potters at St. Catherine's near the Tower. On 11th December, 1744, John Weatherby, glass seller, acquired an interest in a property at Salt Petre Bank, Rosemary Lane, St. Catherines (*Court Books*, entry discovered by J. Ainslie). From 1759 till 24th June, 1760, they were joined by the potter James Abernathy from Wapping (*Public Advertiser* discovered by Francis Burrell).

[4] 'Dragon' pattern breakfast cups and saucers, milk pots and a sugar dish are mentioned in the Bowcock papers from 1756.

frantic 'woman with an umbrella'(1); the bordered 'image' pattern (2)[1] and the 'jumping boy' (3), the latter also occurring on Chaffers' best quality Liverpool porcelain. A harbour-scene pattern (4)[2] appears to have been copied from a Chinese version of a European original. Wasters of all these patterns were discovered by Mr. Toppin on the Bow site as well as wasters of the rare dolphin pattern.[3] The most uncommon Chinese designs occur on magnificent pairs of vases (5) and pairs of bottles with fussily applied floral festoons (6). Then there is the somewhat comical scene of three Jesuit priests on a bridge, one of them riding a yak (7), and the Bow blue and white 'quail' pattern which is an exact copy of the Chinese prototype (8). Flower sprays with rather flattened insects after Meissen examples are frequently found, especially on moulded wares (9) and open-work baskets produced from about 1759. They can be compared with similar coloured designs, such as those on the mug inscribed 'Wm. Taylor 1759', in the Victoria and Albert Museum. The bellied blue and white mug inscribed 'E.P./E.C.' and dated 1757 (British Museum) is one of the very rare examples showing a European landscape scene. Some of the popular less elaborate Chinese patterns typical of the early period were continued, such as the 'banana-tree' pattern and the house with trees like telegraph poles (10).

Powder-blue decorated pieces were a special feature. The earliest known example is the dated Bowcock bowl (11)[4] with its unusually ornate rococo reserves outside and fine figure-painting inside showing

[1] There are frequent references in the Bowcock papers to this pattern, e.g. 'Lord Southwell: Mr. Heylyn has promised him to make an oval tureen, the image pattern, and to be done in 6 weeks without fail'.

[2] A varient of this pattern was produced in the early period sometimes marked with a 'scratch R'.

[3] The Bowcock papers mention a 'blue dolphin pickle stand' for the Duchess of Leeds; however, this may have been one of the scallop shell stands with the figure of a dolphin set in the centre.

[4] In the Entwistle papers (Liverpool Public Library, DQ 6573/26) is a letter dated 21st August, 1922, from Miss K. MacIntire (whose mother originally possessed the Bowcock bowl) stating, 'John and Ann Bowcock were uncle and aunt to my grandfather. They were Liverpool people, John being a sea captain. The bowl was made for them I am told at Shaw's potteries, Liverpool. It was presented to him after one of his voyages. Mrs. Bowcock died and was buried while he was away (of plague). The poor man was never the same after, as the family believed she had been buried alive. They are related to the artist Bowcock and wife whose oil portraits I have. . . .' William Bowcock, the painter, John Bowcock's brother, died at Little Abbey Court, Chester on 14th February, 1800 (*Gore's General Advertiser*, No. 1783, 27th February, 1800).

(1) *Plate* 10B; (2) *Plate* 10C (1). (3) *Plate* 19A. (4) *Plate* 10A (2);
(5) *Plates* 9B, C; (6) *Plate* 17A; (7) *Plate* 10C; (8) *Plate* 13B;
(9) *Plate* 18B; (10) *Plate* 13C; (11) *Plate* 12B.

'John Bowcock landing and sailors dancing with staffs in their hands'. The colour of the powder-blue ground varied considerably from a very dark blackish blue to a much richer and paler colour. The reserves were usually either fan-shaped or circular (1), especially on plates and dishes. A few plates have their upper surfaces completely covered by the blue ground. Powder-blue pickle trays sometimes incorporated a strange cotyledon-leaf and grape-vine theme (2), and bean flowers decorate an example in the Birmingham Museum (3). Centre-pieces (4) and plates are found with a clumsy grape-vine pattern against a background of tendrils and powder blue.

Underglaze-blue transfer-printing was practised at Bow, although this type of decoration is unusual and seems to date from about 1760.[1] Recently a single fragment of porcelain decorated in this manner depicting rocks and weeds has been discovered in Mr. Toppin's collection of Bow wasters. The following blue printed patterns are known:

1. Flower sprays and insects which occur on a pair of immense dishes (5), some dinner plates with shaped rims,[2] a cup and two vases.[3] One vase with an ovoid shape on a pedestal base has an opaque body and is decorated with two large flower sprays including a large rose bud and a bee. One of these flower sprays is also found on late painted wares (6). Variants of both were commonly used at Lowestoft, Worcester, Caughley and Liverpool.

2. Two different scenes said to be from 'The Herdsman and the Spinning Maiden', one of which, sometimes known as the 'Red Cow' pattern, is found on a circular plate with flower sprays round the rim while the other decorates a large mug in the Allman collection.[4] Both these prints are more common on Derby pieces and the author has a small Derby teapot (7) with a print which appears to have been taken from the same copper plate as that used for the Bow mug.

3. An attractive design, 'La Dame Chinoise', occurs on Bow octagonal plates,[5] also on a Derby mug marked with an anchor, a sun face and the word Derby (8)[6], and in sepia on a Worcester mug.[7] It is even

---

[1] For a discussion on the possibility that Holdship may have engraved these prints see pp. 87–8. Printed wares are mentioned as early as 1756 in the Bowcock papers, and almost certainly refer to the much finer overglaze prints produced about that time from copper plates engraved by Robert Hancock.

[2] Dr. John Ainslie, 'Underglaze-blue printing on Bow porcelain,' *The Antique Collector*, April 1957, p. 61, Fig. 1.

[3] *Ibid*, Fig. 4.   [4] *Ibid*, Figs. 2 & 11.

[5] *Ibid*, Figs. 5, 6, 7 & 8.   [6] *Ibid*, Fig. 9, British Museum.

[7] Cyril Cook, *The Life and Work of Robert Hancock*, London, 1948, item 26.

---

(1) *Plates* 12A, C, D, 13A; (2) *Plate* 10D; (3) *Plate* 15A; (4) *Plate* 16C; (5) *Plate* 15C; (6) *Plate* 19C; (7) *Plate* 68B; (8) *Plate* 68A.

found in overglaze black on a hard-paste Bristol cream jug.[1] A copper plate for this design was found at Coalport by Mr. Franklin Barrett, having probably been taken to Caughley by Richard Holdship, who is believed to have gone there for a short time after being at Derby.

4. A 'willow' pattern scene with a Chinaman on a bridge occurs on the other side of the Allman mug (see pattern number 2 above). Two other somewhat similar scenes with swimming swans and pagodas are found on a pair of mugs in the author's collection (1), one having a heart-shaped handle terminal and a turned rim at the base. The pattern also occurs on Derby, occasionally decorating cups with peaked handles (2).

5. A portrait bust of Queen Charlotte on a mug with a heart-shaped handle tag in the Cheltenham Museum (3).[2] The mug has a gilded rim, an unusual feature for Bow blue and white. There are also two full-length standing figures on the mug, one representing Britannia with a spear and shield, and the other Fortune who indicates her own eyes with her right hand and with the other points a sceptre at a single isolated eye (4). The prints on this mug lack the technical perfection of Hancock's original work and they are very much in the style of Richard Holdship.

The porcelain of the middle period is less robust than previously. Cups are generally more capacious, height for height. Footrings tend to be taller and thinner, typically sloping slightly inwards on the outer side, but some are vertical like early examples. Glaze puddles at the footrings are usually a distinct blue colour. Some footrings show evidence of having been slightly smoothed by a grindstone after glazing. Cup handles are frequently grooved or moulded with a central raised rib. They may be painted with simple decorative motives such as dots and dashes or leaves (5). Cream jugs for the most part continue to be bulbous and stumpy. Teapot spouts are no longer steeply arched but have become S-shaped, sometimes with side flutings and the lip cut like a beak. Coffee pots, unlike those of most other factories, have a number of small holes between the body and the spout and they sometimes retain earlier handle shapes (6). Knobs on covers are no longer globular, but have become flattened into a mushroom shape. Cylindrical mugs and coffee cans are sometimes finished

[1] Victoria and Albert Museum. Schreiber Collection No. 779.

[2] Cyril Cook, *The Life and Work of Robert Hancock*, item 91. The portrait of the Queen was engraved by Hancock probably from an engraving by François Aliamet in T. Smollett, *Continuation of the Complete History of England*, 1761, vol. 4, rather than from an engraving by James F. McArdell, published in 1762.

(1) *Plate* 14c; (2) *Plate* 67B; (3) *Plate* 14B; (4) *Plate* 14A; (5) *Plate* 16B; (6) *Plate* 11B;

with a neat ring-like swelling round the body at the base, and most coffee cans have footrings. Painted cell and trellis borders are common, such as that on a two-handled chocolate or caudle cup and cover (1) with pine-cone moulding, and on the documentary ribbed mug dated 1762 (2). Handles are frequently embellished with a heart-shaped moulding beneath the lower terminal, probably copying silver examples. This heart-shaped tag is a typical and common feature of mid-period Bow, although it is occasionally found on Plymouth hard paste and a group of Liverpool porcelain, probably made by William Ball. At Lowestoft the appendage is rare and is not usually heart-shaped but triangular and has a serrated edge. Saucers, plates and dishes often show stilt marks on their upper surfaces, although this characteristic is also found on Lowestoft flat wares. Some plates (3) and dishes have a raised shaped rim like Meissen and Chelsea examples; others are octagonal (4) as were earlier flat wares. Decorative vine-leaf and grape-moulded dishes (5) copy either Chelsea or Meissen prototypes; similar dishes were produced later at Derby. In the mid-period Bow produced a variety of leaf-moulded cream boats (6), mugs (7), chamber candle sticks and pickle trays (8). Basket-moulded wares, such as dishes and sauce boats, are found painted with flower sprays and insects in the Meissen manner. Some sauce boats are moulded with fruit and floral patterns and others have rococo reserves. The Derby factory appropriated some of these designs and seems to have taken moulds directly from Bow examples. Pistol butt knife and fork handles were made to be fitted with metal hafts which, unlike St. Cloud examples, do not pierce right through the handle to the butt end. There are at least six different patterns, many of which are painted with decorations similar to those of St. Cloud.[1]

The porcelain body of the middle period wares is fairly porous and frequently shows slight surface tears through lack of plasticity. The body tends to stain brown where it is not protected by glaze. The glaze is duller, whiter and more starchy in appearance than previously. The porcelain is more opaque to transmitted light, the translucency by artificial light varying from a rather dirty green colour to a warm brownish yellow. Tears in the paste show up as translucent flecks.

In the middle period painters' numerals are common[2] on the bases but are sometimes found under handles and more rarely inside foot-

[1] John Ainslie, 'Knife and Fork Handles,' *The Connoisseur*, March 1953, pp. 14–17.

[2] 60 is the highest number marking a Bow piece in the Victoria and Albert Museum; on a saucer, C846a–1924.

(1) *Plate* 17c. (2) *Plate* 14d; (3) *Plate* 19a; (4) *Plate* 13d; (5) *Plate* 16d; (6) *Plate* 16a; (7) *Plate* 17b; (8) *Plates* 10d, 11a.

rings as on Lowestoft wares. Imitations of Chinese lettering are especially common on flat wares, but some pieces have the crossed-swords mark copying Meissen. A crescent with a face in it is a rare mark which occurs on a Bow basket-moulded plate in the Norwich Museum; it is also sometimes found on Worcester porcelain. Occasionally vine-leaf plates have a capital 'B' scratched underglaze on the base. Some moulded sauce boats have the 'To' mark[1] impressed in the footring.

Production continued during the final few years of the factory's life under the management of John Crowther, in the face of the bankruptcies or deaths of the majority of the proprietors and a serious flood in October 1762. This latter misfortune may have been largely responsible for Crowther's bankruptcy in 1763. 'The china-works at Bow were overflowed', by flood waters from the river Lea, 'in such a manner that the current rushed through the great arch in like manner as the tide runs through the arches of London Bridge'.[2] The London Directories from 1770 to 1775 described Crowther as 'Bow chinaman' having a warehouse at 28 St. Paul's Church Yard. However, shortly after 1775, according to Jewitt, William Duesbury of Derby bought up the Bow factory.[3] Meanwhile the fame of Bow was still world wide and its challenge was felt, even in America where a rival concern was set up about 1770,[4] claiming to make superior tea wares.

During the late period, 1764 to about 1776, the porcelain produced at Bow was mostly of poor quality; eventually even losing that look of sophistication which, to some extent, had counterbalanced the loss of primitive charm. In general the shapes and decorative styles of the middle period were continued; Worcester patterns, shapes and mouldings were frequently copied (1) and Chinese designs and shapes were still in vogue. Although the Robert Crowther plates inscribed 'January 1770' and the mug inscribed 'Joseph and Margret Penny-feather April 1770', are somewhat fussily decorated, they are among

---

[1] Believed to be the mark of a 'repairer' Mr. Tebo. See Arthur Lane, *English Porcelain Figures of the 18th Century*, London, 1961, pp. 87, 121.

[2] The *Gentleman's Magazine*, vol. XXXII, October, 1762. Entry discovered by Mrs. John Frost.

[3] Samuel Keys, who was apprenticed to the first William Duesbury, wrote his reminiscences about 1855. He stated that when the Bow factory closed Duesbury had several beautiful figures and ornaments transferred from there.

[4] Chaffers, *Marks and Monograms*, 14th ed., 1932, p. 969, quotes the *Edinburgh Weekly Magazine*, January 1771, 'By a letter from Philadelphia we are informed that a large china manufactory is established there and that better china cups and saucers are made there than at Bow and Stratford.' This concern was managed by Messrs. Bonnin & Morris, not Duché. It was a failure!

---

(1) *Plate* 18A.

the best products of this last period. Handles sometimes have broad blue scrolls painted on either side of their terminals. Some cups have a pendant point on the under-part of the handle. The heart-shaped handle tags are frequently cross-hatched in underglaze blue, they are usually badly moulded and have become more triangular and stylised in shape. Footrings are often poorly finished and are spotted with black specks. Octagonal plates may or may not have countersunk bases. An octagonal plate in the Victoria and Albert Museum has a capital 'W' mark in underglaze blue on the under side of the rim.[1] A circular plate from the Ainslie collection has an underglaze-blue annular mark with a line through it (I). Tea wares are occasionally marked with a crescent.

Finally the porcelain became so under-fired as to resemble earthenware. It is almost completely opaque and has a grey appearance which lacks brilliance. In this debased state the production of Bow porcelain came to an end after over thirty years of continuous endeavour to make useful and ornamental china which would be less expensive and more acceptable than foreign wares. The measure of achievement is that during its heyday in the mid-eighteenth century Bow had been the most important blue and white china manufactory in Europe.

[1] C698–1924.

(I) *Plate* 19B.

3

LIMEHOUSE, LUND'S BRISTOL AND WORCESTER

The early experiments in porcelain manufacture at the short-lived and mysterious Limehouse factory (about 1745–8) gave the necessary experience which was very soon put to more extensive use, first at Bristol and Longton Hall and then, so we believe, at Worcester and Liverpool. When Dr. Richard Pococke, later Bishop of Meath, visited the Staffordshire pottery villages in the early summer of 1750 he met there one of the potters whom he had previously seen at Limehouse, 'who promised to make the best chinaware, but disagreed with his employers'.[1] Later in the same year when Dr. Pococke was in Bristol he noted that the Bristol china factory had been founded by 'one of the principal manufacturers at Limehouse which failed'.[2]

The Limehouse factory was situated by the side of the Thames in that part of Narrow Street, then called Fore Street, only a few miles away from Bow. The little we know about this factory comes chiefly from advertisements which appeared in the *Daily Advertiser* between 1st January, 1747, and 30th September, 1748.[3] They tell us that the factory was near Duke Shore, but do not reveal the names of the proprietors. However, there is an extract from a letter by Mr. James Middleton of Shelton at an earlier date, 28th December, 1745, addressed to 'William Tams at the Potwork in Fore Street, nigh Duke Shore in Limehouse, London'.[4] Tams is a well known name in the Potteries,[5] and Mrs. MacAlister found the following relevant baptismal entries in the Stoke parish registers:

1748 Stephen Middleton, son of William and Hannah Tams
1753 Stephen, son of William and Hannah Tams of Shelton.

[1] Add. M.S. No. 15,800, British Museum. Letter to his mother, 14th July, 1750, written from Boulness, near Carlisle.
[2] *Ibid.*, 2nd November, 1750.
[3] A. J. B. Kiddell, *Trans E.P.C.*, 1928, no. 1, pp. 19–21.
[4] Ward's *History of Stoke-upon-Trent*, 1843, p. 356. Discovered by Mrs. MacAlister, *Trans E.C.C.*, 1933, no. I, pp. 44–53.
[5] A William Tams was buried at Stoke on 13th June, 1773.

Mrs. MacAlister concluded that Tams' wife Hannah was the sister of the brothers James Middleton and the Rev. John Middleton of Shelton. Another potter at Limehouse was discovered by Mr. Toppin in the registers of St. Anne's, which records the baptism of Elizabeth, daughter of William Ball, potter, Fore Street, and Mary, 8th March, 1747/8.[1]

The recent important discovery of the Limehouse land tax returns[2] gives all the tax payers in Fore Street during the period when the Limehouse factory was in existence. With the help of these lists, the parish registers and a large number of contemporary property deeds as well as the sewer rates and quit rents, it has now been possible to prepare a street plan showing the whereabouts of all the tax-paying occupants of Fore Street, and in most cases their trades and professions.

William Ball the potter lived next to a wharf which lay between Duke Shore Steps and Lime House Bridge, practically opposite Shoulder of Mutton Alley, at number 46 Fore Street,[3] but he did not stay there as a ratepayer for very long.[4] Another riverside property with a wharf was on the other side of Duke Shore Steps but nearer to them; it was occupied by Joseph Wilson and Company who arrived there between July 1744 and March 1745 and left between June 1747 and August 1748.[5] This could possibly have been the site of the Limehouse factory as, apart from some waste land on the other side of the road, it was one of the few places on the built up waterside around Duke Shore where there would have been room for kilns. It has not been possible to discover Joseph Wilson's occupation, although a Joseph Wilson shipwright of Limehouse is mentioned in St. Dunstan's Stepney Baptismal Registers for 1729.[6] However, there were potters by the name of Wilson working in the neighbourhood. Mr. Toppin found an entry in the Limehouse registers[7] for a John Wilson, potter, of Queen Street, Ratcliffe in February 1740/1, who by 1752 seems to have moved to Wapping, and the sewer rates show that a

---

[1] *Trans E.P.C.*, 1931, No. 3, pp. 70–3.

[2] The Guildhall Library, City of London, M.S. 6006.

[3] The houses were re-numbered in 1876.

[4] Joseph Averell, waterman, occupied the property in June 1746. In February 1746/7 John Ball, a shipwright, was there, and William Ball, the potter in June 1747. In August 1748 the property is described as empty, late William Ball. The rates were £12 per annum.

[5] The Land Tax Returns, Guildhall Library, City of London. These dates fit in well with the known dates of the Limehouse factory. The rates were £18 per annum.

[6] 20th September, 1729, Margaret, daughter of Joseph Wilson of Limehouse, shipwright and Mary.

[7] 'A Note on the Limehouse China Factory,' *Trans E.P.C.*, 1931, no. 3, pp. 71 and 72.

LIMEHOUSE, LUND'S BRISTOL AND WORCESTER

John Wilson was in Fore Street, Limehouse, during 1750. In October 1758 a James Wilson, potter, was living across the river at Deptford.[1] Our Joseph Wilson, of Narrow Street, is recorded as having two children who died in 1746 and 1747, and he himself was buried on 15th November, 1752, 'from the Town House'.[2]

The advertisements suggest that the Limehouse factory specialized in blue and white china, but none of its products have been identified. They made useful and ornamental vessels,[3] including teapots, sauce boats and potting pots of various sizes.[4] By June 1747 the wares were reported as being greatly improved, and in the autumn of the next year they were being sold in St. James's.[5] Mr. Pinchbeck even found them worthy of mention in an advertisement dated 28th October, 1747, stating that for strength and enduring the fire they far exceed china or any other ware hitherto invented.[6]

There is a reasonable possibility that soapstone was first used on a commercial scale for porcelain at Limehouse. From there the secret of its use may have been taken to Bristol and Worcester by Lund and then to Liverpool by Podmore, and possibly even more directly to Liverpool by William Ball and William Reid. Soapstone has been found in a few early experimental Longton Hall wares,[7] but for some reason, probably the failure of supply, the use of this ingredient was soon given up in favour of a glassy paste. If soapstone was indeed first used at Limehouse then London can claim to have been the centre at which the three main types of English soft-paste porcelain body were first evolved, and from where the secrets of their manufacture were disseminated.

Soaprock, which was obtained from the Lizard peninsula, is a steatized granite often showing green (ferrous) and red (ferric) mineral veins. It can be fairly hard or very soft. In its soft state it has a greyish white, semi-translucent appearance with a crumbly structure like Stilton cheese. It is distinctly soapy to the touch.[8]

---

[1] G. Wills, 'Ceramic Causerie,' *Apollo*, vol. LXIV, October 1756. In *Apollo*, June 1954, the same author records a Joseph Wilson, Chinaman, of St. Martin's Court, Westminster, for 1747.

[2] The Registers of St. Anne's Limehouse.

[3] *Daily Advertiser*, 20th June, 1747.

[4] *Ibid.*, 30th September, 1748.

[5] *Loc. cit.*

[6] The Pinchbecks were landowners in Limehouse at that time. Land Tax Returns, Guildhall Library, City of London.

[7] This finding has not been confirmed by recent analyses and should at present be treated with caution.

[8] Steatite is a hydrated magnesium silicate. Kaolin is a hydrated aluminium silicate.

The Jesuit D'Entrecolles in a letter dated 25th January, 1722,[1] described a new ingredient that the Chinese were using in the manufacture of a certain class of porcelain in place of kaolin: 'c'est une pierre, ou une espèce de craye qui s'appelle Hoa ché, dont les Médecins Chinois font une espèce de tizanne. . . . Les ouvriers en porcelaine se sont avisez d'employer cette même pierre à la place du kaolin. Peut être que tel endroit de l'Europe, où l'on ne trouvera point de kaolin, fournira la pierre Hoa ché! Elle se nomme Hoa, parce qu'elle est glatineuse, et qu'elle approche en quelque sorte du savon.' He goes on to state that the porcelain made from 'Hoa ché' is scarcer and more expensive than ordinary china and has an extremely fine grain.

Shortly after this, Dr. J. Woodward described steatites, white with veins of red, at the Lizard.[2] Judging from his description he must have considered that he had found the mineral described by D'Entrecolles.[3] He states that this soaprock had already been used in 'several trials that have been lately made for the baking and making this earth into pots, I am satisfied that 'tis not much inferior to that of which porcelain is made, and that the pots formed of it would be near as fine did our potters understand the ordering and management of it so well as the Chinese do'.

Soapstone, like the Chinese 'Hoa ché', could even be used as a medicine in the manufacture of Epsom salts,[4] and the porcelain body made from soapstone at Bristol, Worcester and the Chaffers' Liverpool factory had an extremely fine grain.

The first direct evidence of the use of soaprock in porcelain was at Benjamin Lund's china factory in the Redcliffe area of Bristol.[5] A licence dated 7th March, 1748/9, was granted to Lund to mine at least twenty tons a year with dues of ten shillings a ton for a term of twenty-one years.[6] Dr. Pocock visited the Lizard in October 1750 to see the soaprock mine and noted that the Bristol Porcelain Company was then paying £5 a ton for the mineral, 'being so dear', he adds, 'it must be much better than pipe clay.'

Benjamin Lund was a Quaker and, like Edward Heylyn of the

---

[1] For the most easily available English translation see William Burton, *Porcelain its Nature, Art and Manufacture*, London, 1906, pp. 84–122.

[2] J. Woodward, M.D., *A catalogue of English fossils*, Posthumous publication, London, 1729, vol. 1, Part 1, p. 6.

[3] There appears to be no magnesium in Chinese 'soft-paste' blue and white. Sir Harry Garner, *Oriental Blue and White*, London, 1954, p. 51.

[4] C. A. Johns, *A Week at the Lizard*, 1848, p. 125.

[5] Soapstone had been used in the late bronze and early iron age in Shetland in the clay mix to make crude earthenware pots. J. R. C. Hamilton, *Excavations at Jarlshof*, Shetland, H.M.S.O., 1956.

[6] E. Morton Nance, 'Soaprock licences', *Trans. E.C.C.*, 1935, No. 3, p. 73.

Bow factory, a copper-merchant.[1] He acquired Bristol premises in October 1738, where he erected a workhouse for making brass.[2] Lund may possibly have discovered the properties of soapstone on one of his journeys into Cornwall in search of copper ore before he set up his china factory. Mr. Toppin has shown that Lund together with William Miller, a grocer and banker, began making soapstone porcelain in Bristol at a glasshouse which had previously been worked by William Lowdin.[3] The lease of the premises had been offered for sale by auction on 27th June, 1745. The property, which consisted of several tenements, extended from Redcliffe Street to Redcliffe Backs, close to St. Mary Redcliffe Church, but Lund and Miller appear to have occupied only a part of it.

In November 1750 the Bristol china factory was advertising for young apprentices to learn the art of pottery as practised in Staffordshire, and also to learn how to paint the ware 'in the India or Roman taste'. In the same year they produced a number of white and manganese-decorated figures of Lü Tung-Pin,[4] embossed with the date 1750 and the word 'Bristol' on their bases. In July 1751 the factory was advertising wares made in imitation of foreign china, to be sold at the proprietors' warehouse in Castle Green. No ware would be sold at the manufactory itself and no person could enter the factory premises without prior permission. In January 1751/2 another warehouse had opened next to the Bell Inn in Temple Street. Imperfect ware made during the first experiments was to be sold very cheap.

The output of the Bristol factory is described in a somewhat complicated way by Dr. Pococke. 'They made two sorts of ware', he writes, 'one called stone china, which has a yellow cast, both in the ware and the glazing, that I suppose is made of pipe clay and calcin'd flint. The other they call old china that is whiter, and I suppose this is made of calcin'd flint and the soapy rock at Lizard point, which 'tis known they use; this is painted blue and somewhat like old white china of a yellowish cast, another kind is white with a bluish cast, and both called fine ornamental white china.' In this connection it is interesting

[1] Both Edward Heylyn and Benjamin Lund are mentioned in some bankruptcy proceedings of 12th August, 1745, against William Crisp, who was part owner of the Ranelagh House Gardens and Amphitheatre (Public Record Office, B.1 19, fol. 70).

[2] On the north bank of the river Avon between Hooper's glasshouse and that of Edmund Mountjoy. Lund was the son of a Hammersmith carpenter of the same christian name. He first became bankrupt on 8th December, 1741 (C54/5922/7). His will was proved on 25th February, 1768 (in Somerset House, P.C.C. 70, Secker).

[3] *Trans. E.C.C.*, vol. 3, part 3, p. 129.

[4] These figures seem to have been moulded directly from Fukien porcelain originals.

to compare the very different glaze colours of the three Bristol Lü Tung-Pin figures as well as that of the 'Bristol'-marked sauce boats, both blue and white and enamelled, in the Victoria and Albert Museum.

The documentary 'Bristol'-marked blue and white sauce boats occur in at least three differently moulded patterns (1).[1] They are all fairly long and shallow with widely curved handles and large curled thumb rests. 'Bristol'-marked blue and white cream boats are known in two shapes, a small fluted type on a short four-footed base (2) and a larger hexagonal upright shape found in two differently moulded versions (3).[2] The rococo moulded decoration is sometimes completely different on the two sides of these boats, a feature also found on early Worcester examples. The handles are angled and surmounted by a thumb rest. There are no known Bristol blue and white counterparts of the 'beautiful white sauce boats, adorned with reliefs of festoons which sell for sixteen shillings a pair',[3] although less ornate, high-footed sauce boats were among the earliest products at Worcester. The blue and white decoration on 'Bristol'-marked pieces is fairly limited in subject range; most pieces were decorated by a person who had a fondness for painting a group of three large dots in the middle of Chinese scenes.[4] The underglaze blue is usually dark in colour with a tinge of indigo, but some wares, possibly slightly later examples, are painted with a pale greyish blue. The decoration is nearly always considerably blurred, except in rare cases where the glaze is thinly applied. The landscapes, as on early Longton Hall blue and white, frequently include a pair of mountain peaks, simply represented by two inverted crossed 'L's, and sometimes bordered by a series of large dots (4). This motif remained popular on the earliest Worcester wares when a flagpost was often painted between the mountains. A favourite pattern includes a standing Chinese woman either pointing or holding a bunch of flowers or a fan. Rocks are often painted with spiral lines resembling large snail shells and they are covered with tall weeds like horse tails. Flower sprays, a broad leaf between two thin ones, a scallop

[1] An example in the Worcester Works Museum illustrated F. S. MacKenna, *Worcester Porcelain*, Leigh-on-Sea 1950, Plate 2E.

[2] W. J. Pountney, *Old Bristol Potteries*, Bristol, 1920, Plate XLVIII.

[3] Dr. Pococke's letter dated 2nd November, 1750 (Add. M.S. No. 15,800 British Museum). A number of undecorated and enamel-painted examples correspond to Pocock's description, the enamel-painted sauce boats having been either mostly or all decorated later.

[4] The same mannerism by a different hand is found occasionally on Worcester wares and derives from the Chinese.

(1) *Plates* 20B, C; (2) *Plate* 21A; (3) *Plate* 21D; (4) *Plate* 20B.

shell and precious objects decorate the inner sides of sauce boats and cream boats. Broad blue comma-shaped marks are usually painted on either side of handle terminals, presumably to disguise small fire-cracks which are a common feature. These comma marks are also found on early Worcester mugs and coffee cans, and occasionally on wares from other factories, including Bow, Plymouth, Reid's Liverpool and Lowestoft; in the latter case thin strokes were more often used.

It is possible to separate the small class of blue and white soft paste Bristol porcelain from early Worcester wares by comparing them with the marked sauce boats and cream boats. However, any such differentiation must be made with caution as there was a direct continuity between the two factories. A magnificent mug with spreading base and a strong 'silver-shape' handle is painted in the typical blurred, dark indigo blue (1). Some of the footring has broken off, probably on removal from the sagger after firing, and the broken surface shows dark specks of impurities in the paste. A pair of globular mugs (2), with cylindrical necks after pottery examples, are painted by the same hand as that on the previous mug. A stylized flower bud and stem (or possibly it is a peacock's feather) is painted on the handles; this Chinese motif is occasionally found on early Bow as well as on the strange group of wares provisionally classed as Reid's Liverpool. A shallow, thickly potted meat-paste dish has the characteristic blurred painting and a fire crack in the centre of it (3). A long, shallow sauce boat with a widely curved handle and prominent thumb rest is finely moulded on the outside with a pagoda half hidden by a rock and inside is the typical blurred Bristol painting depicting flower sprays with a scroll and diaper border and a large leaf between two smaller ones.[1] Another sauce boat with simply moulded reserves decorated by the 'three-dot' painter has an angled 'silver-shape' handle with a curved thumb rest (4). Similar handles are found on a pair of thickly potted coffee cans also painted by the 'three-dot' painter (5). The 'three-dot' painter also decorated the small moulded baskets with thin arched handles (6), now rarely accompanied by a fragile spoon formed somewhat like an acorn cup on a twig. There are a number of three-pointed ivy-leaf pickle trays decorated with the pointing woman, and finely moulded with veins underneath. By artificial light the translucency of these pickle trays varies considerably from pale bluish green, which is almost white in the thinner parts, to a greenish yellow or even a straw colour.

[1] Victoria and Albert Museum, C 461–1924.

(1) *Plate* 22A; (2) *Plate* 22C; (3) *Plate* 21C; (4) *Plate* 20A; (5) *Plate* 22B; (6) *Plate* 21B.

ENGLISH BLUE AND WHITE PORCELAIN

The body of Bristol soft-paste porcelain has a fairly hard-looking fine-grained and compact structure, but broken surfaces often show dark specks of impurities. Small firing cracks are common, especially round handle terminals and the raised bosses which offset the handles from the body, and also along mould junction lines. The thicker wares are usually only moderately translucent, frequently showing a bluish green colour by artificial light, but occasionally the translucency is whitish as of the small, fluted, 'Bristol'-marked cream boat (I), or even straw-coloured as the pickle trays mentioned above. There is none of the typical so-called 'glaze shrinkage'[1] on bases as found on most Worcester wares after 1755. The well-fitting, impervious glaze is finely pitted and physically indistinguishable from that used at Worcester, but it tends to be slightly more tinted with cobalt giving a starchy appearance, and areas of black spotting are generally more noticeable. Some green-tinted pooling of the glaze occurs on the bases of large vessels and the glaze is often more thickly applied than at Worcester. Painters' marks in underglaze blue do not occur on these early wares, but some pieces, including a few with the word 'Bristol' or 'Bristoll' embossed, are marked with an incised cross or nick, which are considered to be tally marks used by potters, especially handlers or turners. A few moulded pieces have an incised 'P' and it is tempting to attribute these wares to Robert Podmore, who is thought to have worked at Bristol before joining Dr. Wall at Worcester. A chemical analysis of a sauce boat[2] painted by the 'three-dot' painter shows that the body contains about 40 per cent soapstone, about 8 per cent lead oxide and 2 per cent phosphoric acid. This shows a higher percentage of phosphate and much more lead than is present in any early Worcester wares that have so far been tested.

On 4th June, 1751, a new manufactory of 'earthenware . . . under the denomination of Worcester Porcelain', was founded at Worcester in the grounds of Warmstry House on the banks of the Severn near St. Andrew's Church.[3] The original partnership deeds described the factory as 'the Worcester Tonquin Manufacture', but this name does not appear to have been used to any extent afterwards. The partnership deed states that the 'new Manufacture of earthenware has been

[1] Due to wiping off a narrow margin of glaze in the angle formed by the foot-ring and the base before the glost firing to prevent pooling.

[2] Eccles & Rackham, *Analysed Specimens of English Porcelain*, London, 1922, No. 24, p. 34. Compare this analysis with that of an early Worcester mug, No. 25.

[3] There is an illustration of the factory in the *Gentleman's Magazine*, vol. XXII, 1752, p. 348.

(I) *Plate* 21A.

invented' by John Wall[1] (1708–76) and William Davis[2] (1710–91). 'The full and whole art and secret thereof' was to be written down and put in a box having three different locks. Robert Podmore and John Lyes, who had for some time been employed by the inventors in the said manufacture were to receive special payments to ensure their fidelity.[3] If the venture proved to be a success the partners were to apply for a patent.[4] Fifteen partners are mentioned and by February 1752 there were sixteen partners; these are listed by Mr. Toppin.[5] They included two physicians, one being the famous Dr. Wall, two apothecaries, a goldsmith and a London printer Edward Cave, who owned the *Gentleman's Magazine*. Mr. Toppin discovered important information about the beginning of the Worcester factory in some bankruptcy proceedings.[6] These relate that the Worcester partners had 'established a porcelain manufactory in imitation of Dresden ware in the city of Worcester by way of partnership, and that a porcelain manufactory in imitation of East India china ware[7] was established in or near the city of Bristol by William Miller and Benjamin Lund, which was then generally approved, and that the said partners on considering the state and condition of the said Bristol manufactory had resolved it would be their interest either to procure a union of the said Worcester and Bristol porcelain companies or purchase of the said Miller and Lund their works or manufactory at Bristol and the process thereof and to discontinue the same there, and carry on by the said company at Worcester a manufactory of earthenwares of both China and Dresden . . .'. Consequently the partners had arranged for one of their number, Richard Holdship,[8] a Quaker, to purchase from the Bristol proprietors their stock, utensils and

[1] Eminent physician, stained-glass designer and talented artist whose classical drawings were engraved by Grignion and Ravenet.

[2] A Worcester apothecary and manager of the Worcester china factory.

[3] Podmore and Lyes may have been first at Bristol and if so Wall and Davis would have been able to make full use of their knowledge of the process used by Lund in Bristol.

[4] None was ever granted, possibly because it was left too late before applying and by that time other manufacturers were using a soapstone body.

[5] *Trans. E.C.C.*, vol. 3, part 3, p. 132. There were altogether thirty-seven proprietors between 1751 and 1783 (Toppin, personal communication).

[6] *Trans E.C.C.*, vol. 3, part 3, 1954, pp. 129–40.

[7] 'Dresden ware' and 'East India China' possibly refer to enamelled wares and blue and white respectively. There is very little evidence to show that enamelled wares were produced at Lund's factory in any quantity and the majority of pieces described as such in the past seem to have been made at Worcester or decorated there.

[8] A glover, but described as a 'china maker' in an agreement dated 1764 with Mr. Dewsbury of Derby. The lease of Warmstry was granted to Richard Holdship on 16th May, 1751, and later, with his brother Josiah, he acquired the freehold. He left Worcester about two years before his bankruptcy in 1761 (Public Record Office, B4 22649, 26 May, 1761, a bankruptcy commission against Richard Hold-

effects, as well as their actual process of manufacture on 21st February, 1752. The Bristol proprietors were not to continue to make porcelain or to disclose the secret process to anyone else. Richard Holdship bought the soaprock rights from Lund and in all spent £1,700 of his own money. The other Worcester proprietors agreed to purchase from Richard Holdship 20 tons per annum at least of soapy rock for 20 years at £18 per ton, to be back paid from Christmas 1751. If any soaprock was left over after Worcester had used all they wanted, Holdship was then at liberty to let Lund have the remaining amount for executing a scheme of his own unless the company should within twelve months carry out this scheme themselves. In some recently discovered bankruptcy proceedings dated 23rd February, 1753,[1] the author found that Benjamin Lund is described as a 'china maker now of the City of Worcester'. From this it appears that Benjamin Lund had been supervising the initial developments at the Worcester factory. No wonder then that Bristol soft paste and early Worcester are difficult to separate.

There was an early experimental period from 1751 to about 1755, and a second short period notable for fine painting from 1755 to about 1760,[2] before the Worcester output became standardized as regards quality, shapes and patterns. This standard was maintained almost completely unaltered, except for the increased use of transfer printing, until the factory was taken over in 1783 by Thomas Flight. It is this later marked uniformity that has sometimes led collectors to reject as Worcester some of the early wares in spite of their close similarity to the even earlier soft-paste Bristol, and the consistent development in potting shapes and decoration which relates them to Bristol porcelain.

Very few dated blue and white pieces have survived from the first twenty years at Worcester, although there are a number of examples after 1770. The known blue and white examples are as follows:

A large white moulded tureen dated 1751 in underglaze blue (owner unknown)[3]

A crudely decorated cup inscribed 'T.B. 1753' (British Museum (1)[4]

ship late of the city of Worcester, Glover. Creditor William Barnes of the City of Worcester, Mercer).

[1] Public Record Office, C54,5922.

[2] Some of the finest enamel painting was also done during this period. A number of these enamelled pieces are inscribed with dates from 1757 onwards such as the Lord and Lady Sandys mug, in the British Museum, dated 1759. These documentary coloured wares are useful in helping to date blue and white of similar shapes.

[3] R. W. Binns, *A Century of Potting*, 1877, 2nd edition, p. 23. Possibly a Bristol piece and the prototype of later Worcester examples.

[4] Plate 26B shows a cup decorated by the same hand with the same pattern.

(1) *Plate* 26B (3).

A miniature sugar-bowl, cover and stand inscribed 'C.S. 1758'[1] (from the F. Hurlbutt collection). *The prunus-root pattern*

A cup and saucer inscribed 'W.M. 1766', crescent marked (British Museum). *The blue rock pattern*

An octagonal tea caddy with flower knob on cover inscribed 'Fine Tea 1766' (owner unknown)

A mug inscribed 'Peter Taylor 1769'[2] (Worcester Works Museum)

A number of mugs and coffee cans with dates between 1770 and 1776, one bearing the crest of the Foresters' Company and inscribed 'Saml. Sheriff in Upton 1771' (owner unknown). One of four of these late-dated pieces in the Worcester Works Museum, a mug dated 1776, shows St. George and the Dragon[3]

Three basic potting methods were used at Worcester during the early phase (from 1751 to about 1755), press-moulding, slip-moulding (sometimes called slip-casting), and throwing; any of these methods could be followed by turning and fettling. Bristol moulds were often re-used for moulded wares; consequently it is sometimes difficult to be certain whether to attribute to Worcester or Bristol the capacious, high-footed sauce boats with broad, wavy, everted rims, the attractive fluted and octagonal tea wares (1), and the dainty fluted and hexagonal cream boats. However, the presence of one or more painters' marks in underglaze blue seems to indicate a Worcester origin. Early Worcester sauce boats and cream boats show a fine range of press-moulded patterns, including sprays of flowers and Chinese landscapes. Their rococo scroll reserves are further ornamented with moulded leaves, wheat ears and tendrils, flower heads and fruit, ribbons, shells, birds and cherubs' masks (2). Sauce boat and cream boat handles, as with Bristol examples, usually have prominent curled thumb rests on widely curved or almost square-angled handles. In the majority of cases raised moulded bosses, often rosette shaped, offset the handles from the body. Cos-lettuce leaf sauce boats with arched-over crabstock handles are common in enamel colours but very rare in blue and white (3). Two-handled sauce boats with thumb rests sometimes moulded as monkey heads are amongst the most elegant Worcester creations dating from about 1755 (4). Blue and white salts in the shape of a nautilus shell are even more uncommon than coloured

---

[1] Made for Charlotte Sheriff (F. S. MacKenna, *Worcester Porcelain*, Leigh-on-Sea, 1950, Plate 12).

[2] R. W. Binns, *Catalogue of Worcester Porcelain*, 1884, p. 91, No. 144.

[3] A similar mug with the same decoration, in the Willett Collection Brighton, No. 1404, is inscribed 'A. DUNN Birmingham 1776'.

---

(1) *Plates* 23A, B; (2) *Plate* 28A; (3) *Plate* 33A; (4) *Plate* 30B.

examples. Fine teapots have distinctive knobs which are often mushroom-shaped and crowned with a raised ring (1) or else like an inverted spinning top. A rustic twig knob is found on an unusual teapot (2) of about 1755 shaped like a watering can. Lobed, fluted, ribbed, panelled and basket moulded cups and saucers are matched by cream jugs with silver-shape rococo handles. Beautifully potted eight-sided tea wares have as much charm as their coloured and pencilled counterparts. Twelve-sided tea bowls and saucers in blue and white are rarer than enamelled examples in the *famille verte* style. Some of the moulded tea wares are almost of egg-shell thinness, especially those dating from about 1755, with panels and rococo reserves in which are painted miniature fishing scenes. There are a few massive early tureens of over fourteen inches in length and a large dish or tureen stand (3)[1] from the end of the early period, about 1755. This fine stand has a moulded border with a lizard, birds, fishes and flowers surrounding an elaborately painted Chinese scene. Cornucopiae occur in a variety of moulded patterns and painted designs, sometimes with as many as four painters' marks in underglaze blue. There are three known porringers or bleeding bowls with wide embossed handles, two at the Worcester factory museum and one in the Victoria and Albert Museum, two of which are painted in an unusual primitive style (4). However, most of the blue and white designs on moulded wares are Chinese fishing scenes or floral patterns with no very distinctive features apart from a fondness for eruptive rock formations.

The Worcester paste does not seem to have been readily slip-moulded, since this method was not used to any extent after the early period. However, there is documentary evidence of the use of slip-moulding for teapot spouts up till at least 1771.[2] At Bristol slip-moulding was the common practice for fluted and lobed cups, and, in the early period, the Worcester factory produced a large number of fluted straight-sided coffee cans and a few thinly potted, ribbed and fluted teawares by the same method. Tall blue and white lobed cups with ornate silver shaped handles (5), although rare at Worcester, were also probably slip-moulded.

[1] Some slightly later examples exist which are decorated with coloured enamels and Hancock's transfers of classical ruins. See *Catalogue of the Schreiber Collection*, vol. 1, 1915, Plate 59.
[2] Diary of Captain Joseph Roche, R.M., *Notes and Queries*, 12th Series, No. 59, February 1917, p. 106.

(1) *Plate* 32A; (2) *Plate* 28C; (3) *Plate* 30A;
(4) *Plate* 25B; (5) *Plate* 23A.

Bristol and early Worcester porcelain bearing incised nicks or crosses on the base or footring has been nick-named the 'Scratch Cross' group, a term which fails to differentiate between the two factories and caused confusion when it was discovered that other factories such as Bow and Chaffers' Liverpool also used similar incised tally marks. It seems that on Bristol pieces these marks are confined to a small group of moulded wares such as sauce boats and small baskets (1); but probably even fewer early Worcester moulded pieces such as a superb octagonal bowl (2),[1] bear these incised nicks or crosses. However, the Worcester factory produced a large output of early thrown and turned wares, the majority of which, especially those with handles, have an incised cross or a nick either on the base or on the inner side of the footring, or an incised circle in the centre of the base.[2] Incised marks of this type occur either singly or in combination, often together with underglaze-blue painters' marks. Early Worcester thrown and turned wares are stylistically different from Bristol wares and they have simple practical shapes and clean lines. They tend to be more elegant than contemporary Bow examples; in fact they were unsurpassed by any other English blue and white. The blue decoration is much better controlled than that on Bristol soft paste and is generally a fine pale colour with a definite grey tinge, best demonstrated by comparison with the royal blue colour used on early Bow. Although some examples are now rather scarce, it is possible to separate at least ten standard, imitation Chinese patterns in blue and white:

1. A scene including two swimming ducks and an arched bridge between two islands. *The swimming ducks pattern*

2. A zig-zag paling fence flanked on one side by a peony plant and on the other by an upright rock, from which grows a flowering prunus.[3] *The zig-zag fence pattern*

3. A fence enclosing tall bamboo trees next to a group of upright rocks like posts and an island formed of regular humped boulders topped by a Chinese house (3).[4] *The plantation pattern*

4. One or two sloping fences, one of which is next to a gnarled

---

[1] Cf. H. R. Marshall, *Coloured Worcester Porcelain*, Newport Mon. 1954, Plate 3, No. 47.

[2] Incised marks are sometimes found on Worcester wares which date from the seventeen sixties or later, but the incised circle, a mark made by the turner, is much more common on Caughley. It has been previously overlooked that the alchemists' sign for talc or soapstone is a saltire cross (*Sloane M.S.* 174, British Museum).

[3] F. A. Barrett, *Worcester Porcelain*, London, 1953, Plate 44.

[4] This pattern was used as a transfer print later.

---

(1) *Plate* 21B; (2) *Plate* 23C; (3) *Plates* 24A, C.

willow tree with arched roots. A plant with bent leaves, two mountain peaks with a flag post between them and sometimes a tall Chinese woman and a man fishing from a boat (1). *The willow-root pattern*

5. A short, angled fence abutting onto a rock with circular holes. Out of the rock grows a twisted peony plant. A long-tailed bird on a rush with bent leaves and one or more flying insects (2). *The warbler pattern*.

6. Early examples of the popular prunus-root pattern (3). *The prunus-root pattern*

7. A cormorant on a rock; a man fishing from a boat and a chrysanthemum between two broad paired leaves (4). *The cormorant pattern*

8. A woman playing a side drum followed by a male dancer with a tambourine in a steeply sloping landscape with two mountains (5). *The tambourine pattern*

9. A high rocky island with a house and a willow tree, connected to a smaller island by a bridge. On the bridge is a man with a fishing rod; another man is fishing from a boat (6)

10. An elaborate scene including an ornamental fence, islands, pagodas, conifers, fishermen in boats and a crescent moon facing upwards (7).

Fragments of two of the above patterns, the 'willow-root' and the 'cormorant,' Nos. 4 and 7, were recently found on the Worcester factory site when the area was cleared for development.

Besides these ten patterns there are a number of rare examples all imitating Chinese scenes, some of which appear to be painted by inexperienced workmen (8), for example, the crudely painted coffee cup in the British Museum inscribed T.B. and dated 1753. Another pattern which was used more frequently at Bow, shows an island with a small house and fir trees looking like battle-ship turrets. It is unusual to find these patterns on contemporary moulded pieces as most of them are not easily placed in small reserves. However, a crisply moulded sauce boat in the Victoria and Albert Museum is painted with the 'plantation' pattern, number three listed above, and a pedestal-footed sauce boat bears part of the elaborate tenth pattern.[1] These Chinese patterns are occasionally found with their outlines made more definite by over-painting with iron red; and the colour contrast

[1] Victoria and Albert Museum, Nos. C563–1924 and C827–1925.

(1) *Plates* 26A, 27C; (2) *Plate* 24B. (3) *Plate* 28C (1);
(4) *Plate* 26C; (5) *Plate* 29A; (6) *Plate* 25A;
(7) *Plates* 27B, 29C; (8) *Plate* 26B.

increased by the addition of an overglaze green wash. One sketchy design of a Chinaman on a humped bridge between two romantic tree covered islands is always found over-painted with iron red.[1]

Some mugs and coffee cans have a slightly flared lip and a spreading base which is neatly turned and countersunk underneath. Other mugs have either straight sides or low-set bulbous shapes; both are deeply grooved or waisted just above a small but robust spreading base. A coloured example with typical features and a 'scratch cross' mark is inscribed with the date 1754.[2] Handles are either press-moulded or formed from lengths of clay extruded from a dod box as described by Captain Roche.[3] They are either broadly grooved or widely ribbed, or else D-shaped in cross section, being flattened on the inner side. The lower terminals are usually curved slightly outwards from the lower attachment to the body and are cut off abruptly at right angles; on rare occasions this curve is filled in by a moulded head (1). Large jugs may have an attractive moulded acanthus leaf spray[4] or a mask of a benign aged man on the outside of the lip (2). The mask is usually asymmetrical, the right eye being a little larger than the left one. A similar mask was used throughout the eighteenth century at Worcester and can be compared with the sardonic, grimacing mask used at Caughley, the village simpleton at Lowestoft and the youthful mask at Liverpool. Jugs and coffee pots have neat, practical handles with thumb rests and rounded or curled lower terminals.

The simple elegance of these wares is seen to advantage in the bottles (3), coffee pots, mustard pots (4), finger bowls and stands (5), potted-meat and butter dishes (6). Massive inkwells are bigger and better potted than their counterparts from Bow. Foremost among them all, however, the superb bowls come nearest to perfection. A few early examples decorated with the 'prunus-root', No. 6, have notched rims and full rounded sides. Their footrings are either fairly slender and somewhat undercut or of a broad triangular cross-section. Another attractive type of bowl also with the 'prunus-root' pattern has steeply sloping sides and a wide flat footring. On the other hand small coffee cups have less pleasing proportions, being too thinly potted for their thick, grooved handles. These handles which form

---

[1] *Catalogue of the Herbert Allen Collection*, London, 1917, Plate 8, No. 26.
[2] Dr. H. E. Rhodes, *Trans E.P.C.*, vol. 3, 1931, p. 82.
[3] *Notes and Queries*, 12th series, no. 59, 1917, p. 106.
[4] F. A. Barrett, *Worcester Porcelain*, London, 1953, Plate 44. These fine jugs have sometimes been wrongly described as Liverpool.

---

(1) *Plate* 26A; (2) *Plate* 24A; (3) *Plates* 27B, C; (4) *Plate* 25A; (5) *Plate* 26C; (6) *Plate* 26C.

steeply rising loops are also a typical feature of coffee cans and cream jugs. Footrings on cups and cans are very shallow and often undercut, although some larger coffee cups and the beautiful flared chocolate cups of $3\frac{1}{4}$ inches high have taller footrings of a triangular cross-section. The latter have rounded handles which are slender and flattened on the inner side. Tea bowls and saucers are thinly potted with small rounded, or nearly straight-sided footrings. Cream jugs are uncommon, they have a lip like a sparrow's beak, a long neck and a grooved foot. Teapots have a simple globular shape with a plain roll handle (1) and four or more holes leading to the spout. Large punch pots of nearly three and a half pints capacity have curled thumb rests on their massive handles. Rare circular plates with wide rims and countersunk bases (2) and thickly potted octagonal dishes (3) are, because of their shapes, often mistaken for Bow. An immense octagonal vase and cover (4), of about 1753, is the only known example of this type to have survived from the early period at Worcester.

Many of the blue and white decorator's mannerisms continue those that had been developed at Bristol. Spouts are decorated with Chinese precious objects, bare twigs and large flat leaves; slight scroll or spiral patterns are found on the backs of handles. Blue comma-like marks distract attention from small fire cracks at the handle terminals of mugs and coffee cans. The majority of blue and white designs have clusters of little blue dots scattered over rock, root and tree surfaces. Occasionally three large dots appear in landscapes, but not by the same hand as those on Bristol soft paste. Narrow borders are usually found inside bowls, cups and coffee cans and on the outside of mugs and jugs. Three painted borders were favoured: a diaper and flower-head arrangement, a zig-zag basket-weave and a zig-zag line between flower heads.

Underglaze-blue painters' marks on early wares, are notable for their variety and complexity. Some are so intricate and carefully drawn as to suggest a double function; to identify the painter and to imitate Chinese calligraphy. It is just possible that the three variants of the TF monogram *F* *T* *F* , besides representing a Chinese symbol and indicating different workmen, may also serve the purpose of a factory mark for the Tonquin factory. Rare painters' marks include a large 'A', a mark like a short-bladed dagger, and another like a key. The initials *fh* are found on some of the finely decorated pieces. In contrast one or two arrows through an annulus, three parallel lines, three dots, and a 'P' are fairly common marks. Painters' marks occur on bases and under teapot covers, but are also

---

(1) *Plate* 29; (2) *Plate* 25c; (3) *Plate* 28B; (4) *Plate* 27A.

found beneath handles, on the inside of footrings, inside sauce and cream boats and finger bowls and occasionally on the knobs of teapots.

Even in the early period, from 1751 to about 1755, Worcester had a good quality paste and clear, inpervious glaze in keeping with the neat potting and fine moulding. The occasional presence of glazed-over chips caused by slight damage in the biscuit state is a reminder that production was still hazardous. The glaze is not wiped clear of the footring, leaving a small glaze-free margin[1] as often or as neatly as on typical later Worcester examples. However, there is little or no glaze pooling and sometimes a minute groove can be seen inside footrings where a fettling tool has been used to get rid of excess glaze before firing; a method which was more frequently used at Lowestoft, and at Liverpool by Christian. The translucency by artificial light varies from a blue-green to a yellowish green. A chemical analysis of a 'scratch-cross' type mug[2] gives about 30 per cent of soapstone and 0·67 per cent phosphoric acid.

A few early tea wares, mugs, sauce boats and pickle trays of the type made up till about 1755 are decorated with attractive black or puce-coloured transfer prints with raised lines, the so-called 'smoky primitives'. The Battersea enamel factory, founded in 1753, had first used a number of these patterns on enamels. Some of them were designed by Boitard and engraved on copper by Hancock in 1754[3] with the original intention, it seems, of using them for book plates.[4] Their appearance on Worcester porcelain of 1754 to 1755 suggests that the Worcester factory was able to obtain some of Hancock's copper plates and to use them for initial trials in the then highly secret process of overglaze transfer-printing.[5] It is a reasonable assumption that before Robert Hancock went to work at Worcester,[6] some of the technical difficulties of this new method had been overcome. By that time they were developing the necessary skill to produce overglaze transfers on

[1] Usually known incorrectly as 'glaze shrinkage'.

[2] Eccles and Rackham, *Analysed Specimens of English Porcelain*, London, 1922, No. 25, p. 34.

[3] Cyril Cook, 'Early Prints on Old Worcester Porcelain,' *Apollo*, August 1949.

[4] Cyril Cook, *The Life and Work of Robert Hancock*, pp. 48 and 49 and item 40. See also H. W. Hughes, *Trans. E.C.C.*, No. 3, 1935.

[5] An alternative possibility is that early Worcester was transfer printed at Battersea. Dr. Richard Pococke writing on 28th August, 1754, mentions that '. . . I went to see the china and enamel manufactury at York House, Battersea', *Travels through England of Dr. Richard Pococke*, 1888, vol. 2, p. 69.

[6] Hancock went to Worcester towards the end of 1756 and was a proprietor of the factory from 1772 to 1774. The more generally accepted view that transfer printing on Worcester porcelain did not exist until Hancock's arrival at Worcester does not explain the presence of early prints of about 1754 on early porcelain of about 1754. See also page 88 where a different style of early transfer printing is discussed, also apparently predating Hancock's arrival at Worcester.

porcelain of the superb quality of Hancock's King of Prussia designs, some of which are dated 1757. The technique of printing in under-glaze blue does not appear to have been exploited before about 1760.

From about 1755 the production of a galaxy of fine enamelled patterns tended to obscure the merits of the humble blue and white. The only examples which arouse any enthusiasm in the majority of Worcester collectors are the so-called 'eloping bride' (1) and 'quail' patterns (2),[1] on account of their comparative rarity although some of the latter are possibly of Caughley origin. Indeed, it must be admitted that a large proportion of Worcester blue and white produced after 1760, in spite of consistently good potting, has little interest for the collector, especially when transfer-printed.

The Worcester factory suffered few misfortunes compared with that at Bow, apart from a fire in October 1755.[2] The large number of proprietors proved an adequate safeguard against severe setbacks from individual bankruptcies. The factory prospered and came to rely chiefly on wholesale rather than retail trade. As early as August 1752 the *Gentleman's Magazine* published a view of the factory,[3] together with a short announcement of the sale of a great variety of Worcester ware on the following 20th December at the Worcester Music Meet-ing. The first London sale occurred in the autumn of 1755 when 300 lots were sold in a three-day sale at the Royal Exchange Coffee House.[4] The advertisement states that the proprietors 'do not send riders to vend their ware by pattern or description, but make London their only mart of sale, where the goods will be on view to the trade at London House in Aldersgate Street'.

A wholesale price list of 1755 to 1760 from the Aldersgate ware-house[5] gives some interesting items with the price per dozen. These included King's coffees at 3s. 6d.; teapots, round, fluted, panelled and octagonal in three sizes 15s. to 30s.; wash-hand-basins at 9s. 6d.; chamber pots 4s.; tart and potting pans in three sizes 15s. to 30s.; two-handled sauce boats in three sizes 24s. to 28s.; two sizes of

---

[1] Two different borders are associated with this pattern, a rounded and a pointed dentelle edge.

[2] *Aris's Birmingham Gazette*, 6th October, 1755.

[3] Signed 'J. D. delin,' and 'J. C. Sculp'. Thought to be John Davis, a Worces-ter proprietor and John Cave, brother of Edward Cave, owner of the *Gentleman's Magazine*. The factory plan shows a large yard for coal which suggests that this was the fuel used at Worcester.

[4] *General Evening Post*, No. 3375, 9th–12th August, and No. 3393, 23rd–25th September, discovered by G. Wills. Two further London Sales both in 1769 are mentioned by J. E. Nightingale.

[5] *Catalogue of Worcester Porcelain* exhibited at 30 Curzon Street, June 1959.

---

(1) *Plate* 35D; (2) *Plate* 35C.

cornucopia 2s. 3d. and 2s. 6d.; Dutch jugs two sizes 3s. 6d. and 8s.; milk jugs, round and pressed 8s. to 12s.; vine and fig leaves 4s. to 12s.; scallop shells four sizes 4s. to 12s.; high-footed sauce boats[1] three sizes 14s. to 27s. A 15 per cent discount was allowed for prompt payment. A significant omission is any mention of plates or dishes.

In January 1756 the Castle Green warehouse at Bristol advertised useful blue and white Worcester; cups and saucers at 3s. 6d. a set and quart basins at 10d. each. In 1763 the *Gentleman's Magazine* gave some further interesting and accurate information about Worcester porcelain, describing it as among those wares sold at a cheaper rate than imported porcelain. ' . . . but except Worcester they all wear brown and are subject to crack, especially the glazing, by boiling water. The Worcester has a good body, scarce inferior to that of Eastern china, it is equally tough and its glazing never cracks or scales off. But this is confined to few articles; the tea-table, indeed, it completely furnishes; and some of it is so well enamelled as to resemble the finest foreign china so that it makes up costly sets that are broken without a perceptible difference.[2] But from whatever cause this manufactury has never yet found its way to the dinner table, except perhaps in sauce boats, and toys for pickles and hors d'oeuvres. . . .'[3] Another entry in the same *Magazine* in 1764[4] states that more than two hundred hands were already employed making useful ware, the most durable in Europe. 'Some national encouragement may perhaps be wanting to bring this elegant manufactory to its utmost perfection.'

Between 1755 and 1760 some finely painted patterns were produced; their discreet charm is in complete harmony with the pale greyish blue with which they are painted. Even the boldest designs are less assertive than those done at Bow; they occur on hexagonal vases whose decoration includes tall flowering plants. The 'prunus-root' pattern remained popular, especially for mugs and tea wares and those small bulbous cups having pointed handles with rounded terminals, which are like Derby examples, though thinner. During this period there was an attempt to produce blue and white comparable in quality and design to the enamelled wares, for example the fine brush-work on a pair of vases (1). Chinese figures are especially well

[1] It is interesting to compare this price with that given by Dr. Pococke for the Bristol prototypes, see p. 36.
[2] Coloured Worcester replacements are of great interest to collectors. See H. R. Marshall, 'Notes on the Origins of Worcester Decoration', *Trans. E.C.C.*, vol. 4, part 3, 1957.
[3] Vol. XXXIII, p. 191.   [4] Vol. XXXIV, p. 144.

(1) *Plate* 32c.

drawn, such as the 'lange lijzen' decorating a jug (1). This jug has the typical slight downward tilt of the spout and a well potted practical shape, both of which derive from the early period. Some good quality tea wares are painted with Chinese figures and flowers in alternate panels (2), and a very rare pattern includes a brigand on a horse carrying a flag inscribed 'P C' (3). 'The man waving at birds' in blue and white is an attractive alternative to the better known polychrome version. Bird painting is now at its best as can be seen on an exceptional tureen (4) of 1755, or even earlier, and on a vase (5), part of a garniture, which has a counterpart in enamel colours. Another attractive design with a scroll and flower-head border includes a daffodil, and a stork standing on one leg on a lobed water-lily leaf. Flowers painted in the Meissen style, such as roses, tulips and honeysuckle are found on sauce boats and leaf-shaped pickle trays and also on tea wares, such as the sugar bowls with finely modelled bud and leaf knobs. Landscapes include two outstanding designs, the 'landslide' and 'gazebo' (6) patterns: the former consists of a willow tree with branches hanging down like aerial roots, a chrysanthemum between two broad leaves[1] and a very steeply sloping scene often running down beside the handle (7).[2] The latter landscape depicts a gazebo perched high up in the cleft of a rock, a woman by a house and a man punting. A unique bowl (8) shows a finely painted tree in a panorama including a European harbour scene. Powder-blue decorated pieces, produced from about 1760, lack the richness of their Bow counterparts (9). However, no other European factory was able to equal the Worcester 'cracked ice' patterns scattered with prunus flowers. The somewhat uncommon Worcester version of the 'dragon' pattern shows a more etherial monster than at Bow. Blue and white knife and fork handles are known in three different designs, and egg cups often with diaper and flowerhead borders are found in two shapes, one more cupped than the other.

Moulded wares include fine pedestal cream boats with scalloped sides, the handle moulded as a lamprey and under the lip a pair of intertwined dolphins, a trident and a paddle (10).[3] Moulded hexagonal cream boats are often painted with the 'captive bird' pattern (11). A few barrel cream jugs have silver-shape handles with a short terminal

[1] Similar to the flower in the scratch cross 'Cormorant' pattern, no. 7.
[2] Plymouth also used this pattern.
[3] A crudely moulded version was made at Liverpool.

(1) *Plate* 31c; (2) *Plate* 35B; (3) *Plate* 35A; (4) *Plate* 31A; (5) *Plate* 31B; (6) *Plate* 34B; (7) *Plate* 29B; (8) *Plate* 33c; (9) *Plate* 36A; (10) *Plate* 34A; (11) *Plate* 32B.

tag (1). Pickle trays and asparagus butter boats are found in a variety of leaf patterns, many of them have three small tri-lobed leaves as feet, others with cupped sides have rustic handles and fine acanthus leaf moulding. Among the silver-shape sauce boats are some with fluted sides and others have embossed reserves (2). Tea wares with the 'waved' or 'feather' moulding are usually painted with flower sprays and a floral border. Ribbed trembleuse cups and saucers are copied from St. Cloud examples.

The shapes are now those most typical of the Worcester factory and blue and white and coloured pieces are still finished with equal care. Mug handles tend to be thinly potted and of a plain grooved type or moulded with a central raised rib. Cup handles are usually simply grooved although more ornate silver-shape examples occur, such as one with side grooving, a central node and a thumb rest.[1] Well-formed flower and bud knobs were popular on tea wares. A large acorn knob on covered jars has a counterpart in Tournai blue and white porcelain. The slim footrings of cups are sometimes slightly angled as if they had buckled in firing. A neat glaze-free margin is usually present inside footrings. Little clusters of dark brown or black specks are often found, especially on bases, due to minute particles of dust in small craters formed by burst bubbles where the glaze is thick. The translucency by artificial light shows various shades of green.

The numerous painters' marks are now less elaborate. The 'eloping bride' pattern (3) has its own special imitation Chinese mark consisting of an arrangement of parallel lines at right angles to each other. The crossed swords mark of the Meissen factory is occasionally used. A unique christening can from the Dyson Perrins collection has a cypher of W.P.C. on the base and is inscribed round the sides 'I will drink up the liquor the cup is but small and here's a good health unto Edmund Wall'.

As late as December 1761 the Worcester factory was advertising for more blue and white painters;[2] although at about that time underglaze-blue transfer-printing was introduced. Binns states that in 1770 because of the increasing use of transfers there was a serious strike amongst the artists, with the result that many of them left the factory.[3]

During the last period, 1760–83, the painted patterns include the

[1] S. Fisher, *English Blue and White*, London, 1947, Plate 22.
[2] *General Evening Post*, No. 4394, 10th–12th December, 1761, discovered by G. Wills.
[3] W. M. Binns, *First Century of English Porcelain*, 1906, p. 90. About this time the Plymouth factory was advertising in *Berrow's Worcester Journal*, 22nd

(1) *Plate* 34c; (2) *Plate* 33B; (3) *Plate* 35D.

'Chantilly sprig' depicting a gillyflower which is seen at its best on a fine dolphin centre-piece (1).[1] The so-called 'immortelle', Meissen 'onion' or 'Copenhagen' pattern[2] is found on ribbed wares, the blue often running in the moulded furrows and deeply tinting the glaze. A 'gatehouse' design with a zig-zag fence, which was also used at Longton Hall, is found on tall thickly potted cups with a simple roll handle whose lower terminal runs down the side of the cup. A more attractive pattern is of a bird perched on a ring beside a table on which is a vase and a leaf. The cup and saucer in the British Museum inscribed 1766 bears the 'blue rock' pattern which shows a number of circular rocks and a house on an island next to a fan-shaped cliff.[3] One of the most frequent designs has as its centre a stylized peony flower with a scroll and pine-cone border.[4]

The earliest blue and white transfer printed pieces (there were none before about 1759) include the rare Queen Charlotte mug at Cardiff and the King George III Coronation mug,[5] and a saucer with the equally rare 'teaparty'.[6] By contrast the printed version of the 'plantation' pattern is common on tea wares. Flower sprays derived from prints in the *Ladies' Amusement* decorate a large teapot at Pembroke College, Oxford, said to have been owned by Dr. Johnson. Numerous fruit and flower sprays sometimes including a pine cone were produced from the late 1760's. At their best these floral designs are pleasing enough on the fine crocus pots (2), salad dishes, cabbage-leaf jugs and the rare broth (3) and rice bowls (4), although they are used with less artistry on spittoons and chamber pots. It is frequently difficult to distinguish the later pieces from those made at Caughley. Painted cell borders are common, especially in conjunction with transfer prints. They are even found on the small eye baths and fragile mustard-spoons. The colour of the underglaze blue, both for painted and transfer patterns, is usually darker than that used earlier at Worcester.

February, 1770, for 'a number of sober, ingenious artists capable of painting in enamel or blue'. The engagement of Worcester underglaze painters at Plymouth may account for the large numbers of Worcester patterns on Plymouth wares.

[1] Also common on Caughley porcelain and it is possible that this piece may be Caughley. See p. 110.

[2] F. Severne MacKenna, *Worcester Porcelain*, Leigh-on-Sea, 1950, Plate 13, No. 26.

[3] Bow, Derby, Plymouth and Liverpool used this pattern.

[4] Also used at Bow and Lowestoft and elsewhere.

[5] *Trans E.C.C.*, vol. 5, part 2, 1961, Plate 96.

[6] Cyril Cook, *The Life and Work of Robert Hancock*, London, 1948, item 106. This blue and white example, ex Dyson Perrins, is in the Worcester Works Museum.

(1) *Plate* 37D; (2) *Plate* 34D; (3) *Plate* 37C; (4) *Plate* 37A.

The later moulded shapes include spirally fluted cream boats with steep sides and acanthus leaves at the base, sauce boats embossed with roses and aquilegia (1)[1] and small plates embossed with the rose leaf and buds of the so-called 'blind earl' pattern (2). A fine basket, complete with cover and stand, has the mark 'To' impressed on the base (3). The moulded chrysanthemum pattern on tea wares reveals its full beauty on trans-illumination. This pattern was also used, less effectively, at Caughley.

Although it is unusual to find Worcester footrings that have been ground level after firing, Mrs. Lybbe Powys, who visited the factory in 1771, noted that in one room there were workers grinding bases of vessels to make them smooth.[2] An unexplained feature of the late wares is the frequent presence of a yellow stain just inside the footring at the glaze-free margin.[3] The translucency by artificial light of most of the late pieces is a yellowish green.

After 1760 painters' marks ceased to be used and the crescent mark, the script and capital 'W' and the 'fretted square' came into favour. The crescent mark can be painted or printed and in its painted form it is used together with the square mark on some powder-blue examples. A printed version is cross-hatched on transfer-printed pieces, although this mark is much more common on Caughley.

In 1783 Thomas Flight purchased the Worcester works for £3,000 on behalf of his two sons who were jewellers. From that time the Worcester porcelain can be considered to belong more to the nineteenth than the eighteenth century. The factory received royal patronage in 1788 when George III and Queen Charlotte visited the works. In 1786 Robert Chamberlain had opened his own factory (at first a decorating establishment) about a quarter of a mile away, where the present Royal Worcester Porcelain Works now stand. In 1840 the firm of Flight, Barr and Barr, and Chamberlain and Co. amalgamated under the style of Chamberlain and Co. Later in the century the small separate Grainger factory was also incorporated. The Worcester concern had the necessary business ability to continue through the nineteenth century and even down to the present day. It is the only porcelain factory of those founded early in the eighteenth century that has managed to survive.

[1] Also found on salt glaze, Bow, hard-paste Bristol and even Chinese export ware.
[2] *Passages from the Diaries of Mrs. Philip Lybbe Powys*, London, 1899, p. 125.
[3] Also a feature of Caughley porcelain.

(1) *Plate* 36c; (2) *Plate* 36b; (3) *Plate* 37b

4

LONGTON HALL

Although Longton Hall was a much smaller and less prosperous concern than either Bow or Worcester, it has a unique importance as the first porcelain factory to be established in Staffordshire, and as the only English producer of a large quantity of useful wares made from a glassy paste. The Longton Hall estate lies to the east of the old road from Stone to Newcastle-under-Lyme, in a district long connected with iron-stone and coal workings. In the eighteenth century it was fine park land and even today, although the Hall has been demolished[1] and the trees felled, there are still some green fields and farms, in marked contrast to the crowded and industrious pottery towns nearby. Before it became a porcelain factory Longton Hall was the country home of a family of farmers and iron masters named Lane; then sometime in 1749 or 1750 a certain William Jenkinson rented the Hall from Obadiah Lane and started experiments in china making. It appears that William Jenkinson was connected with the mining industries[2] and he is described as a 'gentleman' in the Longton agreements[3] and as 'Esquire' in his will, but very little else is known about him, especially in respect to his short-lived pottery activities.

On 7th October, 1751,[4] William Jenkinson took William Nicklin and William Littler into co-partnership 'in making, burning and selling the said porcelain ware and all other sorts of wares which the said partners should agree to make or deal in and in painting, japanning, gilding and enamelling thereof'. Jenkinson had already 'obtained the art, secret or mystery of making a certain porcelain ware in imitation of china and was then carrying on a work for making the

[1] In 1939, although the large stables built by Sir John Edensor Heathcote still stand.
[2] His will dated 24th August, 1771, (at Somerset House, P.C.C., Trevor Fol. 410) mentions his patented invention of an engine for raising water out of mines.
[3] The exciting discovery of these agreements is related in *Trans. E.C.C.*, vol. 4, part 3, 1957, and further details are given in B. Watney, *Longton Hall Porcelain*, London, 1957.
[4] The date of the first agreement. The other agreements are dated 25th August, 1753, and 1st September, 1755. There are also two supplemental agreements dated 20th October, 1756, and 1st October, 1757.

same' at Longton Hall. Under the terms of the first agreement his mills, clay, materials, moulds and models were to become the joint property of the three proprietors.

One of the proprietors, William Nicklin, described as a gentleman in the agreements, was a lawyer living at Newcastle-under-Lyme. He held equal shares with William Jenkinson and his part in establishing the Longton factory must have been considerable as William Duesbury, the London enameller, uses the style 'Mr. Nicklin & Company' in his account book for goods delivered in October 1751.[1]

The third proprietor, William Littler (1725–84) was already an experienced salt-glaze potter, and in conjunction with his brother-in-law, Aaron Wedgwood, he is credited with inventing a process for producing salt glaze coloured a brilliant ultramarine. He is described in the agreements as 'late of Hanley Green . . . earth potter'. From 7th October, 1751, he was the resident manager of the Longton factory. Some time before the date of the second agreement, 25th August, 1753, he married, and from the date of the third agreement, 1st September, 1755, his wife Jane was earning a guinea a week for her part in helping to manage the factory's affairs. It is just possible that Littler worked at Limehouse with other Staffordshire potters such as Williams Tams and William Ball before he went to Longton. He could have been the arcanist to whom Dr. Richard Pococke referred in a letter to his mother dated 14th July, 1750, which he wrote after visiting the pottery villages. Dr. Pococke had previously met this potter at Limehouse, 'who promised to make the best china ware, but disagreed with his employers and has a great quantity made here for the oven. . . . He makes what he calls japann'd ware and of this he has made boxes for ladies toilets and several other things; he also makes statues of elephants, lions, birds, etc.: in their natural colour but they are of the stone ware glazed.' It is significant that the Longton Agreements contain further references to the decoration of porcelain by japanning, and that a group of salt-glaze figures, including animals and birds, are thought to have been made at Longton as the pottery counterparts of their early porcelain examples.

Under Jenkinson's influence the Longton factory seems at first to have concentrated on making a large variety of white porcelain figures whose primitive appearance and thick glaze have earned them the nickname of 'snowmen'.

These figures are almost without exception copied from Meissen, Chinese and possibly Chelsea prototypes. In many cases there are contemporary salt-glaze and lead-glaze pottery versions. The former were probably made at Longton Hall and the latter at Thomas

[1] A year later Duesbury refers to the Longton factory as 'Mr. Littler and Comp.'

Whieldon's pottery nearby. A number of wasters of these early porcelain figures have been found on the Longton site since its discovery in 1955[1] and they can now be seen at the Hanley Museum.

When Littler, a practical potter, became manager in October 1751 more attention was paid to the production of domestic wares, although even then most of them were too highly ornamental to be useful, possibly because the intractable paste would not permit itself to be easily thrown or turned. The Meissen factory had set the fashion for vegetable and fruit shapes and at Longton an attempt was made to reproduce these forms, although the relationship is not easily recognizable in their thickly potted and crudely painted plates, baskets, tureens and sauce boats. At first Littler decorated the early wares with his rich ultramarine blue. The pigment, however, ran badly in the soft glaze and only very simple, bold designs were possible. To disguise this serious defect Littler used the underglaze blue as a ground colour sometimes covering all but the under-surface and at other times forming broad borders leaving small reserves for overglaze decoration. Low-fired or possibly unfired gilding was then used to disguise the blurred edges of the borders and reserves and to pattern the blue ground as well as the reserves with sprays of flowers; it is this type of decoration with an underglaze blue ground further ornamented over the glaze that is likely to be the Longton version of 'japanning' mentioned in the agreements. The gilding has now mostly rubbed off these wares, together with any unfired painting which may have been used, leaving them with an unfinished appearance. Sometimes the reserves are painted with flowers or birds in coloured enamels, and occasionally white enamel scrolls and flower sprays embellish the blue ground. However, owing to the recent discovery that Littler opened a china decorating establishment at West Pans near Musselburgh[2] after the closure of the Longton factory in 1760, it is now difficult to be certain which of these early blue and white wares were gilded and enamelled at Longton and which were decorated later in Scotland.

Littler's blue is so distinctive that once seen it is not easily confused with anything else, except possibly Chelsea of the 'gold anchor mark' period which is occasionally found with the decoration incomplete, having only the mazarine-blue-coloured ground. In both cases the soft glaze often forms clear pools of glass and crazing occurs, but the Chelsea blue ground has a darker tint and Chelsea potting is always superior; for example, the wares are thinner and the footrings better finished.

[1] Watney, *Longton Hall Porcelain*, London, 1957, pp. 19–25.
[2] A. Lane, *Trans. E.C.C.*, vol. 5, part 2, 1961, pp. 82 to 92.

B. *Centre-piece, no mark, Longton Hall, about 1752, ht. 5¼ in.*
Birmingham City Museum.
(*See page 57*)

There are no known dated pieces of Longton porcelain, either blue and white or coloured, apart from two mugs both inscribed 1770 from William Littler's decorating establishment at West Pans. Without dated pieces the only criterion available for dividing the Longton output into consecutive periods is the study of the development of style and technique, related whenever possible to contemporary descriptions. No other English factory of the eighteenth century showed such a marked contrast between early and later wares, both in the colour of the underglaze blue and the potting characteristics. The early blue and white was either intended for special occasions,[1] or to be entirely ornamental, but the later wares were made for daily use. The change occurred after a short transitional period about the time of the second agreement (25th August, 1753); there being no further major developments in the blue and white production apart from an increasing tendency towards simplification of potting shapes from about October 1757, the date of the final supplemental agreement, till the closure of the factory in September 1760.

Nearly all the early wares are moulded, strawberry and lettuce leaves being the favourite motifs (1). The leaves are arranged radially round the rims of stands, dishes and plates so as to overlap each other. Such was the passion for strawberry leaves that even tureen ladles have them on their handles. A few stands, shaped as vine leaves, have an intricate moulded pattern of strawberry leaves and pansies (2), although it is almost completely obscured by a broad wash of blue colour and thick glaze. Leaf-shaped cream and sauce boats and the covers of primitive melon-shaped tureens have branching twig handles (3). Moulded floral reserves include the 'lily pattern', some wasters of which were found on the Longton site. This pattern, depicting tiger lilies and anemones, decorates the crested tea service made for the Duke of Rutland.[2] One type of tureen has a curled handle at either end like a strange horned gourd. Various basket-mouldings are a further indication of Longton's pre-occupation with rustic and vegetable forms. Certain rare centre-pieces have trays in the shape of scallop shells set on lumpy bases which represent marine incrustations (4). A coloured example in the British Museum is surmounted by a small figure of Ceres, an important link with the 'snowman' figures. Coffee and teapots of a six-lobed silver-shape have

[1] The earliest recorded advertisement dated 27th July, 1752, in *Aris's Birmingham Gazette*, mentions 'Good and fine ornamental porcelain or china ware, in the most fashionable and genteel taste'.

[2] *The Antique Collector*, April 1955. See also Watney, *Longton Hall Porcelain*, 1957, Plate 23B and C.

(1) *Plate* 38B; (2) *Plate* 38A; (3) *Plates* 38C, 39C; (4) *Colour Plate* B.

either a strawberry, a cherry or a lobed knob, steeply rising S-shaped spouts and plain handles. Thickly potted mugs have a broad band of Littler's blue above a panelled moulding with foliate reserves. Their handles are of the characteristic double-scroll type with the long upper scroll overlapping the lower one; various modifications of this handle were produced later. Fluted and cylindrical mugs and cups with plain or rustic handles are uncommon and they are usually badly potted, especially when made by throwing on the potting wheel.

The early porcelain is thickly potted, heavy in the hand, and rather lumpy, having a pale yellow or greenish yellow translucency by artificial light. A few large air bubbles in the paste show up as circular areas of increased translucency known as 'moons', and the numerous small craters on the surface of the paste have filled with glaze and appear as lighter flecks. Bases are usually flat or slightly concave, and being unglazed are frequently burnt a pale orange colour. Where footrings occur they have, almost without exception, been ground level to remove pools of glaze. Broad radiating scars are usually in evidence due to the use of large stilts as supports in the glost firing. Some pieces are marked in underglaze blue with two crossed 'L's frequently with a short tail of dots beneath. Spectroscopic analysis of eleven early blue and white examples, four of them marked with crossed 'L's, reveals that they are all made from a glassy paste of high lead content with no soapstone,[1] although a few have a small amount of phosphate.

The second agreement brought about important changes in the Longton partnership; the mysterious speculator, William Jenkinson, sold his shares and disappeared; Nathaniel Firmin and his son Samuel, London button makers and gilders, entered the partnership bringing fresh capital. Soon, however, a great deal more capital was required to save the concern from failure and this was provided under the terms of the third agreement (1st September, 1755) by the Reverend Robert Charlesworth of Bakewell. However, the manufactory remained in a precarious state as is stressed by the two supplemental agreements of 20th October, 1756, and 1st October, 1757, and, although the move did not take place, it was agreed as a last resort to transfer the factory to some other place such as Nottingham.

There is a short but definite transitional stage between the early and the later wares when the glaze is still thick and the body heavily potted and lumpy, but the blue colour has a less strident, greyish tint. Better control made powder-blue decoration possible (I), as well as

[1] Analyses which purport to find soapstone should be treated with caution.

(I) *Plate* 39A.

more detailed Chinese landscapes in the same free-hand style as on later wares. Moulded forms have clearer outlines, for example the blue and white sunflower dishes and some peach cups. Cos-lettuce sauce boats, copying a Meissen prototype, were made throughout the factory's life and show a progressive improvement in technique. The early examples have poorly defined moulding, especially the handle, which is curled upwards to represent a flowering and fruiting fig branch. In the transitional stage the figs, one on either side of the handle, are more realistic and less like tassels and the flower on the left side now has recognizable petals. A painted Chinese scene replaces the early floral sprays and includes birds flying in front of clouds, a favourite Longton theme. The later sauce boats have crisp moulding and a clean finish including a satisfactory footring (1). However, the finely moulded leaf veins have caused the glaze and blue to run in the furrows resulting in an undue blurring of the painted landscape.

From 1754 onwards the ornamental leaf and flower shapes are generally decorated in enamel colours. A new line was the production of simply potted chocolate, coffee and tea cups and saucers, painted with a greyish blue which resembles that of early Worcester. Teapots are usually of a practical barrel shape with an acorn or a strawberry knob.[1] The spouts are arched and moulded with scrolls and the handles have a version of the double-scroll shape. The less common globular shaped teapots include a fine example with a cherry knob (2) and another with ribbed moulding and painted reserves (3). Cream jugs usually have a wide lip like a bullfinch's beak compared with the narrow sparrow beak form of Worcester (4). Handles are either a stylized version of the double-scroll shape or else formed from a simple roll of clay with a slight 'kick-up' on the lower terminal, somewhat like Lowestoft. Coffee pots are rare; one example has a heavy crab-stock handle, a wide lip and a carnation as a knob (5). Cups and saucers are 'ribbed, fluted, panelled and plain'.[2] Fine basket-moulding is a typical feature (6) and the ribbed cups are copies of St. Cloud originals (7). Cups are usually tall and rather narrow, their handles are often similar to those on cream jugs mentioned above although another version has a prolonged lower terminal. Mugs, especially their handles, lack the robustness of the earlier specimens (8). The

[1] *Longton Hall Porcelain*, London, 1957, Plate 76A.
[2] *London General Evening Post*, 30th September–3rd October, 1758, announcing the opening of a Longton warehouse in St. Paul's Churchyard.

(1) *Plate* 41B; (2) *Plate* 41C; (3) *Plate* 40C; (4) *Plates* 42C, E;
(5) *Plate* 42A; (6) *Plate* 40A; (7) *Plate* 40B;
(8) *Plate* 42B.

'lily pattern' moulding is continued from the early period. (1). A jug moulded with an auricula plant, carnations and strawberry leaves is one of the few late ornamental pieces in blue and white (2), and in place of the usual chinoiserie on other wares it has an English scene by the 'castle painter'.[1]

There are a large number of standard patterns, many of which have been found as wasters on the Longton site. The best known is the 'folly pattern', depicting a pyramid and a hermit.[2] Wares with this pattern are usually marked with a '5' or a '6' on the base. Ribbed cups in the St. Cloud style are marked with the figure 2 and a fine pair of hexagonal cups and saucers are marked in a monogram of P and L. Some of the Chinese patterns can be distinguished by letters of the alphabet with which they are marked, for instance the pattern on the cream jug (3) is found in conjunction with the letter 'k', the elaborate pattern on the coffee pot (4) is associated with 'e', and a pattern of a gatehouse and face is frequently marked with a capital 'A'. A few patterns are similar to those used at Worcester, for example the 'prunus root' (5), the 'zig-zag fence' and the 'gatehouse' patterns. Painted borders are uncommon except on moulded wares. Occasionally fire cracks between the body and the handle are disguised by over-painting with blue.

The thinly applied glaze is usually somewhat greyish, but may be colourless or slightly opaque. It is soft and silky, and although finely pitted it has a high surface gloss. Sometimes, as on the earlier wares, a line of bubbling and discoloration can be seen at the paste-glaze junction on the footrings in a so-called 'scum line', but a more characteristic feature is the presence of radiating scars under the foot-ring due to 'knife edge' stilt marks. Footrings are often of a squat triangular section. The translucency by artificial light can be compared to that of a thin sheet of paraffin wax, the colour is predominately green, sometimes with a white, yellow or blue tint. Small surface craters due to burst bubbles, and stress tears following throwing lines, are filled with glaze and show up as light flecks. Large imprisoned air bubbles appearing as 'moons' are only found where the paste is thick. All examples, including factory wasters, tested by spectrographic analysis contain a large amount of lead and a little phosphate.[3]

[1] Possibly John Hayfield, who is mentioned in the third agreement. His scenes in coloured enamels often include ruins and castles.

[2] Watney, *Longton Hall Porcelain*, 1957, Pl. 64B.

[3] The previous published analyses of the factory wasters, Watney, *Longton Hall*, London, 1957, p. 23, were subsequently repeated, at my request, by other workers

(1) *Plate* 39B; (2) *Plate* 41A; (3) *Plate* 42C; (4) *Plate* 42A; (5) *Plate* 42D.

After a short life-span of ten years the Longton factory was brought to an abrupt end by the intervention of the Reverend Robert Charlesworth. His agents seized 'upwards of ninety thousand pieces' and took them to Salisbury for the final sale beginning 16th September, 1760. However, Littler managed to keep back sufficient of his unfinished earlier pieces to make it worth his while moving to West Pans where he and his wife decorated them with enamelled crests, monograms and floral sprays, and sold them to the Scottish nobility.

including the institute of Ceramic Research at Hanley. Their findings differed fundamentally from the results I had published and I am now of the opinion that the earlier results should be disregarded. See Watney, 'Porcelain Figures of the Snowman Technique,' *Connoisseur*, vol. CXXXIX, 1957, pp. 149–53, for a further discussion on this subject.

5

LIVERPOOL CHINA FACTORIES

During the first half of the eighteenth century Liverpool witnessed a sudden expansion of its ceramic industry. With a local tradition only for bricks, clay pipes and crude mugs, this late-starting pottery centre had to rely on potters from London, Bristol and Staffordshire to teach the techniques of delft, salt glaze and porcelain. Within the next few years at least twenty pot works had come into being, nine or ten of which are thought to have made porcelain at some stage of their existence. However, as early as the 1760's, the industry had already started to decline almost as rapidly as it had grown up. Neither its earthenware nor its china could compete with Wedgwood's cream ware which flooded into Liverpool via the new canals. Wedgwood even snatched away from the Liverpool potters their main chance of appreciably cutting costs by almost completely monopolizing Sadler's transfer-printing output. Finally, the American War of Independence (1775–83) severely restricted exports, leaving a greatly diminished market for Liverpool's by then largely inferior wares.

This chapter is an attempt to separate the Liverpool porcelains into groups and then to allot these groups to their appropriate factories. This task is made difficult by the rapid succession and proximity of the various factories resulting in close similarities in style between the groups. Unfortunately, documentary evidence is slight and even now when the groups have been defined a great deal of patient research in the Liverpool archives is necessary before attributions can be fully proved.

Liverpool porcelain, such as we know it, can be separated by visual examination into eight main groups and spectrographic analysis of representative examples helps to confirm this classification. Unexpected findings are the presence of soapstone in two groups outside the Chaffers-Christian combine and the absence of soapstone in a group which is considered to be early Chaffers. One of the groups probably made by William Reid can be divided into two sub-groups by analysis, but not readily by the eye, depending on the presence or absence of soapstone.

	The Results of Spectrographic Analysis			
Type of Porcelain	A bone-ash porcelain	No significant amounts of soapstone or bone-ash present		A soapstone porcelain
		A lime-frit or 'glassy' porcelain	A pseudo-hard-paste porcelain	
Factory	Early Chaffers Gilbody Seth Pennington	Early Reid	Wolfe	Later Chaffers Christian Ball Later Reid

The Chaffers, Christian & Pennington Sequence

Throughout the period of china making in Liverpool the same site on Shaw's Brow in the centre of the town was occupied in succession by Richard Chaffers and Company; Philip Christian and Company; then Seth Pennington and John Part, afterwards Messrs. Pennington and Edwards. The output of these factories showing a certain continuity of style has come to be recognized as forming the main Liverpool tradition.

Richard Chaffers and Company (?1754–65)

Richard Chaffers (?1722–65)[1] a Liverpool Roman Catholic, is first described as a potter in the Town Books when he petitioned to be admitted to the freedom of the Borough on 5th October, 1743. A year later, probably when he was aged 22, he married Ann Johnson, also of Liverpool, on 23rd November, 1744.[2] Nothing further is known about his activities until 1747 when the firm of Richard Chaffers & Company is mentioned as the tenant of a pottery with a frontage of 30 yards on Shaw's Brow, now William Brown Street.[3] Later, on 10th October, 1750, John Harrison was bound apprentice to Richard Chaffers, Claypotter, for £15.[4] Chaffers' grandson, John Rosson, in a letter to the Liverpool Mercury, dated 12th May, 1854, states that Chaffers made blue and white earthenware, largely for export, before engaging the services of Robert Podmore.

---

[1] It has not been recorded previously that Chaffers' will was proved at Chester on 29th May, 1800, the value of his personality being less than a thousand pounds. However, Dr. Knowles Boney has discovered a copy of his will in the possession of Lord Cross.

[2] The Catholic Record Society, *Miscellanea*, vol. VII, p. 195. See Knowles Boney, *Richard Chaffers*, Liverpool, 1960, p. 15.

[3] Charles Gatty, *The Liverpool Potteries*, 1882, p. 15.

[4] Toppin, *Trans. E.P.C.* 1929, No. II, p. 44.

ENGLISH BLUE AND WHITE PORCELAIN

On 14th June, 1755, Richard Chaffers and Philip Christian signed a seven-year agreement[1] with Robert Podmore, who was a renegade potter from the Worcester factory. It will be recalled that under the terms of the first Worcester agreement dated 4th June, 1751, Podmore was to receive special payments to ensure his fidelity. His new employers at Liverpool were to allow him a guinea a week as manager as well as one-twelfth share of the net profits. He was to reveal to Chaffers and Christian the secret 'of making earthenware in imitation of or to resemble china ware'.

Rosson's well known account of Chaffers' successful journey into Cornwall to search for soapstone has been copied by Joseph Mayer[2] and later writers. Letters from Gauregan Tippit,[3] Chaffers' agent at Mullion, give more precise information. They show that Chaffers left Cornwall to return to Liverpool shortly before 9th July, 1756. As Tippit sends his compliments to Mr. Podmore it is possible that the latter had been with Chaffers in Cornwall. The first shipment of soap rock was barrelled up and sent to Liverpool at the end of November in the same year. A few days after this, on 10th December, 1756, the first advertisement appeared in the Liverpool newspapers; its *nota bene* recalling a major selling point of the Worcester factory. 'The porcelain or china made by Messrs. Richard Chaffers and Company is sold nowhere in the town but at their manufactory on Shaw's Brow. Considerable abatement is made for exportation and to all wholesale dealers. N.B. All the ware is proved with boiling water before it is exposed for sale.'[4] It is hardly credible that a large stock of soapstone porcelain could have been built up in so short a time and there is now good reason to believe that at least some of Chaffers' early porcelain had a phosphatic body.

An enamelled custard cup,[5] traditionally ascribed to Chaffers, was given by John Rosson to Mayer. This piece belongs to a scarce group with some early features. The porcelain of this group has a hard greyish appearance and is well potted, especially the fine mugs with silver-shape handles. The coloured examples are usually decorated with Chinese figure scenes in bright enamels by a hand whose style closely resembles that of a Longton Hall decorator. The Chinese figures have loosely fitting robes, and on the Liverpool wares there is frequently a large single daisy head in the lower part of the design.

[1] Entwistle Papers, Liverpool Library, and Knowles Boney, *Country Life*, 26th February, 1959, p. 408.
[2] *History of the Art of Pottery in Liverpool*, 1855.
[3] William Chaffers, *Marks and Monograms*, 14th ed. 1932, p. 755.
[4] *Williamson's Liverpool Advertiser*.
[5] J. Mayer, *The Art of Pottery in Liverpool*, 1855, p. 19. This cup seems to have been destroyed in the Second World War.

Unfortunately there are no known dated examples, but a few mugs bear early versions of Liverpool transfers, such as the Masonic Arms[1] which is also found on Longton Hall, 1757–60. Dr. Boney, who possessed a number of the enamelled mugs,[2] has had an analysis performed on one of them[3] which showed that the body is phosphatic and not steatitic. Recent spectrographic tests on other examples, both coloured and blue and white, have confirmed Boney's finding, making it possible to separate this group both by its appearance and composition from Chaffers' soapstone porcelain. Thus it would appear that Chaffers made a phosphatic porcelain for a short while before he became committed to using soapstone on the employment of Robert Podmore and his own discovery of adequate amounts of soapstone in Cornwall.

The blue and white examples are painted in greyish blue which, where it is thickly applied, forms little areas with a matt and roughened surface that are slightly raised above the smooth glaze. Patterns include a man on a bridge (1), island scenes with houses and trees and sometimes figures (2), a ruined arch (3)[4] and a carefully drawn peony and prunus design (4); the latter also occurs on Chaffers' soapstone porcelain. Rocks are represented by simple outlines often rectangular in shape with small clusters of dots or parallel shading lines. Small boulders are frequently kidney-shaped and cliff faces are shown as rectangular areas arranged in a line or in steps, and a few boldly drawn tufts of grass or reeds grow out of the surrounding water. Some trees are depicted by clusters or circles, each with a central dot and a single circle with a dot represents the sun. Diaper and lozenge borders are carefully drawn and wavy 'comma marks' like fluttering pennants are painted on either side of handle terminals. The potting is clean and neat and there are some crisply moulded wares including pickle trays, coffee cans (5) and sauce boats (6).[5] Mugs have silver-shape handles and some have widely grooved feet, very similar to Longton Hall examples.[6] Coffee cans have either flat unglazed bases or neatly turned footrings. The upper terminal of the handle sometimes forms an S-shaped curve (7) to join the body at right angles or it

[1] R. L. Hobson, *Catalogue of English Porcelain in the British Museum*, 1905, fig. 92.
[2] Now in the Williamson Art Gallery, Birkenhead.
[3] Knowles Boney, *Liverpool Porcelain*, London, 1957, p. 165.
[4] Also found on Liverpool delft and Derby porcelain.
[5] This moulding was later used by Pennington.
[6] W. B. Honey, *Old English Porcelain*, London, 1948, Plate 96A and C.

(1) *Plate* 53B; (2) *Plate* 53C; (3) *Plate* 53D; (4) *Plate* 54B.
(5) *Plates* 53A, 54B; (6) *Plate* 53C; (7) *Plate* 53A.

may run straight down the side of the body for a centimetre or more. Tea and coffee pot spouts are well formed and sometimes widely fluted and ribbed. Knobs are usually shaped like an inverted spinning top, but one example represents a convolvulus flower.[1]

The hard-looking body is covered by a thin close-fitting glaze of a grey, slightly nacreous appearance. A few glaze-free patches are sometimes found on bases and slight 'sanding' can be seen. On translumination with artificial light the colour varies from brownish yellow to greyish or whitish green. Numerals, usually 1, 3, 4, 5 or 6, painted in underglaze blue, are found inside footrings[2] or on bases.

There are a few pieces which contain soapstone but which have a number of features in common with the early phosphatic group. Four examples are given here; first, a mug (1) which has the typical grooved foot and silver-shape handle and wavy 'comma marks' of the phosphatic group (2); the painting on it is by the same hand that decorated an early grey tinted teapot in the author's collection. Secondly, a cup which bears the same peony and prunus pattern, the same carefully drawn lozenge and flower-head border and even the same inverted twig motif on the handle (3) as on tea wares of the grey-tinted phosphatic class (4). Moreover, the mug has a numeral on its base and the cup has one on the inner side of the footring. These two pieces, however, are not grey tinted but have the chalky blue-white appearance which is typical of Chaffers' soapstone porcelain. This difference in colour between the phosphatic and the steatitic group is so distinctive that it is even noticeable in a photograph, as can be seen by comparing a cream jug and a coffee can (5), and two sauce boats (6) which otherwise closely resemble each other.

Dated and Inscribed Examples of Chaffers' Soapstone Porcelain

A moulded bowl with a diaper and scroll border similar to one used on the earlier phosphatic group.
Inscribed—'*This comes from your hearts Delight,*
      Who thinks of you boath day and night.
      This bowle is round, it is for you
      If you'l be constanet I'll be true.
      Wm. Benney, Yarmouth
      *Eliz*th *Mershall.*' (British Museum)

[1] Knowles Boney, *Liverpool Porcelain*, London, 1957, Plate 30c.
[2] Also a common finding on Lowestoft blue and white.

(1) *Plate* 54D; (2) *Plate* 54C; (3) *Plate* 54B (2); (4) *Plate* 54B (3); (5) *Plate* 54B (1), 54B (4); (6) *Plate* 54A (1), 54A (2).

A mug inscribed 'Success to Sir William's Plumpers 982'.[1] This refers to the majority vote in the election of Sir William Meredith. The mug is likely to have been made in 1761, the year that this election took place (British Museum)

A jug inscribed 'A free gift to John Fell, China house joiner, 1762'[2] (Bootle Museum)

An inkwell inscribed 'I. H. 1765' (1) (Willsmore Collection)

Chaffers' soapstone porcelain is painted with a brighter, less grey cobalt than the phosphatic group just described. Where areas are filled in with blue, broad brush-strokes are visible causing a streaky effect. There are some well-known patterns which, with few exceptions (2), imitate the Chinese. They include a 'jumping boy' (3),[3] two bowing men on an island (4), a man in a boat plunging almost vertically beside a large spotted rock, and a fine semi-geometric arrangement of flower heads and leaves. There are a number of variations on the theme of romantic islands with fishermen under willow trees and also of peony plants and bamboo growing out of fanciful rock formations. The 'crested bird on a branch' (5) pattern was used for more than twenty years from the beginning of the Chaffers period when the paste contained bone ash, during the time of Philip Christian and into the period when Seth Pennington was the proprietor. Many of the designs appear to have been painted very rapidly and there is a fondness for peppering scenes with dots, a tendency which becomes even more marked during the Philip Christian period. Fir trees are sometimes depicted like wigwams and birds fly in arrow-head formation, often straight upwards. Bridges are supported on tall, thin stilts and pagodas are often of a somewhat squat diamond shape.

The plain, broad strap handle is one of the most common and characteristic features, especially on cups. On coffee pots (6), large jugs (7), and mugs (8) the lower terminal is turned back and cut off leaving a slightly concave end. Grooved handles are occasionally used, but they are somewhat flatter than their Worcester counterparts and not as neatly applied. Simple roll handles are found on tea wares and coffee cans, sometimes with a 'kick-up' of the lower terminal. A neat, silver-shape, broken-scroll handle with a curled thumb rest is found

[1] Knowles Boney, *The Liverpool Bulletin*, vol. 3, No. 3, March 1954, p. 39.
[2] *Apollo*, March 1951, p. 86.
[3] This pattern also occurs in Bow.

---

(1) *Plate* 57B; (2) *Plate* 55B (2); (3) *Plate* 56A;
(4) *Plate* 55B (1); (5) *Plates* 57B, 59A, 59B;
(6) *Plate* 57A; (7) *Plate* 56D; (8) *Plate* 56B.

on a few rare cream jugs; there is an example in the Hanley Museum decorated with the pattern of two men bowing on an island. This type of handle was more commonly used on coloured wares during the Philip Christian period. Another unusual rococo handle is found on cream boats (1) and jugs. Footrings on cups and saucers are often curved on the outside and have a very short, straight or slightly over-hung inner side. This gives a rounded or beaded effect which is very characteristic. Mugs and coffee cans with flat bases usually have a neatly chamfered edge, a feature in common with the earlier phos-phatic group and the later wares of Philip Christian. Coffee pot spouts, because of their weight, frequently dented the bodies during firing. Spouts on large jugs are rather broad and typically rise up above the rim. Plates are rare and usually octagonal (2). Some of the best potted tea and coffee wares have straight sides, such as the fine, six-sided beaker cups which have even been mistaken for Chelsea.[1] Wares with moulded patterns are rather scarce (3) and some contain a small amount of bone ash as well as soapstone, possibly to increase the plasticity of the paste.

The glaze has a similar surface to that of Worcester and there is also a glaze-free ring inside many of the footrings. Entwistle describes the glaze surface as being like a duck's egg shell and its colour as being milky blue. However, the amount of bluing in the glaze varies con-siderably. The translucency by artificial light varies from a yellowish green to a bluish green.

Workmen did not mark their wares with signs as at Worcester, although a few tea wares have a single fine incised line underglaze on the base and, as we have seen, some early pieces have painted numerals. The 'jumping boy' pattern is usually marked with imita-tion Chinese characters and the rare 'dragon pattern' (4) sometimes has a square mark.

Philip Christian and Company (1765-76)

Philip Christian of Lord Street[2] continued to use soapstone at the Shaw's Brow factory after Chaffers' death, but it appears that Chaffers' widow and children retained a considerable financial interest.[3] Then in December 1769, an agreement was made by which Philip Chris-tian, on paying £1,200 in three equal amounts by 30th June, 1771,

[1] Stanley Fisher, *English Blue and White Porcelain*, London 1947, Plate 10.
[2] *Gore's Liverpool Directory*, 1766.
[3] Knowles Boney, *Richard Chaffers*, Liverpool, 1960, p. 35.

---

(1) *Plate* 55B (2); (2) *Plate* 56C; (3) *Plates* 55A, B, C; (4) *Plate* 57C.

was able to obtain full control and thus change the style of the firm to 'Philip Christian and Son', the son being Philip Christian the younger. On 21st July, 1772, he seems to have renewed the licence to dig for soaprock at Predannack near Mullion.[1] When Josiah Wedgwood visited the soaprock mines on 8th June, 1775, he noted that 'Chaffers and Company' were renting a house for £10 a year near a place called Trevas.[2] Less than a year later, however, on 4th May, 1776, Philip Christian and Son sold the remainder of the soaprock lease to the proprietors of the Worcester factory for £500.

Philip Christian and Son stopped making porcelain and moved to Folly Lane as merchants[3] where they purchased a dwelling house and premises with a garden. Philip Christian the elder died on 10th July, 1785, leaving a personal estate worth over a thousand pounds. John Sadler the printer,[4] a Roman Catholic like Philip Christian, was a witness to his will which was proved on 1st August, 1785. Philip Christian the younger died in his sixtieth year on 17th April, 1808. In his will, proved on 30th April of the same year, he mentions besides the property in Folly Lane, two houses in Christian Street.

Dated Wares made by Philip Christian

An inkwell inscribed 'M. S. 1767'(1). (Victoria and Albert Museum.) The pattern on this piece was also used on Christian's moulded tea wares.

A pounce pot inscribed 'Richard Chaffers 1769' (Liverpool Museum. It was destroyed in the last war.) Doubtless made to commemorate the apprenticeship of Richard Chaffers at the age of 14 to Thomas Gill of Liverpool, cooper.[5] Richard Chaffers the younger, a son of the potter, was born in 1755 and died in his forty-sixth year in March 1800.[6]

Christian's soapstone porcelain has several features which distinguish it from Chaffers'. His Chinese scenes tend to be painted with finer outlines and peppered with more dots (2). They are often confined in small reserves surrounded by intricate floral mouldings (3). Willow trees frequently outline the tops of these reserves with rows

---

[1] R. W. Binns, *A Century of Potting*, 2nd ed., 1877, p. 313.

[2] *Wedgwood's Commonplace Book*, in the Wedgwood Museum at Barlaston.

[3] The *Liverpool Directory for 1777*.

[4] John Sadler seems to have experimented with foreign china and Christian's soaprock china body as ingredients for glazes on tiles and earthenware. See *John Sadler's Notebook* in the Liverpool Reference Library.

[5] *Apprentice indenture*, Public Record Office, 57/126, 1769.

[6] *Gore's General Advertiser*, no. 1784, vol. XXXV, 6th March, 1800.

---

(1) *Plate* 57D; (2) *Plate* 58C; (3) *Plate* 58A.

of pendant leaves on horizontal branches like the teeth of a comb. Tea cups have an almost square silhouette and their handles are bent in a wide ungainly curve; whereas Chaffers' cups usually have sloping sides and a steeper and narrower curve to the handles. Footrings tend to be taller and are typically undercut on the inner side. The glaze colour is more constant, being only slightly tinted with cobalt. It is applied thinly, especially on bases of cups and saucers where it often has an uneven dimpled surface.

A handle shaped as a biting snake and a handle with a comma-shaped tag have come to be recognized as typical of Liverpool porcelain. Both these handles, as well as the famous palm-column and leaf moulded teapots, were produced by Philip Christian some years before Seth Pennington copied them. Furthermore, some of the earlier large jugs with mask-moulded spouts were first made of soapstone porcelain by Christian.[1] The Liverpool mask is that of a young heroic face surrounded by scroll mouldings, a marked contrast to that used at Worcester or at Caughley.[2]

Christian used a cobalt which has a pleasing pale grey tint, almost identical to that used at Worcester. Chaffers' blue is darker, partly no doubt because it was laid on more boldly. Christian's use of cobalt for transfer printing, his least satisfactory form of decoration, resulted for the most part in blurred landscapes and undistinguished flower sprays copied from Caughley designs. Nearly all of them were repeated on Pennington's porcelain with even less artistry.

Messrs. Pennington & Part (?1769–99)

The elusive brothers, James, John and Seth Pennington, played a part in the ceramic industry of Liverpool during the latter part of the eighteenth century. A few of the known facts suggest that there was some collaboration between them,[3] but although they called themselves china manufacturers, it is not absolutely certain which of them made porcelain rather than earthenware. However, the bone-ash porcelain now to be discussed would seem to have been the product of

[1] Knowles Boney, *Liverpool Porcelain*, London, 1957, Plate 11A.
[2] See p. 45.
[3] James (*Gore's Directory*) and John Pennington were at the Copperas Hill China Works in 1774 from where, in the same year, a son of the latter was baptized Seth, after the child's uncle (St. Nicholas Church Register). In 1779 John Pennington moved to another factory in Folly Lane (*Liverpool General Advertiser*, Vol. 14, No. 704. 25th June 1779); here he died in October 1786 (St. Peter's Church Register). A month prior to this Seth and Alice Pennington were described as china manufacturers in Folly Lane (St. Peter's Church Register). After John Pennington's death, two of his apprentices, James Turner, indentured 28th January, 1786, and John Evans, indentured 27th August, 1785, were assigned to James Pennington, either John's son, born December 1760, or his brother.

one factory. It forms a remarkably consistent group produced over a period of about twenty years, from the early 1770's till the 1790's.

Seth Pennington,[1] the youngest brother, is thought to have made this porcelain in conjunction with his partner, John Part[2] from Chapel Street. There are three main reasons for this assumption. Firstly, it gives the most satisfactory explanation of the close stylistic links between these wares and those made earlier by Chaffers and his successor Christian, for Messrs. Pennington and Part are known to have taken over the porcelain factory at Shaw's Brow after Christian.[3] Secondly, William Mercer was indentured an apprentice to Pennington and Part in 1778 and a small enamelled plate of this group is inscribed 'W. M. Mercer'. Thirdly, some of these wares are traditionally associated with the name of Seth Pennington (1).

Pennington and Part must have started production of their bone-ash porcelain at Shaw's Brow or elsewhere before Christian sold the soaprock lease to Worcester in 1776. Indeed, a masked jug inscribed 'I.H. 1772' is the earliest known dated piece of this group. It is decorated with the 'crested bird on a branch' pattern that was used previously by Chaffers and Christian. Furthermore, John Sadler gives the recipe for 'Pennington's body' in his note book under the date 1st March, 1769.

Dated Examples made by Pennington and Part

A masked jug inscribed 'I.H. 1772' (2) (Boney collection, Williamson Art Gallery, Birkenhead)

A masked jug inscribed 'Robert Lewis 1773' (Allman Collection)

A masked jug inscribed 'J ^{R} C 1773' (British Museum)

An ink pot inscribed 'I. Heaton 1774' (Harris Museum, Preston)

A punch pot inscribed 'Mary Hargraves, Higham 1775'. (W. E. Hatfield Collection; illustrated *Antique Collector*, August 1957, p. 143 as Lowestoft)

A ship-painted bowl inscribed 'Success to the Issabella 1779' (3) (Liverpool Museum)

A transfer-printed jug with rampant lions inscribed 'Frederick Heinzelman Liverpool 1779' (British Museum)

A mug inscribed 'Jonathan Bate 1779' (Liverpool Museum)

[1] Born on 7th July, 1744, and elected a freeman in 1767 (Entwistle M.S.).
[2] Said to be a relative by marriage of Miles Mason (Entwistle M.S.).
[3] A deed dated 2nd July, 1785, describes this property as 'the china works and dwelling house assigned to Messrs. Part and Pennington.' Then in 1788 they mortgaged the property for £500 (Gatty, *op. cit.*, p. 16).

(1) *Plate* 60; (2) *Plate* 59A; (3) *Plate* 60.

A ship-painted flower pot inscribed 'W. D. 1780' (1) (Watney Collection)

A bowl inscribed 'Prosperity to John Dickinson and all his family 1780' (Allman Collection)

A ship-painted bowl inscribed 'Ralph Farrar 1783' (2) (Allman Collection)

A ship-painted bowl inscribed 'Success to the Will R. Bibby 1783' (Liverpool Museum)

A mug inscribed 'John and Jane Anderson 1783' (Liverpool Museum)

A ship-painted jug inscribed ' W $\overset{M}{\cdot}$ E 1785' (British Museum)

A pounce pot inscribed 'Thomas Bold 1789' (Liverpool Museum)

A masked jug transfer-printed with rampant lions and a sailing ship inscribed 'Fine Ale Luke Lunt 1790' (Liverpool Museum)

At first the cobalt blue used in decorating these wares varied in colour from grey-blue to almost black in the more thickly painted areas. The designs are usually blurred by the blue-green tinted glaze whose high surface gloss gives a shining wet appearance. Where the glaze has pooled at footrings there is the so-called 'thunder cloud' effect.[1] By 1780 the cobalt had lost its greyish tint and become brighter. The glaze tends to be thicker, less glossy and its surface finely pitted. It crazes easily and forms deep, blue-tinted pools at footrings and inside vessels.

Transfer prints, many of them previously used by Philip Christian, are particularly common on this late group of porcelain. They include 'the rural lovers' after a painting by Gainsborough, which is found especially on wares with a high gloss. Three sprays of flowers, each with a different fruit, a medlar, two cherries and a gooseberry, were used early with good effect, but eventually became debased and almost unrecognizable. These fruit and flower sprays were first used at Caughley and then copied by Philip Christian.[2] A mug (3) in the author's collection bears unusually fine prints including roses and other flowers and a large bumble bee adapted from engravings in the *Ladies' Amusement*. A jug with a masked lip inscribed 'Fine Ale Luke Lunt 1790' has an elaborate handle moulded as a biting dragon with a satyr mask on the lower terminal. It bears a print of a sailing ship as well as a print of a splendid rampant lion; both transfers are unique to

[1] Bernard Rackham, *Trans. E.P.C.*, No. II, 1929.
[2] A number of other designs were also taken from Caughley including the Chantilly 'gilly flower' pattern and some Chinese figure scenes.

(1) *Plate* 61B; (2) *Plate* 61C; (3) *Plate* 61D;

this group and decorate some of the more ambitious pieces (1). However, the majority of prints are poorly engraved and the details usually badly smudged. Among the many examples are prints of two stags, a fisherman standing in a sampan holding a fish,[1] two quails, a Chinese woman with a bird on her left wrist, two tall exotic birds in an oriental landscape, and a bunch of bell-shaped flowers with a few 'corkscrew' tendrils. Printed cell and diaper borders are common and tend to become more complex on later wares. A printed scallop-shell and flower-head border is sometimes used to form a reserve containing a small flower spray.

Some of the finest pieces are jugs and punch bowls painted with sailing ships by an unknown artist.[2] Many of the ships were African slavers like *The Will*,[3] but one vessel, the *Polar Star*, was a whaler.[4] There are some tall and elaborately decorated vases with covers surmounted by a flying bird as a knob (2).[5] The same shape of knob is found on a large punch pot with an intertwined handle and painted with an amusing village scene (3). Simpler designs decorate the mass-produced useful wares. Stylized flower heads and buds, often between two bracts, are painted in outline and partially filled in with blobs of blue, and buds painted in profile look like a string of Japanese pith flowers before they open. One flower spray design previously used by Chaffers and Christian[6] is found on tea wares, including tall spirally fluted cream boats with acanthus leaf moulding (4). There are two typical painted borders, one is formed by a bud between two bracts alternating with a small blue dot (5), and the other is simply a row of either dots or dashes.

A few wares such as leaf-shaped pickle trays and a basket-moulded sauce boat still have the same moulded patterns as those originally

[1] Also used at Caughley and known as 'the fisherman and sail' pattern.

[2] John Pennington advertised for decorating his china 'drafts or the likeness of vessels taken and painted in the most correct and masterly manner' (*Williamson's Liverpool Advertiser*, 25th June, 1779). But although he may have been referring to delft there remains the possibility that he, and not Seth Pennington, made this group of porcelain until his death in 1786 when his wife took over the factory.

[3] In December 1785 this ship arrived at Dominica from the Cameroons after a passage of fifteen weeks with two hundred and thirty one slaves and twelve thousand hundredweight of large ivory (*Williamson's Liverpool Advertiser*).

[4] On a bowl in the Liverpool Museum.

[5] Philip Christian made this type of vase earlier, for example the fine garniture painted with biblical scenes from the collection of the Rev. James Clough of Ribblesdale, now in the Liverpool Museum.

[6] This design occurs on a pair of blue and white snuff boxes moulded as a claw of an animal's hoof, in Norman Palmer's Collection, near Oxford.

(1) *Plate* 62D; (2) *Plate* 62A; (3) *Plate* 62B;
(4) *Plate* 58B (3); (5) *Plate* 61A.

introduced by Chaffers on his early phosphatic porcelain (1).[1] For the most part however Pennington copied Christian's later moulded patterns, in many cases apparently using the same moulds. For example Pennington continued the production of fine palm-column and leaf teapots, cream boats with seven arched reserves[2] and tea wares with both floral and panelled moulding. He also used similar silver-shape handles with a terminal comma tag and reproduced the famous handles moulded as a biting snake. Some other moulded wares are crude versions of those made at Worcester. They include small pedestal cream boats with ribbed sides and lamprey shaped handles, tall fluted cream boats with acanthus leaf moulding and wares with the 'feather' pattern. A tall pedestal cream jug was moulded directly from a silver example and even bears the impression of a hall mark on one side.[3]

Pottery counterparts can be found for the unusual sauce boats, or small tureens, shaped like a duck (2), also for sauce boats with large pears and gooseberries moulded on their sides (3), and for the better-known examples with a face, vine branches and 'liver birds' (4).

It is characteristic of this group that most pieces are poorly finished, even to their elaborate silver-shape handles. However, some of the best potted and most robust pieces are the plain globular teapots and tall, fluted coffee pots. The more thinly potted sauce boats with a wet looking glaze have long narrow lips which widen abruptly to form bulging sides. Cream jugs have small pinched lips of the 'sparrow beak' type. The bases of mugs and coffee cans are usually flat and unglazed, leaving an unprotected porcelain body which often stains a pale orange yellow. Footrings on tea wares are at first rather tall and of relatively small diameter. They usually have a narrow triangular cross section. Large scallop-shell pickle trays have three cone feet stuck on to the base like pellets of dough. A few of the later wares are marked with numerals and some enamelled pieces have a monogram of HP on the base in underglaze blue.

In contrast to Christian's porcelain, which usually has a green translucency, these wares show a straw to orange colour on trans-illumination with artificial light. Chemical analysis of the paste reveals that it contains a large amount of bone ash. This is in agreement with John Sadler's recipe for Pennington's porcelain to be found in his note book :[4]

[1] For a late basket-moulded sauce boat see Bemrose, *Longton Hall Porcelain*, 1906, Pl. XLIV, no. 6.
[2] Also used at Worcester.   [3] Dr. and Mrs. Statham collection.
[4] In the Liverpool Reference Library.

(1) *Plate* 53c; (2) *Plate* 59d; (3) *Plate* 59c; (4) *Plate* 62c.

Pennington's Body March 1st 1769
Bone ashes abt. 60 lb.
Lynn sand   40
Flint   35   Fritt
To every 60 of the above 20 lb. of clay.

This recipe would give a body containing about 33 per cent bone ash.

In the 1790's fashions changed, cobalt was no longer used to tint the glaze and Pennington's porcelain began to lose the stylistic identity which showed it to be a product of the eighteenth century. Early in September 1799 the china works were put up for sale by auction[1] and the Pennington and Part partnership came to an end. The Liverpool Directory for the following year lists Pennington and Edmunds china manufacturers, at No. 8 Shaw's Brow, but the 1803 edition gives the new partner's name as Edwards.[2] In 1805 there is an unexpected change, for while Seth Pennington is given as a china manufacturer at 34 Shaw's Brow, Pennington and Son are shown as furniture japanners at 10 Shaw's Brow. One of Pennington's pottery kilns which remained standing for many years was used by emery grinders[3] before the magnificent library, picture galleries and museum were built on that central and commanding position which had long been known as Shaw's Brow.

Thomas Wolfe & Company (1795–1800)

Thomas Wolfe and his partners, Miles Mason and John Luckock, took over in 1795 the Folly Lane factory, which may have been kept in production by Jane Pennington until 1794[4] following the death of her husband John in October 1786. Wolfe and his other Staffordshire partners probably converted this factory for porcelain production.[5] It has been suggested elsewhere[6] that they made a certain group of hybrid porcelain containing some bone ash, but in other respects akin to hard paste. The only known blue and white example is a transfer-printed tea caddy[7] of the same type as the enamelled example in the

[1] Billinge's *Liverpool Advertiser*, 12th August, 1799. The factory was to be sold by auction on 3rd September.

[2] John Edwards, china manufacturer, 103 Dale Street.

[3] A similar fate to the Bow factory '. . . which afterwards became Marshall's emery mills' (J. Marryat, *Pottery and Porcelain*, 3rd Ed., 1868, p. 407).

[4] 'All persons having any demands against Mrs. Jane Pennington of Liverpool China Manufacturer . . .' (*Gore's General Advertiser*, 30th October, 1794).

[5] At the dissolution of the partnership in 1800 the factory is described as 'all that new erected china works with steam engine . . .' (*Gore's General Advertiser* 22nd May, 1800).

[6] Watney, *Trans. E.C.C.*, Vol. 5, part 1, 1960 p. 48.

[7] *Ibid.*, Plate 36c.

Hanley Museum once owned by Enoch Wood and falsely documented by him as having been made by William Littler.

Samuel Gilbody's Factory (?1754–61)

Samuel Gilbody was born on 1st May, 1733.[1] His father, also Samuel Gilbody, was a Liverpool 'clay potter', who owned a pot works next to that of Chaffers on Shaw's Brow. When the father died in July 1752, he left the factory together with the rest of his estate to be managed by his wife Hannah provided she did not marry again. In 1754, a few months before he became of age, Samuel Gilbody the younger married[2] and he almost certainly took over the management of the pottery firm from his mother about that time.[3] The registers of St. Peters Church list Gilbody as living at Shaw's Brow between January 1755 and April 1758, during which period he was successful in making sufficient porcelain to advertise 'wholesale and retail at the lowest prices, china ware of all sorts, equal for service and beauty to any made in England'[4] from his warehouse on the south side of Shaw's Brow. However, his porcelain-making activities were short-lived and although he took two apprentices, first James Adlam about 1753 and then James Akers on 27th September, 1759, he was declared a bankrupt by February 1760.[5] Finally, on 3rd July, 1761, there was the offer for sale of 'the large pot-house situate on Shaw's Brow late in possession of Samuel Gilbody, a bankrupt, also china ware belonging to the assignees of the said Gilbody'.[6]

A distinctive group of Liverpool porcelain is attributable to Samuel Gilbody on the following evidence. Firstly, on 27th July, 1756, he signed the affidavit concerning Sadler's tile-printing experiment by which over 1,200 earthenware tiles were printed in six hours. It would not be surprising therefore to find transfer prints from Sadler's factory on Gilbody's porcelain. In fact this group does bear some early Sadler prints, a few of which are signed by Jeremiah Evans, whose only other signed prints occur on Longton Hall about 1758, and early

[1] *St. Peter's Church Register*. He was a child of his father's second marriage recorded in St. Nicholas Church Register, 24th April, 1731, Samuel Gilbody, potter, and Hannah Waters, spinster.

[2] *St. Nicholas Church Register*, 7th March, 1754, Samuel Gilbody, Potter, and Hannah Dilkinson, spinster.

[3] Under the terms of his father's will he was to have the option to purchase the 'freehold land of inheritance and the buildings thereon' at the age of 21 £50 cheaper than anyone else.

[4] *Liverpool Chronicle and Marine Gazette*, 17th February, 1758.

[5] *Gentleman's Magazine*. Gilbody is described as 'China Facturer, Dealer and Chapman'. His creditor was Thomas Kelley of Liverpool a Merchant. (Public Record Office B4/16, p. 33.)

[6] *Williamson's Liverpool Advertiser*, 3rd July, 1761.

Chaffers of the same date. The famous Gilbody mug, which until recently was thought to have been destroyed in the last war, bears a transfer print of Frederick, King of Prussia, signed 'Gilbody maker, Evans Sct'. It is consequently disappointing to find on examination that this mug appears to be of Worcester origin.[1] It is known that Sadler sometimes decorated Worcester[2] and one must suppose that the Gilbody-Evans signed print was used on this mug inadvertently.

Secondly, as the two pioneer Liverpool porcelain factories of Chaffers and Gilbody were next door to each other, it might be expected that their wares would show some points of similarity. Indeed, a fine bird painter and a painter of semi-comical chinoiserie enamelled some pieces of this group and both artists also decorated the early phosphatic group attributed to Chaffers as well as some of his earliest soapstone examples.

This group of porcelain is a small and individual one, showing two phases of development in potting technique comparable to that of early and middle period Longton Hall. The very scarce early pieces tend to be heavily potted and covered with a thick under-fired glaze. They are decorated with poorly defined blue patterns, overglaze *rouge de fer* and gilding. The later pieces consists mostly of fine-quality enamelled and overglaze transfer-printed wares, the blue and white examples being especially hard to find. The glaze, which is extremely soft and glossy, scratches easily. It is either colourless or tinted a pale grey and is usually well controlled, although often leaving a few bare patches on bases.

The blue and white designs (I) are well painted in a pleasing greyish blue and, as with the enamelled examples, they are sometimes by an artist who decorated early Chaffers' porcelain and had a fondness for painting a single daisy head under scenes. Handles usually show mould marks on their backs. A blue and white coffee can has a small thumb rest on an otherwise plain handle, but some coloured and transfer printed pieces have more elaborate silver-shapes.[3] Footrings have shelving inner-sides, and long, thin stilt marks are found under plate rims, usually accompanied by a little fawn-coloured sanding. The translucency is almost colourless by artificial light, but sometimes there are numbers of rust-coloured specks. Cracks stain brown

[1] Spectrographic analysis has confirmed that the porcelain is steatitic like a typical Worcester sample. Illustrated by Knowles Boney, *Liverpool Porcelain*, London, 1957, Plate 35a.

[2] See an interesting article on this subject by Dr. Knowles Boney, *Apollo*, Vols. LXXIII and LXXIV, March and April 1961.

[3] Watney, *Trans. E.C.C.*, vol. 4, part 5, 1959, pp. 20–25 and Plates 13, 14, 15, 16.

(I) *Plate* 52B.

as in phosphatic bodies and spectrographic and chemical analysis confirm that the porcelain contains bone ash.

Messrs. Reid & Company (?1755–61)

William Reid with his partners Daniel McNeal[1] and John Baddeley[2] may have been the first potters to make porcelain in Liverpool; they certainly published two advertisements in 1756 a few months before Chaffers, who is generally credited with being the first in the field. Reid's factory, which he called 'the Liverpool China Manufactory',[3] stood with its own colour mill on Brownlow Hill, a few minutes walk from the centre of the town. His warehouse was at first in Castle Street near the docks; it was later moved to Castle Hey, shortly afterwards renamed Harrington Street.

During the factory's short life Reid frequently advertised for apprentice painters, for example even his first advertisement[4] was for young persons with capacities for drawing and painting. Moreover the artist Ralph Wilcox,[5] who had just completed his apprenticeship to Dunbibin and Company, the Liverpool delft potters, is said to have worked for Reid and was with him when he failed. Two apprentices, John Robinson[6] and John Schroeder[7] are both described as potters when they petitioned for their freedom on 26th September, 1765. The former had served seven years' apprenticeship with William Reid & Company and the latter had served seven years with Daniel McNeal and Company.[8]

William Reid, described as late of Liverpool, became a bankrupt on 8th June, 1761; this was largely the result of shipping losses, for he was part owner of at least one ship which met with misfortune.[9] Josiah Wedgwood, one of the creditors, took an active part in recovering his own debts and those of Reid's other creditors at Burslem.[10] Wedgwood was almost certainly responsible for the winding up notice of 4th

---

[1] Mentioned as a partner in *Williamson's Liverpool Advertiser*, 19th June, 1761.

[2] Mentioned as a partner of Reid in *Wedgwood's Experiment Book*.

[3] *Williamson's Liverpool Advertiser*, 19th November, 1756, and 3rd November, 1758.

[4] *Ibid.*, 24th September, 1756.

[5] With his wife Sarah, the daughter of Thomas Fry, he later helped to decorate the famous Russian service for Wedgwood.

[6] Possibly the same John Robinson who worked as an artist at Seth Pennington's factory, see J. Mayer, *History of the Art of Pottery in Liverpool*, 1855, pp. 22–23.

[7] A *Leed's Directory for 1813* gives John Schroeder, potter.

[8] Daniel McNeal is described as late of Liverpool merchant dealer and chapman when he became bankrupt on 23rd June, 1761. The creditor was Edward Leigh of Cheadle Gent. Public Record Office index 22649.

[9] 'The Racehorse,' see Watney, *Trans. E.C.C.*, vol. 4, part 4, 1959, p. 19.

[10] *Ibid.* In January 1768 he wrote to Bentley asking him to inquire about matters in Liverpool and as to how the lawsuit was progressing in Ireland.

December, 1761, in the Liverpool Advertiser. 'To be sold by public auction on the 5th of January next at 6 o'clock, all those new erected buildings now used as a china manufactury with the colour mill and premises appurtenant thereto, situated on Brownlow Hill near Liverpool and lately occupied by Reid and Company, held by lease under the corporation of Liverpool. Any person desirous to view the premises may apply to Mr. Wedgwood at Burslem or to Mr. John Dobson in Liverpool. There is now on sale at Mr. Reid's shop, the upper end of Harrington Street, best blue and white cups and saucers at 3s. per set, second best do. at 2s. per set. Enamelled coffee cups from 6s. to 2s. a dozen. And all sorts of china cheap in proportion.' Wedgwood in his experiment book which dates from 1759, noted under experiment 65B that Isle of Wight sand, bone ashes, chalk and Purbeck clay[1] were the ingredients being used for the Liverpool china made by Messrs. Reid and Baddeley.

The small group attributed to Reid[2] is unlike any other Liverpool porcelain, but the opaque tin-containing glaze is a strong indication of a Liverpool origin, linking it with delft and tin-glazed stoneware. The primitive appearance, the comparative rarity and the lack of stylistic development suggest an early short-lived factory, such as was Reid's. In one respect this curious group parallels that of Chaffers as both have a few seemingly early examples which have no soapstone in them. The presence of soapstone in the majority of these pieces is a most unexpected finding and it is even more surprising to discover the remarkable similarity in style to Lund's Bristol porcelain. In fact, it is debatable whether this group was made at Limehouse, Bristol or Liverpool.[3] However, the enamelled examples have a bold, rather amateur style of decoration which is fully in keeping with a Liverpool attribution.

Reid's second advertisement dated 19th November, 1756,[4] mentions 'all kinds of blue and white ware, not inferior to any made in England, both wholesale and retail'. Indeed, this group consists mostly of blue and white, especially pickle or sweetmeat trays moulded directly from scallop shells (1), and large lion-masked and paw-footed sauce boats reminiscent of Bow examples (2). Teapots are unusually small and especially attractive (3). A number of pieces have salt-glaze counterparts, for example, a tall, acanthus-moulded vase with a grotesque mask (4), and cream boats moulded with rows of overlapping

---

[1] 'Pearl ashes' are added in pencil and then crossed out.
[2] Watney, *Trans. E.C.C.*, vol. 4, part 5, 1959, pp. 13–20.
[3] *Loc. cit.*   [4] *Williamson's Liverpool Advertiser.*

---

(1) *Plate* 43A; (2) *Plate* 44A; (3) *Plate* 46; (4) *Plate* 44C.

acanthus leaves. Tea caddies formed as boys' heads (1) are among the novelties produced by this extraordinary factory. The small blue and white figure of a dismal hound (2), the only known Liverpool figure, has an enviable pedigree, for it came from Lady Charlotte Schreiber's collection and was passed to her daughter Blanche, Countess of Bessborough, and then to her granddaughter Olwen, Lady Oranmore and Browne.

A scallop shell (3) and a fine tureen (4) are strikingly decorated with similar European landscapes and figures by a hand seemingly used to painting on delft. The same ambitious artist, possibly Ralph Wilcox, was especially fond of painting fruit, such as grapes, apples and pears, with carefully shaded contours. His characteristic rose sprays are found inside the tureen, on a dry mustard pot (5) and with other flowers on a covered cream jug (6). In contrast the Chinese figure scenes have a naïve charm best seen on a large covered vase,[1] a beaker (7), a sauce boat (8) and an attractive teapot (9). Chinese symbols decorate another fine teapot (10) as well as leaf-shaped pickle trays (11), many of which are bordered with a row of three plumes wound round with ribbons.

Imitation Chinese decoration is often so close to that on soft-paste Bristol as to be almost indistinguishable from it; for example, the chrysanthemum plants and flower sprays which decorate Reid's sauce boats and his small globular vases with tall, thin necks. Both factories were fond of painting broad leaves and scallop shells on pickle trays and sauce boat rims. Broad leaves are also found on teapot spouts and at the side of handle terminals. Furthermore a stylized peacock's feather, copied from Chinese export wares, is a favourite motif on handles and spouts; it was occasionally used on early Bow, on another group of Liverpool porcelain attributed to William Ball and much later on Caughley.

There seems to be little difference on visual examination between those pieces containing soapstone and those without it; in both cases under-firing and a small amount of tin often make the glaze rather opaque. In general, however, those with a bluish-white glaze are likely to contain soapstone while those with a darker grey colour and a more primitive appearance are non-steatitic. The latter pieces, especially the flat wares, are often mis-shapen and badly blistered.

[1] *Trans. E.C.C.*, vol. 5, part 2, 1961, Plate 83A.

---

(1) *Colour Plate* C; (2) *Plate* 45A;
(3) *Plate* 43A; (4) *Plate* 43D; (5) *Plate* 43B;
(6) *Plate* 44B; (7) *Plate* 45C; (8) *Plate* 44A;
(9) *Plate* 46B; (10) *Plate* 46A; (11) *Plate* 45B.

C. *Two tea caddies, steatitic porcelain, William Reid's factory, Liverpool, about 1756, ht. 5¼ in. Winifred Williams.*
(See page 80)

They are practically opaque with an orange translucency showing only in the thinner parts. The tureen (1) is one of the largest and best potted pieces of the non-steatitic group. Other examples include the rare blue and white versions of the prunus cup (2), whose crabstock handle begins as moulded roots at the lower terminal and ends by spreading out from the upper terminal as flowering branches to encircle the cup. A few of the steatitic pieces, especially some of the scallop shells, are better fired and less opaque, showing a green translucency by artificial light.

It is reasonably certain that William Reid and Company, who were outside the Chaffers-Christian group, obtained their soapstone directly from the Lizard. On 1st January, 1760, Viscount Falmouth granted a soaprock licence to John Baddeley[1] of Shelton and William Yates of Newcastle-under-Lyme for ten years. The soapstone they mined in Cornwall would have been shipped to Liverpool where, as we have previously noted, one of the licence holders, John Baddeley,[2] was already in partnership with William Reid at the Liverpool China factory.

William Ball (?1755–69)

There are a number of indications that William Ball was not a native Liverpool potter. He was apparently never a freeman of Liverpool and there is no record of any apprentices becoming indentured to him. Indeed, this elusive potter does not even appear to have advertised his china wares in the Liverpool newspapers. He is, however, listed in the first Liverpool Directory of 1766 as a china maker in Ranleigh Street and the entry is repeated in 1767 and 1769 but not afterwards. The first mention of a pottery in Ranleigh Street occurs in St. Peter's Parish Register which gives the birth of Jonathan, son of Thomas Dennett, clerk at the pot house in Ranleigh Street, on 19th December, 1755; a later birth and baptismal entry for Dennett in 1757 is mentioned by Price.[3] It is possible that William Ball the potter at Limehouse[4] left London for Staffordshire in 1748 and after a few years opened the pot house in Ranleigh Street, Liverpool. This supposition must await confirmation, but one factor which militates against an early solution is that there were at that time a number of Balls in Liverpool and Staffordshire: consequently we have to be

---

[1] *Trans. E.C.C.*, vol. 1, No. 3, 1935, p. 79.
[2] He became a bankrupt a few days after Reid on 16th June, 1761, and is described as late of Shelton, potter, dealer and chapman. The creditor was John Plumbe of Liverpool.
[3] *John Sadler*, 1948, p. 102.   [4] See p. 32.

---

(1) *Plate* 43D; (2) *Plate* 43C.

certain that we are not dealing with two potters with the same name.

The group of porcelain which is here ascribed to William Ball has certain features in common with Bow products and others reminiscent of Longton Hall wares. The group includes some of the finest Liverpool wares, especially those decorated with polychrome transfer prints overpainted with enamels. This type of decoration is also found on a few Longton Hall Britannia figures, and monochrome prints from the Liverpool copper plates, similarly embellished with enamels,[1] were used on Champion's hard paste porcelain at Bristol.

The earliest inscribed piece has the date 1756 in underglaze blue on the base (1). The only other documentary examples are a few tea wares[2] and a large covered jug,[3] in underglaze blue over-painted with iron red and gilt, which bear the date 1764. These dated wares have importance as regards attribution since they cover a period when only two Liverpool porcelain factories were in continuous production, namely the Chaffers Christian combine and that of William Ball.

The blue and white is easily distinguishable from other Liverpool wares. It appears to be freshly painted in a 'sticky blue' as it is decorated in an unusually bright cobalt and covered by a soft glaze with a high surface gloss. Among the close resemblances to Bow are many of the mannerisms used for depicting a similar choice of oriental patterns (2). A number of potting shapes also appear to derive from Bow, for example the fine pedestal sauce boats (3), the cylindrical coffee cans (4) and the bellied mugs, one of which, in the author's collection, even bears a heart-shaped handle terminal.[4] Imposing rococo sauce boats, some with fine snake-moulded handles, are the most characteristic products (5), one of which[5] has a Liverpool delft counterpart. This factory produced an unusually large variety of wares including tall covered jars (6), chamber candlesticks (7), mortars (8), goat and bee moulded jugs (9) and leaf moulded pickle trays on conical feet[6] and trinkets such as snuff boxes.[7] The attractive teapots sometimes have bold rococo handles (10). The flat wares (11), cornucopiae (12) and vases (13) are among the best potted and decorated pieces.

The blue and white decoration is usually inspired by scenes on Chinese porcelain, but a few pieces are decorated with European

---

[1] *Trans. E.C.C.*, vol. 5, part 1, 1960, p. 44.   [2] *Ibid.*, p. 44.
[3] *Ibid.*, Plate 34B.   [4] *Trans. E.C.C.*, vol. 5, part 1, 1960, Plate 29E.
[5] *Ibid.*, Plate 30D.   [6] *Ibid.*, Plate 31E.   [7] *Ibid.*, Plate 28C.

---

(1) *Plate* 50c; (2) *Plates* 47B, 49D, 50c; (3) *Plate* 47A;
(4) *Plate* 49D (2); (5) *Plates* 47, 48c; (6) *Plate* 52A; (7) *Plate* 50A;
(8) *Plate* 51B; (9) *Plate* 50B; (10) *Plate* 49c; (11) *Plates* 48B, 49A, 51c;
(12) *Plate* 48A; (13) *Plate* 51A.

scenes in a style reminiscent of painting on delft. A well-known example is the mug[1] with equestrian figures copied from an engraving in the *Ladies' Amusement* after a drawing by L. Walker. Another small group has painted flower sprays and insects in the Meissen manner such as a spoon tray in the British Museum inscribed 'H.W.'. An interesting punch bowl inscribed round the inside with a drinking song 'set by Mr. Yates' was recently illustrated in Sotheby's sale catalogue.[2] It is probably the bowl described as Bristol in 1873.[3]

The potting of this group shows certain features in common with that of Longton Hall, although its paste is always much less translucent. The translucency in artificial light varies from bright green to yellowish brown. Surface tears in the paste appear as light flecks and, as on Longton wares, sometimes form linear defects in the throwing lines. The glaze is usually very smooth and sometimes crazed. Footrings tend to be poorly finished and on some flat wares they appear to have been applied by hand and not turned. Cup handles often have a D-shape section, but are poorly formed and roughly applied. These wares give an intense white fluorescence with short wave ultra-violet light somewhat similar to early Longton wares. Spectographic analysis of ten examples shows that the paste is steatitic with the occasional presence of a slight trace of phosphate.

There is no doubt that in the mid-eighteenth century the production of a soapstone porcelain was considered a major advance towards a closer imitation of the Chinese; its successful use had already been demonstrated at Bristol and then at Worcester. William Ball's soapstone recipe must have been a closely guarded secret, for he appears to have used this ingredient in his paste at least as early as Chaffers without attracting any publicity. It is possible that the initial experiments with soapstone were carried out at Limehouse where Benjamin Lund and William Ball could have shared a knowledge of the recipe. Unfortunately no soaprock licence has yet been discovered for William Ball, but Morton Nance who recorded the licences[4] was fully aware that others may have been granted by landlords, such as members of the Vivian family, whose relevant deeds he had been unable to trace.

[1] *Catalogue of The Schreiber Collection*, Victoria and Albert Museum, vol. I, 1915, Plate 83.
[2] 10th May, 1960.
[3] H. Owen, *Two Centuries of Ceramic Art in Bristol*, 1873, pp. 14, 15.
[4] *Trans. E.C.C.*, vol. 1, no. 3, 1935.

6

DERBY

John Heath,[1] a merchant banker, and a young china maker named Andrew Planché, were probably the founders of a small china factory which was set up in leasehold premises near St. Mary's Bridge, Derby, about 1750. This factory concentrated on producing figures whose exceptionally fine modelling rivalled that of the contemporary Chelsea 'raised anchor' and the first 'red anchor' marked figures. Only a few domestic wares were made in this early period. They probably include the three well-known white cream jugs[2] which are decorated with applied clusters of strawberries and leaves and strawberry flowers. Planché's training as a goldsmith and jeweller[3] no doubt influenced his choice of shapes not only for these cream jugs but also for some rare salt cellars and sauce boats in the form of exotic shells[4] with marine encrustations.

Blue and white wares were apparently not produced until William Duesbury[5] became a partner in 1756 and the factory expanded along the Nottingham Road.[6] Even then, unlike most English eighteenth-century porcelain factories, Derby made comparatively little blue and white. Furthermore, apart from an unduly large proportion of moulded sauce boats and cream jugs (I), the early output is typified by ornamental pieces such as pot-pourri (2)[7] and open-work baskets (3),

[1] He became a bankrupt in March 1779.

[2] One inscribed 'Derby', the second 'D. 1750' and the third 'D'.

[3] Apprenticed to the jeweller and goldsmith Edward Mountenay of London from 3rd July, 1740, until 3rd July, 1747.

[4] Ll. Jewitt, *The Ceramic Art of Great Britain*, 1878, vol. 1, p. 328, fig. 706. Sauce boats of this type, both in the white and enamelled, have in the past been variously ascribed, especially to Plymouth by Jewitt. A shell salt from the MacAlister Collection is now in the British Museum.

[5] An important enameller, especially of figures, who had had his own business in London between 1751 and 1753 before working at the Longton Hall factory for two years prior to taking up his new duties at Derby.

[6] Further leasehold properties were taken over in April 1756 and November 1756. See F. Barrett, *Trans. E.C.C.*, vol. 4, part 5, 1959, p. 26 *et seq*.

[7] These were sometimes known as chestnut baskets.

(I) *Plate* 65c; (2) *Plate* 64b; (3) *Plate* 64c.

and plates (1) sometimes embellished with applied flower heads and painted with intricate borders. The unusual care that went into the production of these wares at Derby may have been due to the fact that the glassy paste was difficult to work, and thus Duesbury only found it worth while to make pieces that were somewhat pretentious and correspondingly expensive.

No dated blue and white examples are known prior to 1770 and other means have to be relied on to classify the wares. As is also the case with the enamel-painted figures and vessels, the majority of blue and white pieces have three or more circular glaze-free patches on the base, known as 'patch' marks, caused by supporting the vessel in the sagger on bobbs of clay. A small blue and white cream jug (2) and a miniature cup and saucer in the author's collection have an unusually primitive appearance and were probably made early in 1756. They are without 'patch' marks on their bases but were fired on broad stilts like Longton Hall pieces.[1] However, the glaze is not strictly comparable with that on contemporary enamelled wares such as the teapot bearing the incised date 1756 underglaze on the base.[2] The two Derby sale advertisements for 1756 do not mention blue and white, but Jewitt lists some when describing the contents of 42 large boxes sent to London in 1763.[3] Amongst these were fluted sauce boats, blue strawberry pots, blue guglets and basins; other interesting wares, not necessarily blue and white, included sage-leaf boats, open-worked spectacle baskets, fig-leaf sauce boats, vine-leaf plates (3), butter tubs, honeycomb pots and polyanthus pots.

Wares bearing 'patch' marks were made up till about 1770, including some which contain soapstone, but the majority were produced earlier from a glassy paste between 1756 and 1764[4]. Typical of the early 'patch' mark group are sauce boats in different shapes and sizes moulded with pears and cobnuts (4). These and other sauce boats with various silver-shape mouldings have been copied directly from Bow examples and they are always less crisply moulded than their prototypes. Sometimes they even have a poorly formed heart-shaped terminal to the handle. Derby was fond of knobs formed as cherries and strawberries, especially on butter dish (5) and chocolate or caudle-cup

[1] Possibly due to the influence of William Duesbury who had recently left the Longton Hall factory. But stilt marks are found on many items including the earliest Derby figures.
[2] The Cecil Higgins Museum, Bedford (F. Hurlbutt, *Bow Porcelain*, London, 1926, Plate 15).
[3] Ll. Jewitt, *The Ceramic Art of Great Britain*, 1878, vol. 2, p. 69. [4] See top of page 87.

(1) *Plate* 64A; (2) *Plate* 63A; (3) *Plate* 65D; (4) *Plate* 66A; (5) *Plate* 66D.

covers (1). This feature was probably also derived from Bow whose tureen and cover with a cherry moulded knob (2) was reproduced almost exactly. Derby mugs are distinctive and tend to be tall with widely arched handles whose terminals curl upwards (3). The octagonal butter tubs (4) have a practical simplicity in contrast to the ornamental pickle trays (5), 'wine tasters' (6), and centre-pieces (7). Among the rarities are a chamber candlestick (8) and a trinket stand (9). Blue and white cups, including those with peaked handles (10), are uncommon, but early saucers are even scarcer—in fact none have yet been discovered which can be dated before 1760.

Between 1756 and 1764 the paste and glaze of the blue and white, unlike those of the coloured wares, shows little variation. The glaze is usually full of small bubbles and its surface is uneven. It is sometimes thickly applied and at other times brushed on so thinly that the design remains slightly raised above the almost matt surface. Patterns had a strong tendency to blur in the soft glaze, but where the glaze had been thinly applied this defect was minimized. The wares are often thickly potted and rather lumpy and the paste appears remarkably white through the glaze. Flat wares especially show circular translucent areas; these are due to air bubbles and known as 'moons'. There are sometimes more of these 'moons' to the square inch in Derby plates than in any other porcelain. The translucency in artificial light is usually a cloudy straw colour with varying tones of green. Footrings had to be ground level as a result of glaze drips. Handles, especially on large sauce boats and mugs, tend to be thick and practical, and there is frequently a small hole in the paste under the lower handle terminal. The underglaze blue often has a strong ultramarine or violet tone and this vivid colour contrasts with the very white body to produce a rather harsh effect. The usual romantic symbols of the Chinese landscape, such as pagodas and islands covered with rocks, trellis fences and pine trees, are carefully but rather stiffly portrayed in a style reminiscent of needlework (11). These, together with the highly stylized flower paintings, are in marked contrast to the minutely observed moths and butterflies.[1] No amount of trouble has been spared in painting the intricate Chinese borders which were a veritable obsession of this factory (12).

[1] J. L. Dixon, *English Porcelain of the Eighteenth Century*, London, 1952, Plate 32B.

(1) *Plate* 66c; (2) *Plate* 18c; (3) *Plate* 69B;
(4) *Plate* 65B; (5) *Plate* 66B; (6) *Plate* 66B;
(7) *Plate* 65A; (8) *Plate* 63B; (9) *Plate* 63c;
(10) *Plate* 67A; (11) *Plate* 63D; (12) *Plate* 68D.

In 1764 Richard Holdship[1] signed an agreement with Messrs. Duesbury and Heath to supply soaprock and to reveal the secrets of making soapstone porcelain 'according to proof already made by him at the Derby works'.[2] Holdship was also to introduce the other Worcester speciality with which he had been intimately connected, namely that of transfer-printing.[3] About this time a few examples with a glassy paste were decorated in underglaze blue transfers, and these were probably Holdship's first attempts at Derby. They include some designs previously used at Worcester but for the most part they are less skilful re-engravings; for example a version of the 'zig-zag fence' pattern, the 'plantation' pattern, a pair of Chinese river scenes,[4] and birds, including two swans (1).[5] Most of these 'Worcester' prints are likely to have been copied from engravings by Robert Hancock and re-engraved by Richard Holdship.[6] There is a possibility, however, that a few of the designs were originally Holdship's own work at Worcester, since we know that at Derby he not only engraved copper plates but also had his own process 'for printing enamel and blue'. He undoubtedly acquired these skills before going to Derby.

As might be expected these 'Worcester' designs are also found on a small group of Derby (2) typical examples of which contain soapstone. One of the designs, the so-called view of 'Sutton Hall', can be seen in underglaze blue on a lobed dish,[7] and in overglaze black on an election mug for 1768 marked with the word 'Derby' and an anchor as a rebus for Holdship.[8]

[1] A former partner in the Worcester porcelain factory who left Worcester in 1759.

[2] R. W. Binns, *A Century of Potting in the City of Worcester*, 2nd ed., London, 1877, p. 115, gives details of the process of manufacture given by Holdship to John Heath and William Duesbury at Derby, 31st December, 1764. Holdship gave recipes for two types of ware: the first containing soapstone in the body and foreign china and tin ashes in the glaze, the second 'in imitation of Nanquin being an opaque body', containing bone ash in the body, and not only foreign china but also borax in the glaze.

[3] Ll. Jewitt, *The Ceramic Art of Great Britain*, vol. 1, pp. 232–3 and vol. 2, p. 88.

[4] F. Brayshaw Gilhespy, *Crown Derby Porcelain*, Leigh-on-Sea, 1951, fig. 124. An analysis showed a glassy paste containing 8·18 per cent lead oxide.

[5] Cyril Cook, *The Life and Work of Robert Hancock*, London, 1948, item 93.

[6] Some of these transfers are also found on Derby creamware. G. Godden, *E.C.C.*, vol. 3, part 4, 1955, lists four prints on cream ware which have the anchor rebus for Holdship.

[7] Aubrey Toppin, *Trans. E.C.C.*, vol. 3, part 1, 1951, Plate 28A.

[8] It does not appear to have been previously noted that the other side of this mug bears an engraving adapted from a design by Samuel Wale R.A., said to be engraved by Hancock at Worcester. It is one of the few designs which are associated with an anchor rebus mark on Worcester porcelain. (Cyril Cook, *Supplement to The Life and Work of Robert Hancock*, 1955, item 143.) Also Toppin, *Trans. E.C.C.*, vol. 3, part 1, Plate 27.

(1) *Plate* 67D; (2) *Plates* 67C, 68C.

The copper plate of this design was later found at Coalport where another plate, also with a design used at Worcester and Derby, was discovered.[1] The attractive engraving on this latter plate, known as 'La Dame Chinoise', was adapted for a small mug now in the British Museum (1). It is marked with the word 'Derby', a sun and an anchor in underglaze blue. This design, together with three other patterns, a Chinese island scene with swans (2), a boy riding a buffalo, and the underglaze blue version of the 'red cow' pattern, are found not only on steatitic Derby porcelain of the mid 1760's but also on Bow porcelain of the early 1760's. In at least one case the same copper plate appears to have been used at both factories, to decorate a Bow mug[2] and a Derby teapot (3). The most likely explanation of this link-up is that Richard Holdship worked for a short time at the Bow factory before taking his copper plates to Derby in 1764. He could easily have done this during the period when there is no record of his activities, which extends from the time he left Worcester in 1759, having sold his share, until 1764, when he was at Derby.

The association of a number of transfer prints with Holdship at Derby and possibly also at Bow raises the question as to how far he was responsble for the original introduction of these designs, in particular the 'red cow' pattern at Worcester. This design, which cannot reasonably be claimed as a Hancock engraving, is found on some of the earliest Worcester pieces.[3] If Holdship was indeed the originator of this engraving it is likely that he may have also initiated the process of transfer printing at Worcester about 1754,[4] well before the arrival of Hancock in late 1756 or early 1757, although the latter undoubtedly eclipsed any such amateur efforts with his own brilliant achievements.

[1] Franklin A. Barrett, *Caughley and Coalport Porcelain*, Leigh-on-Sea, 1957, Fig. 40. Also Cyril Cook, *op. cit.*, item 26. Holdship may possibly have visited Caughley after being at Derby but there is no good evidence of this.

[2] John A. Ainslie, Underglaze blue printing on Bow Porcelain, *The Antique Collector*, April 1957, Fig. 11.

[3] H. E. Marshall, *The Antique Collector*, April, 1959, Fig. 13.

[4] Probably with the help of his brother Josiah Holdship. P. Entwistle, M.S. 15/161 Liverpool Reference Library, records a letter, dated 14th July, 1796, from Martin Barr of the Worcester factory to Ralph Wedgwood, which is in the Wedgwood Museum at Barlaston and concerns the application for patent rights. Barr writes, 'Pray remember that that worthy honest man Josiah Holdship who invented printing at Worcester lost, merely for want of prudent care upwards of £13,000 which he was possessed of when he found out that art.' We know that when Richard Holdship was later at Derby he valued his press at ten guineas and his copper plates at a large amount. He had, he said, been offered several hundred pounds for his process for printing enamel and blue (Ll. Jewitt, *Ceramic Art in Great Britain*, vol. 2, p. 89).

---

(1) *Plate* 68A; (2) *Plate* 67B; (3) *Plate* 68B.

Only a few underglaze blue transfer prints are apparently peculiar to Derby. Amongst these are various flower sprays also found on Derby creamware, and an unusually bold design of flowers standing in a large shallow bowl. A Chinese scene including a catamaran is found on tea wares, plates and pickle trays, and another similar scene, including houses and pagodas has a later, less attractive painted version (1).

The use of soapstone at Derby, from 1764 to 1769, made it possible to pot wares more thinly than with the earlier glassy body. As a result more cups and saucers were made as well as fine globular teapots and tall tapering coffee pots to match (2). Shapes are simplified and the wares are neatly finished. A few Worcester shapes were copied, such as small pedestal cream jugs[1] with ribbed sides and those leaf moulded pickle trays with handles which are sometimes called 'artichoke butter boats'. Footrings no longer needed to be ground level and flat wares are no longer riddled with air bubbles. The body still has a very white appearance and the translucency by artificial light remains a cloudy yellow tinged with green. The glaze is much better controlled, smoother and tighter fitting; the surface however is sometimes sanded with fine black specks. The glaze is usually soft and colourless, but on later examples it is harder and tinted a bluish grey closely resembling that on Worcester porcelain (3). The shades of cobalt vary from almost black to a brilliant royal blue, and the designs, whether transfer-printed or painted, still tend to blur in the glaze. The occasional clear outline is a well merited reward for consistently careful drawing.

From the 1770's onwards there seems to have been a number of experiments with the body and the glaze for all types of wares, but none of these was particularly successful for blue and white. The quality fell off considerably and the paste and glaze eventually became as characterless as those of most late eighteenth-century and early nineteenth-century porcelains. A certain William Taylor 'painted only blue under the glaze on biscuit. That failed, and he asked permission to paint on the glaze, and paid his foot-ale for it'.[2] Added gilding became a common feature in an attempt to enliven the blurred patterns which for the most part were painted in a bright indigo, or else, as a novelty, in two shades of blue. The designs with their scale and cell borders are usually painted to look like transfer

[1] These never seem to have a lamprey moulded handle as on the Worcester examples.
[2] Wallis and Bemrose, *The Pottery and Porcelain of Derbyshire*, Derby, 1870, p. 12. Taylor was, however, still an underglaze blue painter in 1791 when, according to Joseph Lygo, Duesbury's London agent, he decorated a plate for Mr. Digby (F. B. Gilhespy, *Derby Porcelain*, London, 1961, p. 75).

(1) *Plate* 70D; (2) *Plate* 69A; (3) *Plate* 70B.

prints, and indeed they have been mistaken for them. For example there is a painted teapoy (1) which is described by Haslem as having been in the possession of Miss Duesbury, a grand-daughter of the founder of the works. He wrote, 'it is covered all over with a printed pattern, and has the Derby mark, all in blue, under the glaze. This piece is of a much later date than 1764, and the blue is of a better quality than was made at that time. On the cover the name of Duesbury is scratched in the glaze, it is said by himself, from which it might be inferred that the piece was an experiment, rather than that such goods were then manufactured at Derby.'[1] Nevertheless, transfer-printing undoubtedly continued to be used after Holdship left in 1769, for instance in 1771 John Lodge[2] engraved some plates including one of Chinese figures. A fine jug with a mask moulded lip[3] bears a transfer-print of the town's crest, a stag at lodge, and a teapot[4] shows the continued use of the 'catamaran' pattern.

After 1770 numbers of shallow, fluted sauce boats were made and wide saucer dishes were fairly common. Tea bowls and saucers often had a double ogee shape and cup handles had pointed terminals or else were square-ended and moulded with bands across them (2). Some of these late shapes such as the large dishes (3), small pickle trays and asparagus servers[5] resemble those of Caughley. Patch marks no longer occur and wares show signs of having been fired on stilts and spurs. Factory marks are found for the first time. The crown with the letter 'D' beneath may date from the occasion in 1773 when George III is supposed to have visited the factory, although it was probably used a few years previously as a mark of royal patronage. The script 'N' either incised or painted is found alone or in conjunction with the crown and 'D' mark. The 'N' mark occurs on an unusual mug in the Bootle Museum (4), on asparagus servers and on a few silver-shape cream jugs. The crown and cross batons with six dots over a script 'D' is thought to have been used shortly after 1782,[6] especially on pieces

[1] John Haslem, *The Old Derby China Factory*, 1876, p. 24.

[2] Ll. Jewitt, *The Ceramic Art of Great Britain*, 1878, vol. 2, p. 89.

[3] A. L. Thorpe, 'Some Early Derby Porcelain', *Connoiseur*, vol. CXLVI, Dec. 1960, Plate 20.

[4] F. Tilley, *Teapots and Tea*, Newport, 1957, Plate XXVI, Fig. 83.

[5] It is difficult to imagine how these servers were used but they are said to have been spaced out on a dish to hold individual bundles. They are now frequently known as knife rests. They are sometimes marked with impressed letters such as 'M' or 'L'.

[6] The date on a documentary enamelled jug with a mask lip of Admiral Rodney bearing the crown over 'D' mark without the batons.

(1) *Plate* 70D; (2) *Plate* 70C; (3) *Plate* 69C;
(4) *Plate* 70A.

decorated in the French style with floral sprigs in Smith's overglaze blue enamel.[1]

Bone ash was introduced into the Derby paste about 1770[2] after the Chelsea factory had been taken over and the so-called 'Chelsea-Derby' period commenced. However, for some blue and white wares there appears to have been a reversion from a steatitic to a glassy paste; in particular for early pieces marked with the crown over 'D' (I). Later examples with this mark contain 40 per cent or more of bone ash.[3] Joseph Lygo gives some interesting details about the supply of raw materials for Derby porcelain.[4] He shows that continual difficulty was experienced in obtaining suitable supplies of cobalt. In 1786, for example, he writes: 'There are no other samples of blue to be got at present, enclosed is a list of prices of different cobalts from Irish and Hitchens, they showed me many different styles of Mr. Turner's, both from smalts and cobalts. I understand they have served him for some time, the cobalt at fifty shillings produces a strong colour under the glaze.' In 1790 he refers to broken Nankin china being used in the glaze and being sent to Derby by water from the India warehouse. In 1792 bone ashes were hard to get and not well burnt. In 1795 it was difficult to obtain imported smalts in the pure state as the East India Company was exporting them to China.

Christie's sale catalogues of the late 1770's and 1780's list a fair quantity of blue and white in the sales of Chelsea and Derby porcelain.[5] The smaller wares include asparagus servers, pickle leaves and scallop shells, knife handles, artichoke cups and egg spoons. On a larger scale are cheese and vegetable stands, salad dishes, sweetmeat stands and sauce boats. Then there are 'double-shape' coffee cups and a large coffee pot of the 'blue Nankin' pattern and coffee cans with saucers. The 1783 sale is of particular interest because Dr. Johnson, presumably Dr. Samuel Johnson, bought a number of lots among which were some blue and white. This is in spite of the fact that on his visit to the Derby factory in 1777 Dr. Johnson had asserted that he could have had 'vessels of silver of the same size as cheap . . .'. One lot he bought for seven shillings consisted of six scallop shells, six artichoke cups and six asparagus servers. He paid four shillings and sixpence for a pair of

[1] Said to be invented by William Smith, one of the first apprentices of William Duesbury.

[2] William Bemrose, *Bow, Chelsea and Derby Porcelain*, 1898, p. 112.

[3] Eccles and Rackham, *Analysed Specimens of English Porcelain*, 1922, p. 31.

[4] His letters to Duesbury in the Derby Public Library.

[5] J. E. Nightingale, *Contributions towards the History of Early English Porcelain*, Salisbury, 1881.

(I) *Plate* 70c.

potting pots 'blue and white landscape' pattern. A pair of butter tubs, covers and stands, enamelled 'blue Chantille' pattern cost him six shillings and another lot of six French shape cups and saucers 'enamelled fine blue and white' cost fourteen shillings.

Derby blue and white, unlike Duesbury's other lines, could hardly have been a commercial success. In spite of continual experiments he was unable to achieve a consistent standard of production, the wares being either outstanding or else little better than seconds. After his death in 1786 underglaze blue decoration seems to have been used very infrequently and then mostly for special orders.

7

LOWESTOFT

Local collectors have long been particularly susceptible to the endearing qualities of Lowestoft porcelain. This is little wonder as no other English china evokes quite the same sense of belonging to a particular place. For example, the birth plaques (1) made for hanging in the East Anglian cottages and the host of other pieces inscribed with good Suffolk and Norfolk names. It is not difficult to imagine those first porcelain souvenirs of the seaside, the 'trifles' from Lowestoft (2), Yarmouth and elsewhere being sold direct from the factory, in the village shops and at Bungay fair. Then there are the fine pieces decorated with accurate pictorial records of a coastal battery, of the lighthouses and windmills, of the Lowestoft Nonconformist Chapel and of St. Margaret's Church both before and after the extension of the churchyard. An important enamelled bowl depicts the exciting action of a sea battle with the Dutch fleet,[1] while in contrast other pieces show the less spectacular everyday activities such as boat building (3) and smoking herrings (4).[2] Even the Lowestoft blue and white which is decorated in the Chinese manner and which formed a major part of the output is unmistakably provincial in appearance. It was largely decorated by unskilled but self-confident painters, for the most part women and children,[3] who by a clumsy interpretation of the oriental scenes produced their own distinctive fantasies.

Isaac and Edmund Gillingwater, one time hairdressers in the High Street, were the first historians of Lowestoft. Their book,[4] published by Edmund Gillingwater, gives the only known contemporary account

[1] *The Catalogue of the Lowestoft Bicentenary Exhibition* at Ipswich, No. 189. The Battle of Camperdown, 11th October, 1797.
[2] *The Universal Directory 1795* 'Walker and Browne China Manufacturers and Herring Curers'.
[3] Robert Allen is said to have been employed as an underglaze blue painter at the age of 12.
[4] *An Historical Account of the Ancient Town of Lowestoft*, the preface dated 1790.

(1) *Plates* 75c, 81b, 83b; (2) *Plate* 86a; (3) *Plate* 79a; (4) *Plate* 76c.

of the origin of the porcelain factory. They relate how the discovery of a deposit of suitable clay led to some preliminary trials first at a china factory near London, presumably Bow, and then on the Gunton estate just outside Lowestoft by Hewling Luson[1] the landowner. In the following year, 1757, four Lowestoft men, Robert Browne,[2] Philip Walker,[3] Obed Aldred,[4] and John Richman[5] bought some property on the South side of Bell lane, now Crown Street, where they set up their china factory.[6] From the outset they made their wares with a bone-ash paste, apparently using a recipe almost identical to that which was the original discovery of the Bow proprietors. This could hardly have been a coincidence and there may be some truth in the family tradition[7] that Robert Browne discovered their secrets by disguising himself as a workman and taking up temporary employment at the London china manufactory. Furthermore, Gillingwater states that workmen from the London manufactories had been

[1] A member of an interesting Nonconformist family who were related to Oliver Cromwell. Bankrupt 9th October, 1761, creditor John Spicer of Lowestoft, Yeoman (Public Record Office Bankruptcy Index 22649 Fol. 160). On that date he is described as of Gunton in the county of Suffolk, Merchant. The Gunton estate was purchased in 1762 by Vice Admiral Sir Charles Saunders, K.B.; Hewling Luson had probably left Lowestoft by that time. The *London Gazette* of 25th January, 1762, describes him as late of Gunton. However, he did not lose all connection with Lowestoft for he owned herring boats there continuously from 1748 until his death in 1777. In the same year his son, Hewling Luson junior, was married at Lowestoft.

[2] Reputed to be a chemist and the manager of the porcelain factory. He died in 1771 aged 68. Described as a Yeoman in his will (in Somerset House, P.C.C. Trevor 143). His executors were Philip Walker, Gentleman, and Obed Aldred, Bricklayer. His son, Robert Browne the younger, inherited his fourth part or share in the china business.

[3] He had a practical knowledge of making glazed pan-tiles at his brick kiln at Gunton (*Norwich Mercury*, 28th June 1760. A. J. B. Kiddell, private communication). The major shareholder in the porcelain factory having two of the four shares. He died in 1803, aged 81. In his will he mentions his copyhold land at the northern end of Lowestoft which was once part of Hewling Luson's estate (P.C.C. Marriott 499). His Coat of Arms is given in Gillingwater, p. 423.

[4] Described as a merchant in his will (P.C.C. Calvert 381). He appears to have died a fairly wealthy property owner in 1788 aged 67. After his wife's death in 1791 his fourth part share in the china factory went to his grandson Samuel Higham Aldred, the eldest son of Samuel Dixon Aldred.

[5] A merchant who, like the rest of the partners, had an interest in the local herring fisheries. He became a bankrupt on 18th November, 1756, when he was described as a merchant of Lowestoft, the creditor being William Kingsbury of Bungay, Maltster. *The Ipswich Journal* for 16th April, 1757, describes him as late of Lowestoft (N. H. P. Turner, private communication) but he seems to have returned to Lowestoft shortly afterwards. 'John Richman died by a pistol shot' 1st October, 1771 (*Lowestoft Parish Registers*).

[6] The factory's water mill built on leasehold land in Gunton ravine is mentioned in the wills of Browne, Walker and Aldred as part of the joint assets.

[7] Ll. Jewitt, *The Ceramic Art of Great Britain*, vol. I, London, 1878, p. 443.

employed at Lowestoft. One of these was James Mottershead, a china
painter who seems to have worked at Bow, then at Lowestoft and
afterwards in the Potteries at Hanley.[1]

The Lowestoft factory is particularly well documented. Excavations
on the factory site in 1902 and 1903 produced a large quantity of
moulds and wasters, many of which were admirably illustrated in
monographs by Spelman[2] and Crisp:[3] these form the basis for future
identifications. A greater number of dated pieces were produced at
Lowestoft than at any other English porcelain factory and their close
sequence has been recorded in an authoritative study by Kiddell.[4]

This was followed by three important papers by Hunting[5] who used
his own unrivalled knowledge of the subject to give a clear picture of
the artistic development from the earliest days.

It is convenient to divide the output of the Lowestoft factory into
three periods coinciding with a number of major changes in style, but
one factor which complicates such a classification is the factory's habit
of re-issuing their early potting shapes at a much later date.

The Early Period (1757–1760)

The primitive wares which compose this group were first described
by Hunting.[6] They have a pleasing delft-like appearance, sometimes
with a marked pink undertone to the greyish blue glaze. It is tempting
to ascribe this similarity to delft to the Dutch influence which for
generations had been particularly strong in East Anglia, but it is
probably the fortuitous result of under-firing the body and glaze. The
early shapes, while frequently copying Chinese porcelain and English
silver prototypes, were remarkably little influenced by contemporary
English porcelain. The following are some of the few remaining
pieces of this early group. They include beautifully thrown baluster
vases with covers surmounted by a bird-shaped knob: the bird-shaped
knob is also found on a sucrier (1) giving a clue to the teapot from the
same service. Tall beakers with flared lips can be matched with wasters

[1] A. J. Toppin (personal communication). The Registers of St. Mary Stratford
Bow 1765 to 1767. See also Chaffers, 14th ed., pp. 846 and 853. Also Ll. Jewitt,
vol. I, p. 452.
[2] W. W. R. Spelman, *Lowestoft China*, 1905.
[3] F. A. Crisp, *Lowestoft China Factory*, 1908.
[4] A. J. B. Kiddell, 'Inscribed and Dated Lowestoft Porcelain', *Trans. E.P.C.*,
No. III, 1931.
[5] D. M. Hunting, 'Miniature Lowestoft China', *The Antique Collector*, November 1949; 'Lowestoft China Teapots', *The Antique Collector*, December 1951;
'Early Lowestoft', *Trans. E.C.C.*, vol. 3, part 1, 1951.
[6] 'Early Lowestoft', *Trans. E.C.C.*, vol. 3, part 1, 1951.

(1) *Plate* 73A.

from the factory site. Two splendid coffee pots (1) have high domed lids and steeply rising spouts, features which were to become more exaggerated in the later wares. Some coffee cups and cans (2) have unusually primitive loop handles in marked contrast to the thin, fragile scroll forms which are found on other early pieces,[1] but not to any extent afterwards. A robust hand-basin (3) with a neatly curled rim, and the ewer that went with it, were the prototypes of examples made in the mid 1760's. An elegant two handled porringer with a reversible saucer-type cover was re-issued with slight alterations as an enamelled piece about twenty years later. Early plates are exceptionally rare, and even in later years only a few seem to have been made. On the other hand circular patty pans and moulded pickle trays in the form of leaves and scallop shells appear to have been popular, and they must have been considerably easier to produce than the only known early spoon tray (4).[2] There are a small number of open-work baskets (5) dating from about 1760 and a few moulded sauce boats (6), probably made a year or so earlier. Only recently Mr. G. Godden of Worthing has discovered some early knife-handles.

Certain embossed tea wares were made prior to the well-known examples moulded with the dates 1761 and 1764 and the initials 'I.H.' They differ from the later pieces in the boldness and clarity of the moulding (7) and in certain small features of the design, the most noticeable of which is the absence of large chrysanthemum flowers and broad leaves. On the tea and slop bowls a single line of beads encircles the reserves instead of the later two or three graded rows of beads, and there is a floral moulding instead of moulded scroll work above the footring. Cream jugs at first appear to have had a plain loop handle with a slightly curled upper terminal; this was soon followed by an elaborate scroll handle with a finely formed thumb rest, which was replaced in later services by a more practical shape. Cups of the early services have handles with particularly well-formed thumb rests and the typical Lowestoft feature of a cocked-up lower terminal. Pairs of rectangular tea caddies with broadly chamfered corners are inscribed with the name of the appropriate type of tea on small reserves surrounded by moulded festoons over-painted with blue. Hunting mentions that these vessels were re-issued about ten years later, but with less attractive decoration. Three standard Chinese scenes are painted in underglaze blue in the circular reserves on the sides of pieces from

---

[1] See a fine bell-shaped mug, D. M. Hunting, *op. cit.*, Plate 30B.
[2] A slightly later example is at Number 4 South Quay, Yarmouth.

---

(1) *Plate* 71A; (2) *Plates* 72A, D; (3) *Plate* 71B; (4) *Plate* 72B; (5) *Plate* 73B; (6) *Plate* 73C; (7) *Plate* 75A.

the early service, and the same scenes decorate the later services. Saucers have an extra central reserve painted with a prunus spray in profile and surrounded by a moulded floral border in the early service, and a moulded leaf design in the later examples. The early tea bowls and basins have two painted borders, a loose scroll design and a trellis and flower-head pattern, on either side of the rim. The services moulded with the date 1761 are decorated with a bolder and more compact scroll design, but the trellis and flower-head border is much the same as before although it was sometimes replaced by a broad blue border with flower-head and scroll reserves in white. The 1764 service has a single border, the so-called 'key and cell' pattern.

At first great care was used in painting the designs on non-embossed wares, showing a pleasing sense of individuality and an appreciation of form and balance which was not achieved later. The outlines are finely drawn and filled in with pale blue tints. There is none of the slapdash triviality of the later stock patterns. However, the decorative motifs have a limited range and they are easily recognizable with a little experience. They consist for the most part of trailing plants with the root stock often hidden by a large chrysanthemum or peony flower. Water fowl are strangely contorted as though suddenly stopped in mid flight by a shot[1] and huge insects hover over the scene.

The rare early coffee pots (1) include in the decoration the figure of a woman painted with the same innocent direct confrontation which is found in modern 'primitive' painting. Sauce boats (2) and open-work baskets (3) are decorated with rather disjointed Chinese scenes.

Already at this early stage certain mannerisms were developing which eventually became the typical features of Lowestoft porcelain. Willow trees were often painted with pendant dotted lines between their branches, presumably to represent catkins (4). There was a fondness for depicting flower heads and buds in profile, not only as part of the main decoration but also as embellishments for handles and spouts. A spray of three leaves is a common decorative feature on thumb rests. Fine single lines were often painted at the sides of spouts and handle terminals, and round the feet of pickle trays. Painters' numerals appear on bases and more characteristically on the inside of footrings. Among the potting features a heart-shaped terminal is an exceptional rarity. It occurs on one of the two known early coffee pots and on a few later wares when the edges of the heart are usually serrated. The delicate hand-made open flower knob on the coffee-pot

---

[1] This mannerism was copied from the Chinese and is also often seen on English delft.

(1) *Plate* 71A; (2) *Plate* 73C; (3) *Plate* 73B; (4) *Plate* 72C.

lid is not found later although it may have occurred on contemporary teapots and sucriers.[1] Both the bird-shaped knob and the ribbed bulbous knob continued to be used in the early 1760's.

The Middle Period (1761–1770)

This was a period of greatly increased production when a comparatively large number of pieces were inscribed with dates, especially after 1765. Unfortunately the decorations on the majority of the documentary pieces are either somewhat insignificant designs or else unusually fine topographical scenes, thereby limiting their usefulness in dating standard patterns. The earliest date is on a birth tablet (1) inscribed 1761, although the style of decoration indicates that this particular example may have been produced a few years later than is suggested by its inscription. Birth tablets, which are a peculiar feature of Lowestoft, were made throughout the factory's life, the last two examples being dated 1799. An unusually large tablet (2) dated 1782 is decorated on the reserse side with a transfer print. The backs of others show a variety of painted decorations including a fox, a man and a woman in contemporary costume, Chinese scenes, floral sprays and a sailing lugger (3). The only known combined birth and memorial tablet is inscribed 'Martha Liffin born August 17, 1794' on one side and 'Mary Liffin died May 4, 1795' on the other. Inkwells were also a favourite production. They were made in the early period before the first dated example of 1762 (4) until the last dated example inscribed 'John and Sarah Drinkald 1798'.[2] The first dated bell-shaped mug, 'Ann Hammond Woodbridge April 9th 1764' (5), has a Chinese scene including fishermen, a pagoda and willow trees in the typical Lowestoft style. It has the painter's numeral '3' on the base and is signed 'Rich'd Phillips' under the handle. Another mug showing John Cooper smoking his herrings is dated 1768 (6). It is also marked with the figure '3' and has the initials R.P. under the handle.[3] The varying styles of drawing by the 'number 3' painter, presumably Richard Phillips, form an interesting comparison (7). The most accomplished and also the most prolific blue and white artist painted some outstand-

[1] Spelman illustrates what appears to be a fragment of a sucrier cover with this knob from the factory site (*Op. cit.*, Plate XLVIII).

[2] From the Passmore Collection, now in the British Museum.

[3] This painter's hand is also seen on a pedestal bowl inscribed 'Trulls Best Virginia. Norwich October 14th, 1766' and on a punch bowl made for 'Thos Bonner, Halsworth, Carrier 1764'; both are marked with the numeral '3' (Kiddell, *Trans. E.P.C.*, no. 3, 1931, Pl. 5).

(1) *Plate* 75c; (2) *Plate* 81b; (3) *Plate* 83b; (4) *Plate* 74a;
(5) *Plate* 76b; (6) *Plate* 76c; (7) *Plates* 71b, 74c, 76a.

D. *Punch-bowl, inscribed 'Elizath Buckle 1768', painter's
numeral 5, Lowestoft, diam. 11 in. J. H. Nurse Collection.
(See page 99)*

ing pieces marked with the figure '5'. For example, the magnificent Elizabeth Buckle punch bowl dated 1768 (1). The design is adapted from an engraving in 'An Embassy to the Grand Tartar Cham, Emperor of China', entitled 'Chinese Priests and Monks'.[1] The bowl is said to have been decorated by the painter Robert Allen for his aunt. Most of the fine blue and white pieces with local topographical views also bear the numeral '5', the tally mark of this artist. He, probably Robert Allen, was especially fond of depicting Lowestoft church[2] as on a teapot inscribed 'S. C. 1767'.[3] Another such piece is a powder-blue plate in the British Museum, and there is also a fine ewer and bowl which includes St. Margaret's among the coastal scenes.[4] His painting of a windmill occurs on an attractive teapot inscribed with the miller's name 'Jeas. Fisher 1769', and as with previous examples this is also marked with the figure '5'. A circular plate in the Victoria and Albert Museum is inscribed on the back 'R. W. N. 1768'; it has no painter's number but is decorated with a similar Chinese scene to that on an apparently unique tureen marked with a '5' (2). A rare dated piece bearing a standard pattern is the Elizabeth Johnson teapot inscribed 'Feb 3 1768' and marked with the figure '6',[5] and this pattern except for a few rare exceptions is always marked with this figure.

About 1761 the wares were better fired and consequently they are more translucent than the earlier pieces. However, their pleasing glassy quality was a short-lived achievement. The best examples include thinly potted sauce boats (3) with crisp moulding in a variety of patterns.

The 1761 embossed services are of two types, those with rectangular and those with circular or oval reserves.[6] The same moulds with an

[1] John Nieuhoff, *An Embassy to the Grand Tartar Cham, Emperor of China*, 1st English ed. 1669, by Ogilby, p. 220, engraving by W. Hollar. 'But the most strange garb is that of the begging priest, who has commonly a gown on of several colours, and full of patches: upon his head he has a cap, which on both sides hath long feathers to defend him against the sun and rain: in his left hand he carries a bell, upon which he continually strikes till something is given him, or that you are gone out of sight. They seldom go about begging, but sit upon the ground with their legs across like our tailors.'

[2] Robert Allen was later to paint the east window of St. Margaret's Church.

[3] D. M. Hunting, 'Lowestoft China Teapots', *The Antique Collector*, Dec. 1951, Fig. 3.

[4] A. J. B. Kiddell, 'Lowestoft China in the Collection of Mrs. Russell Colman', *Connoisseur*, September 1937, Plate IV.

[5] Hunting, *op. cit.*, Fig. 3. Among the documentary pieces bearing numerals this is the only known example with a numeral other than '3' or '5'.

[6] For further details see D. M. Hunting, 'Lowestoft China Teapots', *The Antique Collector*, Dec. 1951.

(1) *Colour Plate* D; (2) *Plate* 78A; (3) *Plate* 74C.

altered date were used for the 1764 services, only the teapots still retained the original 1761 date (1). These re-issued teapots can be distinguished by their somewhat less attractive paste and glaze, plain roll handles, slightly arched spouts and their single painted key and cell border. Their covers may retain the ribbed bulbous knob or it may have been replaced by an open flower or an acorn.

The non-embossed tea wares are commonly decorated with a variety of imitation Chinese scenes including a lively one of a boy on a bridge[1] that may have been derived from a design by the artist Jean Pillement. Another attractive pattern in a similar style shows a trailing peony, whose flower petals are shaded with bold cross-hatching, growing from a root stock represented by a mass of fanciful scrolls. Powder-blue decoration is first found on an exceptionally large punch pot[2] inscribed 'H. C. 1763' under the handle. The cover has a typical bird knob and crude gilding has been used in an attempt to hide the irregularity and lack of sharpness of the reserves. This lack of symmetry of the reserves is a common feature of Lowestoft powder blue (2). There are no known Lowestoft examples with fan-shaped reserves such as are frequently seen on Bow. The Lowestoft blue ground nearly always has a somewhat greyish tint that lacks the rich, even, granular effect of their Bow counterparts. Among the best pieces are coffee pots made in three sizes, with long narrow spouts that rise steeply in an 'S' curve.

Some more of the Lowestoft potting shapes and mannerisms of the 1760s are as follows. Coffee cups, shallow teacups and bowls usually have a footring of triangular cross section with a fairly shallow inner side; by contrast cup footrings in the 1770s are often of a broader triangular cross section, and bases have a smaller diameter frequently with a marked conical bulge in the centre. Cup bases are glazed, as are those of all other wares including inkpots, but there is often a small area where the glaze is thin and where a fine granular effect, like grains of salt, interrupts the shiny surface. In some cases the angle between the footring and the base appears to have been cleared of excess glaze before firing, by a sharp instrument leaving a fine groove;[3] this feature being especially common on the later transfer-printed wares. In other cases the slight glaze pools are tinted clear blue or turquoise. Thumb rests on cup and jug handles tend to be less well

---

[1] Hunting, *op. cit.*, Fig. 2H.
[2] In the Norwich Museum, length 20″. This was produced only about four years after the first Bow examples with this decoration.
[3] This method was also used at Philip Christian's Liverpool factory.

---

(1) *Plate* 75B; (2) *Plates* 77A, C.

formed in the later examples, and the cocked-up lower handle term-inal remains one of the most distinctive features. In the mid 1760's painted lines at the sides of handles and spouts are occasionally replaced by feathered strokes. Cream jug handles frequently have a slight pro-tuberance or hump half way down the outer side, although this feature disappears about 1768, the date of the Elizabeth Johnson tea-pot. Large jugs about 9 inches high were made with five different types of moulding. The earliest example[1] has unusually vigorous relief moulding of bunches of grapes, flowers and leaves. Cornucopiae (1) were made with two different mouldings which have their almost exact counterparts in Bow porcelain, although the Lowestoft examples are more highly translucent. A documentary sauce boat (2), dated 1770, has been taken from a rather worn mould; it is embossed with chrysanthemums in the style of the so-called 'James Hughes', 1761–4, tea services that have already been discussed. Pap warmers or *veil-leuses* dating from the late 1760's onwards were one of Lowestoft's special productions, for apart from pottery examples such as those in Bristol and Liverpool delft, they were not made in porcelain to any extent elsewhere in England.[2] They consist of a two-handled food bowl or *écuelle* with a cover surmounted by a candle nozzle. This container rests in a high cylindrical base with a pair of shell moulded handles between a pair of grotesque, or more rarely, mitred masks. The burner which fits inside a window in the base is a small two-handled *godet* for oil with a removable cover pierced by a central hole for the wick.[3] Lowestoft feeding cups (3) also have counterparts in delft. Those made in the late 1760's have straight spouts, but some of the later transfer-printed examples have S-shaped spouts.

Teapots occur in a wide range of sizes from miniature upwards and include a fine barrel shape. Their covers and those of the cream jugs display a variety of neatly shaped knobs[4] such as a stylized mushroom, an acorn, or an open flower with a stalk between a pair of oak leaves.[5]

One of the most common painted borders on all types of wares, especially in the middle period, is known as the 'husk' pattern. It

[1] *Connoisseur*, June 1957, p. 61.

[2] A red anchor marked Chelsea example was once owned by the late C. T. Fowler and is now in the Drake Collection, Toronto.

[3] A biscuit wick holder from the factory site, now in the Norwich Museum, is illustrated by Spelman. *op. cit.*, Plate XXIII, Fig. 2.

[4] D. M. Hunting, 'Lowestoft China Teapots', *The Antique Collector*, Dec. 1951, Figs, 1, 2 and 3.

[5] The cover of the teapot inscribed 'Jeas. Fisher 1769' has the paired leaves and stalk, but the flower head is now missing.

(1) *Plate* 74B; (2) *Plate* 80A; (3) *Plate* 78C.

consists of a row of dome shapes with or without a clear outer zone, tufted by three whiskers (1).

It was undoubtedly the comparative cheapness of the raw materials and the good firing qualities of the bone ash body that enabled the Lowestoft potters to experiment with so many varieties of shape and size. They concentrated entirely on blue and white until after 1770 and for a small provincial factory[1] the potting was of a remarkably high standard. Few other rival concerns could have found it worth while to produce pieces such as the pap warmers or even the large hors d'oeuvre dish with segmental partitions fired in one piece.[2] Compared with the Bow factory, however, they produced relatively small numbers of plates (2) and dishes.

The Late Period (1771–1803)

In 1771 the Lowestoft factory entered a new and intensive phase of production following the death of Robert Browne senior. In the previous year a London warehouse had been opened under the management of Clark Durnford[3] in an ambitious attempt to compete in a wider market. An increased awareness of rival concerns led to a certain amount of imitation especially of Worcester. Transfer printing was introduced and the blue and white painted examples lost much of their previous charm. With few exceptions the best artists were occupied with coloured wares, although a talented flower painter, 'the tulip painter', occasionally decorated blue and white. A few pieces including a jug (3) and some flat-sided, circular flasks (4) have outstanding scenic paintings possibly by the number 3 or number 5 painter, or even the local artist Richard Powles (1763–1807).

The first documentary transfer-printed piece is a bell-shaped mug inscribed 'Willm. Mewse Southwould 1771'.[4] It has a painted cell border and transfer-prints of butterflies and flower sprays in the Worcester style. In the following year Lowestoft showed that it

[1] At the height of their prosperity only 60 to 70 hands were employed compared with 300 at Bow.

[2] H. C. Casley, *Procs. of the Suffolk Institute of Archaeology*, vol. XI, 1903, Plate 1, left-hand bottom corner. Now exhibited at No. 4 South Quay, Great Yarmouth.

[3] Clark and Mary Durnford, china merchants, are shown in a London newspaper and the London directories to have traded from a number of different warehouses between 1770 and 1797. These include No. 4 Great St. Thomas the Apostle, Cheapside, an address in Doctor's Commons and another at the New Wharf, Whitefriars.

[4] In the Bristol Museum. A coffee pot inscribed 'John Baker Yarmouth 1772' with similar decoration is illustrated by Kiddell, *Trans. E.P.C.*, no. 3, Pl. ivb.

(1) *Plate* 79c; (2) *Plate* 78b; (3) *Plate* 85d; (4) *Plate* 79a.

could find its own original transfer designs by decorating a bowl inscribed 'John and Ann Glasspool, Blundstone 1772' with one of the largest and most detailed prints ever used. It depicts a sportsman and dog putting up a partridge (1) and is said to have been engraved by Gamble of Bungay. Hunting states that there are about thirteen different transfer-printed Lowestoft services and probably over half of these have original designs. They include the so-called 'Good Cross Chapel' (2), 'Two dromedaries on a raft', 'Two pheasants' (3), 'A wolf and an exotic bird' and 'A squirrel and a Chinese woman' (4). A rare variant of the last-mentioned pattern has a counterpart in enamel colours. Four flower sprays (5) and a chinoiserie design (6) after Pillement are especially attractive but many of the designs are poorly engraved resulting in many broken lines and lack of depth in the shading. Some of the later examples, such as the crowded scene of pagodas and trees like the 'willow' pattern, have added washes of blue in the Caughley and Derby manner. A neatly painted blue and white zig-zag border is found mostly on printed wares; it is in marked contrast to the wide variety of rather clumsy and over elaborate borders on the majority of late painted tea and coffee services.

The two most distinctive painted designs of the late period are the 'Robert Browne' pattern (7) and the 'dragon' pattern.[1] The former consists of blue-scale zig-zag panels alternating with flower sprays and pieces are often marked with an open crescent. The dragon differs from the Bow and Worcester version by having a pair of projections like the flattened mandibles of an insect, sometimes painted in two shades of blue; this was a speciality of the painter who marked his wares with a 'V' on the footrings. His best examples have outstanding merit and miniature pieces of this pattern have a particular charm.

The potting shapes of the late period are unusually diverse and the unrecorded shapes that still come to light (8) act as a warning against too rigid generalization. Teapots usually have a fat bun-shaped knob or else a moulded flower bud with paired leaves, but re-issues with earlier type knobs are known (9). The handles are of the plain roll type and, in most cases, the spouts have an S-shaped curve with neatly placed straining holes in the body. A typical example is the 'Mary Crowfoot 1778' teapot[2] from the Hunting Collection, which is painted with one

[1] W. W. R. Spelman, *op. cit.*, Plate LXXVI, Fig. 3.
[2] D. M. Hunting, 'Lowestoft China Teapots,, *The Antique Collector*, Dec. 1951, Fig. 4P.

---

(1) *Plate* 85B; (2) *Plate* 83A; (3) *Plate* 84A;
(4) *Plate* 84C; (5) *Plate* 86B; (6) *Plate* 84B;
(7) *Plate* 80B; (8) *Plate* 77B; (9) *Plate* 86D.

of the forty or so variations on Chinese garden and river scenes. Sucriers and butter dishes may either have typical thick and deeply indented oak leaves on their covers or long, flat leaves with fine veining in the Worcester manner. Large jugs sometimes have the Lowestoft version of a mask-moulded lip showing a bearded simpleton (1). Very late jugs have a long curved lip. Handles on jugs and mugs show a wide variation and include an indented or ear shape, a broken or double scroll and an angular type. More rarely they are ribbed in the Worcester manner and very occasionally a grooved handle is found on late pieces. An applied leaf below the handle is an unusual but distinctive feature associated with ear-shaped handles (2). Coffee pots occur with a broad lip fitted with a strainer, although these vessels were also probably used for punch as is suggested by the inscription on one example.[1] Sauce boats often have moulded shapes derived from Worcester prototypes and one late variety has shallow fluted sides (3) like Derby and Caughley pieces. Open-work baskets with applied floral rosettes mimic Worcester even to having similar transfer-prints.

Lowestoft made a phenomenal number of small objects including eye baths (4), pounce pots (5), caddy spoons (6), knife handles, salad-oil jugs (7), egg cups (8), bottles, and pots for dry and wet mustard (9). A robust salt cellar painted like a Bow piece is inscribed 'M x S 1772'[2] and a later more fragile type has mask and paw feet (10). Small cream boats (11) embossed with rural scenes including sheep and cows are likely to have been taken directly from a salt-glaze original, but the mould makers of Lowestoft were still capable of producing good crisp original designs such as a chamber candlestick moulded with honeysuckle (12) or a leaf-shaped pickle tray moulded with fruiting currants. Other pickle trays are sometimes difficult to distinguish from their Bow prototypes, and small-handled artichoke butter boats are close copies of Derby. Lowestoft's large output of miniature tea wares is fully discussed by Hunting.[3] For the most part their shapes and patterns are but smaller editions of the standard productions.

Some late fluted tea wares are decorated in a much brighter blue

---

[1] A. J. B. Kiddell, 'Lowestoft China, Collection of Mrs. Russell Colman', *Connoisseur*, Sept. 1937, Plate XV.

[2] In the Norwich Museum.

[3] D. M. Hunting, 'Miniature Lowestoft China', *The Antique Collector*, Nov. 1949. Caughley and Bow were the only other factories to produce any quantity of miniature wares.

---

(1) *Plate* 85A; (2) *Plate* 85C; (3) *Plate* 86C;
(4) *Plate* 82A; (5) *Plate* 82D; (6) *Plate* 82B;
(7) *Plate* 81A; (8) *Plate* 82C; (9) *Plate* 83C;
(10) *Plate* 81C; (11) *Plate* 79B; (12) *Plate* 79C.

than was used previously, and a proportion of these have rims coloured brown with underglaze manganese. The latter feature also occurs on tea wares with one of the standard Chinese pagoda and island patterns. Two patterns copied from Meissen are marked with the crossed swords (I) and the open crescent mark appears on some painted and transfer-printed pieces. Painters' numerals do not occur after about 1773 and the highest known numeral is 17. Letters of the alphabet are used concurrently with numerals but not before the later 1760's. The glaze on the late pieces is still often remarkably clear and brilliant and the translucency is often good. The paste tends to be more porous and to stain brown more easily on footrings and in cracks. Saucers usually show three 'stilt' marks on their rims as are found on Bow.

A number of reasons have been put forward for the closure of the Lowestoft factory in 1803, but the most cogent must surely have been the death of Philip Walker early in the same year. It was largely through his interest and financial backing that the factory was brought into being and thrived as a flourishing concern for so long.

(I) *Plate* 80c.

8

CAUGHLEY

'Caughley was admirably situated for the manufacture of china, from the fact that coal lay about twenty feet from the surface, and clay for seggers at a less depth even; at the same time there was a navigable river with barges passing up and down, then at all hours of the day, to bring other materials, or to convey goods to distant towns and cities.'[1] The Caughley factory was on the south side of the river Severn near Broseley just under forty miles upstream from Worcester. The site was on a hill about a mile from the river and part of the Caughley Hall estate.[2] Here about 1754 Ambrose Gallimore, a relative of the late landowner, took on a sixty-four-year lease of a small pottery which appears to have been in existence for a few years previously; included in the lease was a colliery to supply fuel for the kilns. Porcelain was not made at Caughley until after 1772 when Thomas Turner[3] from Worcester became Gallimore's partner and the works were considerably enlarged. On 1st November, 1775, a local newspaper announced that 'the Porcelain Manufactory erected near Bridgnorth, in this County, is now quite completed, and the proprietors have received and completed orders to a very large amount. Lately we saw some of their productions, which in colour and fineness are truly

[1] John Randall, *Broseley and its Surroundings*, 1879, p. 305. Randall was an artist at the Coalport factory.

[2] Owned by the Browne family, one of whom, Edward Browne, was buried at Benthall on 15th March, 1750. Will proved 19th July, 1753, the estate left to his wife Jane. Ambrose Gallimore, later Turner's partner, was a witness to the will (in Somerset House, P.C.C. Searle 333).

[3] The son of the influential Rev. Richard Turner LL.D. Born 1749 and apprenticed to his father, described as a writing master, at the age of 12 on 28th October, 1761. Admitted a Freeman of the City of Worcester on 14th January, 1771. He married firstly Ambrose Gallimore's daughter Dorothy in 1783; she died in 1793. At Caughley he became an important local figure as a county magistrate, a bailiff and the chairman of the Court of Equity. He was on good terms with the local gentry, especially the Foresters of Willey; Lady Katherine Forester, daughter of the Duke of Rutland was a god-mother to one of his children. He died intestate at Caughley in 1809, the administration of his goods being granted to his second wife Mary Turner. In her will, proved 16th May, 1816 (in Somerset House, P.C.C.), she states that her late husband had left a very small personal estate but considerable real estate.

elegant and beautiful, and have the bright and lovely white of the so much extolled Oriental.'[1]

Although Thomas Turner is said to have previously worked at Worcester there is no indication that the new Caughley venture was a subsidiary of the Worcester factory. Indeed, the early relationship between the two factories was almost certainly one of keen rivalry. A study of Salopian porcelain indicates that among Turner's first objectives was the manufacture of very large quantities of useful blue and white more economically than was possible at Worcester. He was in an advantageous position for most of the raw materials and by using less of the expensive soapstone in the body[2] and concentrating on transfer-printing, he sought to undersell his Worcester competitors whose wares he copied as closely as possible.

The Worcester soaprock licence had expired in 1770[3] and in November of that year there was an advertisement for the lease of the Gew Graze mine near the Lizard.[4] In the meanwhile the Worcester company had taken out another permit to dig for soaprock nearby on Predannack Common in the parish of Mullion.[5] It is likely that Turner attempted to obtain the next licence to work the Gew Graze mine but the Worcester partners prevented him by renewing their own licence for that mine for a short term of seven years from 19th June, 1773. Turner had to wait and in the meantime he probably relied on Cornish merchants to send him soaprock.[6] However, in 1776 he was prudent enough to secure a fourteen-year licence for the Gew Graze mine to take effect in 1780, when the Worcester licence expired, or earlier should the latter factory surrender its rights prematurely.

James Giles, 1718–80, the independent London decorator and china dealer, has a number of entries in his account book for Thomas Turner from April 1773 to November 1775. At first the heading is 'Mr. Thos. Turner at Worcester'[7] and in 1774 Giles debited him for some copper plates.[8] In February 1775 six boxes of Worcester china were sent from

---

[1] Chaffers, *Marks and Monograms*, 14th ed., 1932, p. 766.

[2] Eccles and Rackham, *Analised Specimens of English Porcelain*, London, 1922, pp. 34–8. A single specimen of Caughley contained about 22 per cent soapstone compared with 35–45 per cent soapstone in specimens of Worcester.

[3] The licence had been originally granted to Benjamin Lund on 7th March, 1748/9.

[4] *London Evening Post*, 3rd November, 1770, *Trans. E.C.C.*, vol. 1, no. 5, p. 53.

[5] R. W. Binns, *A Century of Potting in the City of Worcester*, 2nd ed., 1877, p. 310.

[6] A John Nancarrow of Breage near Helston, a friend of William Cookworthy, was part owner of the licence granted in June 1773.

[7] Turner had already left Worcester for Caughley by 1773, but see below.

[8] These would be blank copper plates that were sent by Giles. Previous writers have misinterpreted this entry to mean that Turner had sent Giles engraved copper plates.

Turner to Giles and in March of the same year there was a box from Salop. From June 1775 Turner's address is given as Caughley Hall. He is charged for a complete set of Derby china and after that for twelve boxes of sundry Worcester which Giles sent to Mr. Hussey.[1] On the credit side is over £158 for Worcester china sent on sale or return but only £6 2s. 6d. for Salopian white. These accounts suggest that Thomas Turner may either have had a stock of Worcester porcelain or else his own decorated wares were being called Worcester. The entries from June 1775 are the first indication that Turner had his original warehouse at Worcester, and this is confirmed by a newspaper announcement quoted below.

Early in 1772, the year when Thomas Turner left Worcester for Caughley, there had been a sale of the Worcester factory. Robert Hancock, 1731–1817, had become a Worcester proprietor as a result of the subsequent changes in management. However, an indenture dated 31st October, 1774, shows that the other partners soon bought back Hancock's sixth share because of certain 'controversies, disputes and differences'.[2] Turner at once took advantage of this situation and made an agreement with Hancock, the result of which can be assessed from a contemporary newspaper announcement.[3] 'SALOPIAN China Warehouse, Bridgnorth. R. Hancock begs leave to acquaint the public and particularly the considerable dealers in china ware, that having disposed of his share in the Worcester work, he is now engaged in the Salopian China Manufactory, on such terms as enable him to serve the trade at the most moderate rates. He has already an ample assortment of the blue and white, and will with all possible expedition proceed in the enamelled or burnt in china. The sole province of dealing in this manufactory, except in the London trade, being assigned over by Mr. T. Turner and Co. Hancock, country dealers (sic) will find it turn to their account to be supplied by him in the same manner as they were by Mr. Turner from Worcester.—Wanted a diligent clerk at the above warehouse. Likewise a person who has been used to china printing.— Letters directed to R. Hancock, at the Salopian China Warehouse, Bridgnorth, shall be duly attended to.' It is not known when Hancock left Caughley but he is stated to have been living at Oldbury near Birmingham in 1780.[4] While he was working at Caughley he decor-

---

[1] William Hussy, Chinaman, of 5 Portugal Street, was at that time Turner's London agent.

[2] R. W. Binns, *A Century of Potting in the City of Worcester*, 2nd ed., 1877, Appendix.

[3] *Aris's Birmingham Gazette*, 3rd July, 1775.

[4] A. R. Ballantyne, *Robert Hancock and his Works*, 1885, p. 8. It should be noted, however, that there is another Oldbury about a mile from Bridgnorth. Nevertheless in 1791 Hancock's address was Moat Row, Birmingham, *Trans. E.C.C.*, vol. 1, no. 2, 1934, p. 43.

ated a large amount of porcelain using underglaze and overglaze transfers as he had done at Worcester.[1] Turner's London trade was carried on mostly through his warehouse at No. 5 Portugal Street.[2]

Apart from the close copies of Worcester, Turner was evidently greatly attracted by Chantilly porcelain and it is said that he went to France in 1780[3] to bring back with him some skilled French potters. One of these, François Hardenburg, was later at Derby as a modeller from 1788 to 1789.[4] Among the finer examples of Salopian manufacture which closely resemble Chantilly are a few rare pieces marked with an incised H (I), and it is highly probable that these were made by Hardenburg. Turner succumbed to the French influence to such an extent that he even had his new residence Caughley Place built like a château.

The unsatisfactory suggestion put forward by a number of writers that biscuit wares were sent from Messrs. Flight and Sons at Worcester to Caughley to be printed in underglaze blue, stems partly from remarks made by Jewitt[5] and partly from the difficulty in separating wares of the two factories. On the other hand there is abundant evidence to show that quantities of Salopian blue and white and plain white were sent to Chamberlain's decorating establishment for gilding and enamelling.[6] Binns states that in 1789 over £2,000 worth of goods were received by Chamberlain from the Caughley works. In the same year Chamberlain recorded his disappointment at being sent only a small quantity of blue and white; 'we are every day disobliging our customers and injuring ourselves for want of them'. The recent discovery of some undoubted pieces of Caughley, including one of their 'willow' patterns, on the original site of the Worcester factory sug-

[1] It is frequently but incorrectly stated that there is very little evidence of Hancock's work on Salopian wares, with the result that many of these wares still pass as Worcester.

[2] Previously Lisle's Tennis-court, then Lincoln's Inn Fields Theatre where *The Beggar's Opera* was performed in 1727–8. It appears that William Hussy first occupied this warehouse as Turner's London agent. Jewitt mentions a bill dated 24th January, 1794, and headed 'Salopian China Warehouse. Bought of Turner and Shaw'. The *London Directories for 1797* have the entry 'Thomas Turner, Salopian China Warehouse, Portugal Street, Lincoln's Inn'. By 1798 Turner had moved his warehouse to 103 Hatton Garden and Josiah Spode had left 43 Fore Street, Moorfields, to occupy the Portugal Street premises.

[3] He was certainly strongly influenced by Chantilly patterns long before 1780.

[4] Ll. Jewitt, *The Ceramic Art of Great Britain*, vol. 2, p. 110. He left Turner's Manufactory in debt to Ann Oakes of the Turks Arms, Broseley, and was dismissed by Duesbury for repeated idleness and ignorance.

[5] *Op. cit.*, vol. 1, p. 271.

[6] Between 1785 and 1788 Chamberlain's factory was solely a decorating establishment.

(I) *Plates* 89A, B.

gests that Messrs. Flight and Sons also dealt in Caughley blue and white.

The Caughley factory had a lead over Worcester in the production of dinner services since they seem to have soon mastered the art of making large quantities of plates and dishes economically. For example, in February 1780 a sale at Christie's consisting mostly of Bristol porcelain offered 'one complete Salopian table set, 126 pieces, the new Salopian sprigs', and it was this lot that fetched the day's highest price. The next day there was listed another 'Salopian table service with Chantilly sprigs containing 115 pieces'.[1] The 'Chantilly sprig' was one of Turner's earliest patterns and it was certainly one of his favourite introductions. It took the form of an oeillet or gillyflower and two forget-me-nots surrounded by smaller flower sprays and an occasional insect (1).[2] This pattern occurs in both finely painted and printed forms and it is found on a mug marked with a hatched crescent and incised with the date July 31st 1773.[3] The rather heavy potting of the widely grooved handle is one of the features that suggest a Caughley origin, and it is likely to have been among the first pieces made by Turner rather than made at Worcester, which is the present attribution. Another Chantilly pattern copied by Turner is composed of widely spaced, sketchy sprays of flowers and cross-hatched sprigs (2), à l'épi or à la brindille. It is found on tea and dinner wares which may be edged with blue or gilt on brown and which are sometimes even marked with a hunting-horn in imitation of the Chantilly factory mark (3). Chantilly plates with wide basket-moulded rims, known as the 'osier' pattern, were closely copied, some were painted with blue sprigs and others were sent to London for enamel decoration and many of these still pass as Worcester because of their fine potting. The 'Copenhagen' or 'immortelle' pattern which occurs on ribbed tea wares with an open crescent was another standard production, but other Caughley painted floral designs are uncommon (4). Painted scenes are somewhat unusual (5) apart from two variants of a Chinese pattern of islands and sailing boats, one of which, a highly simplified design, is especially common on miniature wares, while the other is copied from Worcester. There is also a more detailed pagoda, willow tree and island design which is found on square and fan-shaped dishes

[1] J. E. Nightingale, *op. cit.*, pp. 108 and 110.
[2] Also Stanley Fisher, *English Blue and White Porcelain of the 18th Century*, London, 1947, Pl. 41.
[3] Victoria and Albert Museum, *Catalogue of the Schreiber Collection*, vol. 1, 489.

(1) *Plate* 37D; (2) *Plate* 89; (3) *Plate* 90A;
(4) *Plate* 87B; (5) *Plate* 90B (1).

often with the word 'Salopian' impressed.[1] A Worcester 'lange lijzen' pattern is copied very closely and it is likely that some examples of the 'quail' pattern are Caughley and not Worcester. Powder-blue decoration is in the Bow and Worcester tradition with fan-shaped and circular reserves, although the ground is frequently pale and peppered with dark blue specks. One unusually complex Chinese design has panels of floral and symbolic motifs[2] against a background of powder blue. Another pattern which is peculiar to Caughley attempts to reproduce the Chinese 'oil-spot' effect resulting in a bright, strident blue ground closely patterned with small circles.[3] The 'Queen Charlotte' or 'lily' pattern with super-added gilding closely copies that found on late Worcester; in both cases the regularity of the painted design gives the impression of transfer-printing. The boldly painted Caughley 'blue dragon' was the last and one of the least common of the English eighteenth-century painted versions of the Chinese and should not be confused with the printed 'Broseley dragon' pattern mentioned below. According to Chaffers a man named Adams was a blue-painter at Caughley.

Turner's fantastically close imitations of Chantilly were to some extent over-shadowed by his very large output of transfer-printed wares. The early use of Hancock prints makes separation from Worcester extremely difficult, especially in the many cases where potting shapes are practically indistinguishable. An exceptionally fine early jug (1)[4] with a mask moulded lip is an important documentary piece because its mark 'Gallimore Turner Salopian' confirms the partnership between Gallimore and Turner at Caughley. It is decorated with three blurred transfers, a compact bunch of fruit and flowers in front and on opposite sides a seated figure of Britannia and a recognizable Hancock print of Fame.[5] Three Hancock transfers illustrated by Cook are probably only found in blue and white on Caughley and not on Worcester. They are firstly a version of 'Parrot and Fruit',[6] then 'La Pêche'[7] and its companion 'La Promenade Chinoise'.[8] A rare

[1] C. Clifton Roberts, 'Salopian China, part 2', *Connoisseur*, vol. LV, 1919, p. 223, Pl. 1, Nos. 3 and 4.

[2] F. Barrett, *Caughley and Coalport Porcelain*, Leigh-on-Sea, 1951, Fig. 52.

[3] Barrett, *op. cit.*, Fig. 53.

[4] Another unmarked example in the Victoria and Albert Museum.

[5] Cyril Cook, *The Life and Work of Robert Hancock*, London, 1948, item 33.

[6] Cook, *op. cit.*, item 79. An original copper plate of this design is at Coalport. Barrett, *op. cit.*, Plate 32.

[7] Cook, *op. cit.*, item 81. An original copper plate of this design and the next one were found at Coalport in 1862 by Jewitt.

[8] Cook, *op. cit.*, item 88.

(1) *Plate* 87A.

version of 'La Terre' (1)[1] is paired with one of the two better-known chinoiseries depicting a seated lady with a hand to her ear and a small child standing beside her holding toy bells or else a three-lobed fan.[2] Among the finest Caughley prints are two shooting scenes (2)[3] reminiscent of paintings by George Stubbs (1724–1806), and there is also a rare fox-hunting print with the inscription 'We shall catch him anon' (3); these three were almost certainly engraved by Hancock. His 'milkmaids'[4] decorate both Worcester and Caughley and there are a number of minutely detailed views of classical ruins on late Caughley pieces which are in the style of some of Hancock's Worcester designs. His more successful Italianate scene which includes a tower and a circular building with columns is only found on Caughley. Some of the earlier fruit and flower engravings are likely to have been Hancock's work at both Worcester and Caughley, including a sensitive design of fine sprays of lilies on either side of a large open rose and the most accomplished examples of the standard 'pine cone' or 'mulberry' pattern. A popular print of three large birds in a stunted tree may have been among Hancock's last engravings for Caughley (4).

Turner seems to have continued to use some of Hancock's plates after the latter had left Caughley but he also engraved his own and is said to have had a number of apprentice and assistant engravers working under him. These included the famous Thomas Minton, Edward Dyas,[5] William Davis,[6] John Walton,[7] Richard Hicks[8] and Thomas Lucas.[9] Turner produced a number of chinoiseries, at least ten of which were variations on the perennial theme of islands, pagodas and willow trees (5). Perhaps the most distinctive, the 'fisherman and sail' pattern, depicts a fisherman standing in a sampan holding his catch with a cormorant on a rock nearby.[10] Turner is

[1] Compare Cook, *op. cit.*, item 108.

[2] This latter transfer occurs on one of the earliest dated pieces inscribed 'R. Parr 1776' (Victoria and Albert Museum).

[3] Barrett, *op. cit.*, Fig. 27.   [4] Cook, *op. cit.*, item 73.

[5] Later at Coalport. He helped to perfect a technique for the manufacture of printers' rollers.

[6] Said to have introduced four printing presses at Caughley.

[7] John Randall, *op. cit.*, p. 305.

[8] Mentioned by Jewitt, *op. cit.*, vol. 2, p. 185. Also by Mankowitz and Haggar, *The Concise Encyclopedia of English Pottery and Porcelain*, London, 1957. He afterwards made blue printed earthenware in Staffordshire.

[9] Simeon Shaw, *History of the Staffordshire Potteries*, re-issue 1900, p. 214.

[10] An original copper plate of this 'fisherman and sail' pattern at Coalport is marked No. 1. Pennington's factory at Liverpool copied this and a number of other Caughley prints.

---

(1) *Plate* 90B (2); (2) *Plate* 90C (1); (3) *Plate* 88A;
(4) *Plate* 87C; (5) *Plate* 88D.

traditionally associated with two famous transfer-printed designs: the 'Broseley dragon' and the 'willow' pattern. However, it has not been possible to discover any version of the former design which was made before Turner left the Caughley factory in 1799. The 'willow' pattern was not really an original Caughley chinoiserie, but merely the crystallization of a number of similar transfers used at the English porcelain factories from about 1760.[1] This romantic vision of Cathay gained full popularity in its final form as a result of the mass production of cheap earthenware by Staffordshire potteries in the nineteenth century. The creation of a suitable legend heightened the appeal and ensured its continuity. The 'flying bat' pattern[2] only occurs on late Caughley usually in conjunction with a disguised numeral mark.

In a totally different style is the somewhat scarce print of a group of European country figures including a man smoking a pipe and riding a donkey. The erection over the Severn of the first cast-iron bridge by the neighbouring Coalbrookdale works in 1792 is commemorated by a number of inscribed jugs (1) which are decorated with an accurate topographical print. The memory of a local volunteer force, the Brimstree Loyal Legion, is perpetuated by another jug.[3] It bears the royal coat of arms as used before 1st January, 1801, at which time the *fleurs de lys* of France were removed from the royal shield of Great Britain.

Imitations of Worcester and Chantilly potting shapes make up the major part of the Caughley output. Some wares were thinly potted but they were often more robustly fashioned than Worcester. However, similarity of paste, shape and decoration can make differentiation difficult. The finish may be exceptionally neat although footrings and bases are not always up to the best Worcester standards. There are a large variety of wares from outsize cabbage-leaf jugs with mask moulded lips and large salad bowls down to complete miniature services. Apart from open-work baskets and pickle trays, few ornamental pieces were made, although it is still possible to find examples of the small useful wares such as inkwells (2), pounce pots (3), egg cups, eye baths, asparagus trays or knife rests, mustard pots (4), spoons and ladles. The mask on jugs is of an old man usually with a sardonic

[1] John Ainslie, 'Underglaze Blue Printing on Bow Porcelain', *The Antique Collector*, April 1957, Fig. 10.

[2] Franklin Barrett, *op. cit.*, Fig. 22.

[3] *Schreiber Cat.*, No. 790. A similar jug was doubtless made for the Wenlock Loyal Volunteers as copper plates for the royal arms and appropriate inscription still exist. Thomas Turner was an officer in the Volunteers at Broseley (J. Randall, *op. cit.*, p. 237).

---

(1) *Plate* 87D; (2) *Plate* 88C; (3) *Plate* 88C; (4) *Plate* 88B.

grimace whereas the Worcester counterpart has a benign appearance. Inscribed puzzle jugs copied from earthenware are a rare Caughley speciality (1).[1] Cream jugs are usually of the slim Worcester 'sparrow beak' type with a grooved handle, others have a robust barrel-shaped body and a plain roll handle or an elaborate broken scroll with a terminal tag. A lamprey moulded handle is found on a few small pedestal creamers. Sucriers, tea and coffee pots may have large flower-head knobs or else unlike Worcester a distinctive stud-button type.[2] Footrings on tea wares may be triangular in cross section but they are more frequently straight-sided and taller than Worcester examples. Sometimes one or more bold concentric circles have been incised in the base. Teapot handles are often kinked inwards above the lower ter-minal, but a late moulded type copies a Chinese original with a heart-shaped thumb rest. Mug handles are usually either widely grooved or they are strap-like with two shallow lateral grooves. Sometimes these handles are moulded with an overlapping flattened thumb rest like a belt end.

The underglaze blue varies considerably in colour; sometimes a fine pale greyish tint was achieved and at other times an intense violet blue[3] especially on later wares. Turner was always experimenting to find the most popular shade of blue and two of his trial mugs have survived (2).[4] Borders vary from a simple painted edging of blue to elaborate transfer copies of Chinese butterfly and diaper patterns, or crowded juxtapositions of diaper and floral motives alternating with miniature European views. Many of the later wares are lavishly decorated with gilding. The translucency is typically a cloudy orange colour by artificial light, but it is not generally realized that some Caughley has a definite greenish tint.[5] The glaze has many Worcester characteristics although generally less cobalt was used to colour it, especially for imitations of Chantilly. This results in a creamy white appearance, but even when the glaze is definitely tinted it does not have the greyish blue-green of Worcester. Furthermore, the Caughley

[1] A later example is illustrated by Jewitt, *op. cit.*, vol. 1, Fig, 586. It is inscribed 'John Geary Cleak of the old Church Brosley 1789' and 'Mathew ch V v 16'.

[2] C. Clifton Roberts, *Connoisseur*, vol. LV, 1919, Pls. XIV and XV. Also Cyril Cook, *op. cit.*, item 51, there wrongly attributed to Worcester.

[3] Some of Flight's Worcester porcelain also had this colour.

[4] Stanley Fisher, *op. cit.*, Pl. 37. Joseph Lygo's letters to Duesbury for 1786 contain the following entry: 'There are no other samples of blue to be got at present, enclosed is a list of prices of different cobalts from Irish and Hitchens, they showed me many different styles of Mr. Turner's both from smalts and cobalts. . . .'

[5] The translucency should always be tested with a standard electric light bulb as when bright sunlight is used many more wares show a green tint like Worcester.

(1) *Plate* 87B; (2) *Plate* 90C.

glaze gives a less brilliant effect and in the majority of cases the under-glaze blue looks flatter and less luminous. On bases the glaze is often rather speckled by fine spots of cobalt and other impurities in suspension, and inside the footring there is a glaze-free ring usually stained yellow, often more strongly than on Worcester.

From the outset Salopian porcelain frequently bore a factory mark. The letter 'S', with or without an 'x' or an 'o', is commonly found, and also a capital 'C' for Caughley; more rarely, on plates and dishes, the word 'Salopian' is impressed. Occasionally a small incised star occurs by itself or accompanying the 'S' mark. Disguised numerals from 1 to 8 indicate a late piece. The Worcester crescent was closely imitated in its various forms, especially the cross-hatched variety on transfer-printed wares. Sometimes letters of the alphabet are incorporated with the crescent mark. The Worcester 'W' mark was used, especially the ornate script form, and also apparently the Worcester 'fretted-square' mark.[1] The 'hunting-horn' of Chantilly painted in blue is known on tea wares.

In October 1799 Thomas Turner gave up the manufacture of porcelain and the Caughley works were taken over by the Coalport proprietors Edward Blakeway, John Rose and Richard Rose. Turner assigned over the factory as a going concern including the stock of unglazed goods and his copper plates. The Caughley pottery was eventually dismantled, the last buildings being pulled down in 1821.

[1] C. Clifton Roberts, 'Salopian China, part 4', *Connoisseur*, 1920, p. 26.

9

PLYMOUTH, BRISTOL AND NEW HALL

The European potters and ceramic chemists of the eighteenth century were determined to copy Chinese hard paste and they were keenly aware that their soft paste was a substitute, even though often an attractive alternative, for the real thing. The brilliant researches of Tschirnhausen and Böttger in Germany led to the discovery of the Chinese secret in 1709 and to the formation of the Meissen factory and its satellites. France and England had to wait for at least another half century before their own arcanists were able to find both a satisfactory technique and a suitable supply of native raw materials. This was in spite of the fact that from 1717 Francis d'Entrecolles' first-hand description of the Chinese method was available together with actual samples of Chinese kaolin and petuntse.[1] Thus the basic principal which was the firing of a mixture of refractory clay with vitrifiable ingredients was established in France[2] and England long before it was found possible to put the theory to commercial use.

In England tentative attempts were made to use kaolin from North America, and we have seen that it was mentioned as *unaker* in the specification to the first Bow patent in 1745.[3] Also in 1745 an unknown mining prospector from Virginia had shown the Plymouth chemist William Cookworthy experimental samples of porcelain, possibly from Bow, and stressed the importance of the use of kaolin to ensure success. However, the Bow factory apparently soon gave up their attempts with

[1] S. Shaw, *The Chemistry of Porcelain Glass and Pottery*, 1837, p. 407 relates that Dr. William Sherrard, about the time of the publication of d'Entrecolles' letters, brought samples of kaolin and petuntse from Paris and presented them to the Royal Society. They were subsequently transferred to the British Museum. See N. J. G. Pounds, 'The Discovery of China Clay', *Economic History Review*, 2nd series, vol. 1, no. 1, 1948.

[2] M. de Réaumur, *Idée Générale des différentes manières dont on peut faire la porcelaine. Hist. de l'Académie Royale des Sciences*, 1727, pp. 185–203, and 1729, pp. 325–44.

[3] Pp. 13, 14. Samples of this clay were also obtained by Richard Champion from his brother-in-law Caleb Lloyd in 1765 and in the following year by Wedgwood via Mr. Vigor, but at a later date from his own agent in Carolina, Thomas Griffiths.

kaolin and invented instead a more workable mixture containing 'virgin earth'.[1] This term, 'virgin' or 'pure earth', had a definite meaning to eighteenth century chemists, and it included substances such as bone ash and gypsum, or calcium sulphate, which are known to have been incorporated in the Bow formula.[2] This use of virgin earth is likely to have been the direct outcome of a renewed search for refractory substances to make hard paste in line with the teachings of Réaumur (1683–1758), which were based on d'Entrecolles' discoveries.

In 1722 d'Entrecolles described an alternative method employed by the Chinese to make porcelain using 'hoa ché' in place of kaolin,[3] and he suggested that this soapy stone might be found in parts of Europe where kaolin was not indigenous. There is little doubt that this description led to the use of soapstone by Benjamin Lund and to the manufacture of his steatitic porcelain at Bristol from about 1749.

It was left to William Cookworthy[4] to continue the direct line of research which ended in his discovery of both kaolin and petuntse in Cornwall and his establishment of a factory to make the coveted hard paste. William Borlase was aware of Cookworthy's experiments when he wrote his book[5] in 1758. He describes moorstone from Tregonnin near Helston which is 'of the same nature with the Oriental Granite' and which was used for building[6] and by Mr. Cookworthy 'who has tried many experiments this way and has found it most proper for making porcelain'. The granite has a ground 'of a white opake grit, tender almost as clay, interspersed with granules of quartz, cinereous, transparent, laminated, small from the eighth of an inch and under.

[1] Herman Boerhaave M.D., *Elements of Chemistry*, translated from the original Latin by Timothy Dallowe M.D., London, 1735. The term earth was used in describing 'the principles or elements of which compound bodies consist . . . a simple, hard, friable fossil body, fixed in the fire but not melting in it, nor dissoluble in water, alcohol, or air. . . . It remains so fixed and immutable in the most intense fire, that when it is entirely alone it is not possible to put it in fusion.' See also p. 16.

[2] P. 17.

[3] See p. 34.

[4] A pious Quaker born at Kingsbridge 12th April, 1705. At the age of 14 apprenticed to Silvanus Bevan, 'the Quaker F.R.S.,' a London chemist of 2 Plough Court, Lombard Street. The firm was later Allen and Hanbury's. He returned to Devon and set up as a wholesale chemist and druggist in Nut Street, Plymouth, under the style of Bevan and Cookworthy and later in partnership with his brother Philip. Died 16th October, 1780. Will proved P.C.C. Webster 125. He was buried in the Quaker burial ground, Treville Street, Plymouth.

[5] *The Natural History of Cornwall*, 1758, p. 99.

[6] For example, the portico of Godolphin House and the New Church at Helston. Cookworthy is said to have discovered the important St. Stephens deposits of china stone by noticing it in the tower of St. Columb nearby. There is another tradition related as early as 1797 that Cookworthy first noticed the fusible properties of this granite at a bell foundry in Fowey (Lady Radford, *The Devonian Year Book*, 1920, p. 31).

The stone is soft and easy for working, especially when first raised, but afterwards hard and lasting; extreamly white when newly wrought, but apt to contract a mossy green hue in time.' Borlase also describes the levigation of a refractory white clay[1] which was found twenty feet under the surface and which was then only used for making bricks for smelting-houses, 'enduring the most intense fire of the furnace better than any other within equal reach of the workmen.' He suggests, however, that this clay might be a useful ingredient for making porcelain, and adds that a clay of this type was to be found at Tregonnin Hill. Cookworthy must have been aware of this refractory white clay and its use in constructing tin-smelting furnaces before May 1745. At that date he mentioned his treatise on furnaces[2] in a letter describing his meeting with the discoverer of china earth in Virginia. It could not have been long afterwards that he guessed that the refractory Cornish clay was in fact kaolin. On his business trips through Cornwall he often stayed at Godolphin near Tregonnin as the guest of John Nancarrow,[3] who was the local tin-mining superintendent and 'a scientific person'. It was doubtless through this friendship that he came to recognize the deposits of both china stone and kaolin at Tregonnin.[4]

In Cookworthy's brief account[5] of this method of making hard-paste porcelain written before 1768 'lest I should not live to carry it into manufacture', he describes his discovery of the two essential ingredients at Tregonnin nearly twenty years previously and then some untried but promising deposits in St. Stephen's parish. He mentions that the stone with greenish spots, as described by d'Entrecolles, was the best for making glaze, but for a softer glaze vitrescent material such as lime and fern ashes could be added just as the Chinese did. The body consisting of equal parts of washed kaolin and petuntse was first baked to a soft biscuit, then painted with blue and covered with liquid glaze before being subjected to the major firing. Large vessels could be dipped in the glaze tub without a prior biscuit firing in the

[1] *Ibid.*, pp. 63, 64.

[2] This was probably published in a contemporary journal. Cookworthy is also likely to have known of the attempts to make crucibles from Cornish clay and granite for the tin smelters at Calenick near Truro by Jacob Lieberich. The latter was granted a premium by the Royal Society of Arts in 1759 and another in 1766 for his discovery (G. Staal, 'Calenick Crucibles', *The 124th Annual Report of the Royal Cornwall Polytechnic Society*, 1957).

[3] John Prideaux, *Relics of William Cookworthy*, 1853, p. iv. John Nancarrow also had an interest in the soap rock mines at the Lizard, see p. 107, footnote 6.

[4] Wedgwood mentions in 1775 that a Mr. Carthew of St. Austell claimed to be the first person to notice the fusible properties of growan clay when some of his furnaces built of this material were taken down: 'the clay was by the fire, become true porcelain' (*Proceedings of the Wedgwood Society*, 1956, no. 1, p. 49).

[5] George Harrison's *Memoir of William Cookworthy*, 1854, Appendix v, more easily available in Ll. Jewitt, *Life of Josiah Wedgwood*, 1865, pp. 226–31.

Chinese manner. Cookworthy's description of firing his experimental wares is of special interest as he found it impossible to obtain satisfactory results with coal-fired kilns, especially when bags were used, but had to employ a wood-fired brown stoneware kiln of the thirty-six hole type, which alone produced the necessary amount of upward draught in the centre of the kiln to avoid smoke staining.[1] This was achieved by burning billets of wood before and directly under the chamber which contained the ware so that the flames could ascend and play round the saggers.

In spite of his forebodings and at considerable expense[2] Cookworthy eventually in 1768 in his 63rd year established his Plymouth factory at Coxside adjoining the Sugar-House in Mr. Bishop's timber yard, with his china shop in Nut Street.[3] There were fourteen shares of which Cookworthy retained three, the rest being divided as single units amongst various relatives and Quaker merchants including Richard Champion of Bristol.[4] A short-term lease was granted by Thomas Pitt, afterwards Lord Camelford, for obtaining china stone and clay from a moor called Carlogass near St. Stephen's parish and this was renewed for 99 years on 12th December, 1770.[5] Cookworthy obtained a patent on 17th March, 1768, and the specification was duly enrolled on 14th July in the same year.[6] The factory at Plymouth was a small one as only from fifty to sixty persons were employed,[7] but there was a good demand for the porcelain both at home and in

---

[1] Champion in a letter to Caleb Lloyd, 7th Nov., 1765, mentions a new work just established for making porcelain from Cornish stone and clay '. . . But in burning there is a deficiency; though the body is perfectly white within, but not without, which is always smoky'. In another letter of 28th Feb., 1766, to Lord Hyndford Champion relates that this manufactory in Bristol was abandoned as the impurities in the glaze could not be driven off even in the greatest fire they could give it. Cookworthy may have been concerned in this early attempt. See Sarah Champion's statement of Jan. 1764 (H. Owen, *Two Centuries of Ceramic Art in Bristol*, 1873, p. 15).

[2] Lord Camelford writing to R. Polwhele, the historian, on 30th Nov., 1790, stated that they had expended between two and three thousand pounds.

[3] William Burt's *Review of the mercantile, trading and manufacturing state, interests and capabilities of the port of Plymouth 1816*, p. 174, mentioned by John Prideaux, *op. cit.*, p. 5. Jewitt, *Ceramic Art of Great Britain*, vol. 1, p. 326, states that the works were 'at the extreme angle which juts into the water at Sutton Pool. Some parts of the buildings still exist, and are used as a shipwright's yard.'

[4] A full list is given by Lady Radford, *op. cit.*, p. 36 and by Honey, *Old English Porcelain*, 2nd edit., 1948, p. 225.

[5] See Wedgwood's reasons why an extension of the term of Mr. Cookworthy's patent would be injurious (Ll. Jewitt, *The Life of Josiah Wedgwood*, 1865, p. 246, and Lady Radford, *op. cit.*, p. 41).

[6] This specification gives less exact details than those recorded in his earlier memorandum but he adds that magnesia alba could be used as an alternative vitrifying agent for the glaze.

[7] William Burt, *op. cit.*

America, even though it was often far from perfect. Cookworthy marked many of his wares with the alchemical sign for tin, no doubt as a reminder that he made his original discovery of kaolin and petuntse through his close acquaintance with tin mining and smelting methods. However, conditions at Plymouth must have been unexpectedly difficult, for in just over two years the manufactory was transferred to Castle Green at Bristol in the hope that it would flourish where the potting tradition was much stronger. William Cookworthy moved to Bristol with his factory which was still called Cookworthy and Company, but from this time onwards Richard Champion[1] began to take an increasingly prominent part in the management. Champion's drawing of a wood-fired kiln[2] is of special interest as it is of the type described by Cookworthy in his memorandum. The kiln depicted in vertical section and ground plan consists of a cylindrical seven-foot-high glost or high-temperature oven with a biscuit or low-temperature firing chamber above. Directly beneath is the thick-walled furnace having a vertically divided projection of three and a half feet to increase the effective capacity for burning billets of wood. The drawing is dated 16th October, 1770, and was almost certainly made at the time of the last firing at Plymouth before the kiln was dismantled. A note beside the drawing adds 'the last burning of enamele Nov. 27 1770', and to commemorate this event there still exists a Plymouth jug[3] with a faint inscription in red which includes the same important date.

Eventually by a deed of assignment dated 6th May, 1774, William Cookworthy transferred to Richard Champion the full patent rights, although the Bristol rate books show that the firm was already styled Richard Champion and Co. in September 1773.[4] But even before that, in January 1772, the new apprentices were indentured to Richard Champion and his wife Judith. Champion, a young man with

[1] A Quaker merchant born 6th Nov., 1743, died on 7th Oct., 1791, near Camden, South Carolina. When applying for an extension for the term of the Cookworthy patent Champion states in his evidence before Parliament 'that he has been almost from the beginning concerned in the work . . .'. For very full details of Champion's life see H. Owen, *Two Centuries of Ceramic Art in Bristol*, 1873.

[2] Owen, *op. cit.*, Pl. 2. There wrongly described as Champion's enamelling kiln. Compare Champion's drawing with the later engravings of the Sèvres wood-fired kilns Plates 1 and xli and the English stoneware coal-fired kiln Plate xxiii in the *Atlas* to A. Brongniart, *Traité des Arts Céramiques*, Paris, 3rd ed., 1877

[3] *British Museum catalogue* vii 50 a. Decorated in the famille verte style with the 'kylin' pattern, see Mackenna, *Cookworthy's Plymouth and Bristol Porcelain*, Pl. 26, where a teapot of this pattern is shown with the rare double mark for tin in red and blue.

[4] In October 1773 Champion's sister wrote of Cookworthy 'that the China business which brought him to Bristol is settled. I hope satisfactorily to both parties. . . .'

ambition, was now in full control but he was faced with a difficult situation. The cost of china clay and stone had been doubled owing to a royalty which he had to pay Cookworthy after completion of the deed of assignment. He must have foreseen that he could easily be ruined if the patent was to expire at the end of its natural term in 1782 when other potters would be free to obtain the Cornish materials to make hard-paste porcelain, doubtless at less than half the price which he would still be committed to pay. The remedy was an early application to Parliament for an extension of the patent, and this he made in February 1775. A bitter struggle then ensued between himself and Josiah Wedgwood,[1] the latter doing everything in his power to oppose the granting of further patent rights, even attempting to prove that the existing patent was invalid. The case came before the House of Lords and Champion was obliged to offer two major tactical concessions in an attempt to undermine Wedgwood's opposition; he proposed that the china clay and stone should be available to other potters, but only for making earthenware, and that he would provide the House with a new specification of his method of manufacture. The Bill was eventually passed towards the end of May 1775, but while the Act gave Champion his fourteen years extension of patent rights, it also incorporated as law the two proposals which Champion had been obliged to make. This result was only a partial victory for Champion and its achievement must have severely strained his limited financial resources. Wedgwood on the other hand was jubilant and at once set off for Cornwall with another Staffordshire potter, John Turner. It was this momentous journey which determined the future of the potting industry in Staffordshire by making available comparatively inexpensive supplies of Cornish clay and stone.[2]

The cold glitter of the English hard paste demanded a high standard of decoration to make it attractive and Champion certainly produced some beautiful things ornamented with coloured enamels and exceptionally fine gilding. However, the successful English porcelain factories of the period found it necessary to devote an increasingly large proportion of their output to useful blue and white, partly no doubt to

[1] Hugh Owen, *Two Centuries of Ceramic Art*, Ch. V, for full details.

[2] From a small estate in St. Stephens owned by Mr. Trethawy, where the clay and stone was leased for ten guineas a year. Later another agreement for these materials at a similar cheap rate was made with Mr. Carthew of St. Austell. This should be compared with the prices paid by Champion, apparently an average of £30 a year in royalties alone between 1774 and 1778 so that his materials actually cost him twice this amount, that is £60 a year on a tonnage basis compared with Wedgwood's 10 guineas a year for an unlimited amount of clay and stone. (R. J. Charleston, 'The end of Bristol, the beginning of New Hall: some fresh evidence,' *Connoisseur*, vol. CXXXVII, no. 553, April 1956, p. 186, and *Procs. of the Wedgwood Society*, 1957, no. 2, p. 94.)

counter the growing competition from the vast quantity of cheap creamware from Wedgwood's new factory at Etruria. Champion was unsuccessful in the manufacture of blue and white in any quantity and we have his own words describing his difficulties.[1] Speaking in the third person he says, 'There is one branch of the manufacture, the blue and white, upon which he has just entered, this branch is likely to be the most generally useful of any: but the giving of a blue colour under the glaze, on so hard a material as he uses, has been found full of difficulty. This object he has persued at a great expense by means of a foreign artificer; and can now venture to assert that he shall bring that to perfection which has been found so difficult in Europe in native clay.'

Three years later in August 1778 Champion has 'assigned his property to trustees for the benefit of his creditors',[2] and a Commission in Bankruptcy, dated 29th August, 1778,[3] was declared against him, to be temporarily suspended at the petitioner's request on the same day, no doubt on the intervention of his influential friends such as Edmund Burke and the Duke of Portland.[4] After 1778 the Bristol factory continued to make hard-paste porcelain under Champion's management until 1781, although the output was on a lesser scale than previously,[5] and in September 1781 Champion stated that he then carried on the smallest work.[6] With little hope of continuing at Bristol with any success Champion planned to set up a large company in Staffordshire which besides having its own manufactory would allow its members to make use of the patent rights in their own works on payment of a fine to the parent company.[7] His plan was opposed by Wedgwood, and the Staffordshire potters were hesitant about forming a company which would be burdened with the price that Champion had to pay for the Cornish clay and stone when they could easily obtain these materials more cheaply on their own account.[8] Conse-

[1] Owen, *op. cit.*, Champion's reply to Wedgwood's memorial, p. 128–9.

[2] F. Severne Mackenna, *Cookworthy's Plymouth and Bristol Porcelain*, Leigh-on-Sea, 1946, p. 43.

[3] Major W. H. Tapp, 'The Art of James Banford, Painter of Derby Ceramics,' *Connoisseur*, vol. XCIX, February 1937, p. 2.

[4] Owen, *op. cit.*, pp. 96, 114.

[5] After 1778 there was a marked fall off in Champion's requirements of raw materials (R. J. Charleston, *loc. cit.*, p. 186).

[6] *Ibid.*

[7] Champion's orginal plan was possibly to form a central manufacturing company using his expensive supplies of Cornish materials which would be subsidized by fines paid by the members to make hard paste porcelain in their own works from cheaper supplies of clay and stone.

[8] Champion sought to have the cost of his materials reduced to make them competitive with those otherwise available in Staffordshire. It is possible that he was partly successful in this as the New Hall factory was later able to sell prepared

quently Champion was forced to curtail his original plan[1] and he eventually left Bristol for Staffordshire in November 1781 to establish his new manufactory at Tunstall. However, shortly after this, in April 1782, he finally severed his connections with the potting industry and became the Assistant Paymaster to the Forces.

The Staffordshire Company moved from Tunstall to Shelton Hall, known as the New Hall, under the style of 'Hollins, Warburton and Company,[2] Manufacturers of Real China'. Here they were successful in producing an astonishing quantity and variety of hard-paste tea wares amongst which were some strident blue and white patterns. The New Hall hard paste apparently continued to be made for some time after Champion's patent had expired in 1796, until it was finally outmoded by the advent of bone china.

Many of Cookworthy's potting shapes have a formidably robust appearance, especially the thrown wares such as cups (1), mugs (2), tea and coffee pots (3), and vases, where the intractable material has dictated the simplest of outlines. They were fortified by their mechanically strong construction against a tendency to warp in the violent fire to which they were subjected. The Plymouth wares were indeed fired to such a high temperature that even the rococo moulded sauce boats (4) and shell salts (5)[3] have a petrified remoteness which is in marked contrast to the sensuous quality of the finest soft paste. Nonetheless, their rarity and their romantic origin evoke respect, especially perhaps the first dated example (6) of 14th March, 1768[4], which was almost certainly painted and initialled 'C.F.', for 'Cookworthy fecit', by Cookworthy himself. Cookworthy exploited the stubborn characteristics of his hard paste to practical advantage in making a fine mortar (7), and again with his massive ink wells,[5] but he found it virtually impossible to fire flat wares, and at the most he only managed to produce

glaze called 'composition' to other potters (Jewitt, *A Life of Josiah Wedgwood*, 1865, p. 261). However, no more materials were mined after 1785 on Mr. Pitt's estate at Carlogass on which the 99-year lease had been obtained by Cookworthy in 1770 (Lady Radford, *op. cit.*, p. 41).

[1] 'I have now entered into an agreement with ten potters only', Charleston, *loc. cit.*, p. 186.

[2] John Daniels joined the firm at a later date when his name was included in the firm's bill heading.

[3] This was possibly made at Bristol.

[4] There is an anniversary blue and white tankard in the Schreiber Collection, no. 757, inscribed 'Josiah and Catherine Greethead March 13 1769'.

[5] Mackenna, *Cookworthy's Plymouth & Bristol Porcelain*, Pl. 18.

(1) *Plate* 92A; (2) *Plate* 95D; (3) *Plates* 93A, B, C, D; (4) *Plate* 92B; (5) *Plate* 94B; (6) *Plate* 91A; (7) *Plate* 91C.

a few saucers (1) to pair with his cups. He made sets of seven hors-d'oeuvre dishes (2),[1] complete with spoons to fit on circular wooden stands, but the majority of the more fanciful leaf moulded pickle trays (3) were probably produced later at Bristol under either Cookworthy's or Champion's management. His mugs tended to be tall with a low-set bulbous body and a flared-out rim, but he also made straight-sided cider mugs (4). Rather stunted jugs with a mask representing Winter moulded under the lip are likely to have come into production at the time of the move from Plymouth to Bristol.[2] The rare wet-mustard pots[3] copying a Worcester prototype and the pounce pots were probably made only at Bristol. The practical Worcester shapes were, however, adopted at an early date as a basis for the design of tea and coffee pots including their covers, and standard Worcester blue and white patterns were used to decorate them. Handles often have a bold central rib, others are grooved; but a distinctive type, also found on Bristol cups and coffee cans, has a simple curved outer surface with marked flattening of the inner side. The more fragile and ornate handles for sauce boats with double scrolls and a row of bosses for the thumb rest (5) were probably mostly from the Bristol factory. Occasionally a moulded heart-shaped tag is found under the lower terminal and blue-painted scroll marks are sometimes present on either side of the handles at their junction with the body.

Cookworthy appears to have succeeded in making more blue and white than his successor Champion, and in his anxiety to use entirely native materials he may possibly have decorated his wares with Cornish cobalt, especially as he is credited with being the first person to have refined the local crude ore.[4] But whatever the origin of his blue he scarcely ever managed to prevent it from becoming blackened through over-firing. This deficiency necessitated the sparing use of cobalt and his most successful designs have only a finely 'pencilled' outline with the minimum amount of shading. Some of the earliest pieces are decorated with a simple floral motif including a daisy (6), and this flower was incorporated in one of the more complex borders. Many Plymouth pieces show signs of smoke and iron-staining and brown-coloured sanding. Spiral ridges are found on thrown wares and this peculiarity due to the poor plastic quality of the paste is known as

[1] *Schreiber Catalogue*, p. 130, No. 715.
[2] There is a dated polychrome example in the British Museum inscribed November ye 27th 1770'.
[3] An example in the Plymouth Museum.
[4] Ll. Jewitt, *A Life of Josiah Wedgwood*, 1865, p. 232.

(1) *Plate* 92A; (2) *Plate* 91B; (3) *Plate* 94C;
(4) *Plate* 95D; (5) *Plate* 94A. (6) *Plate* 92D.

'wreathing'; this also occurs on Bristol and New Hall. The glaze is completely fused with the body and small fissures passing through the glaze and into the body are a fairly common feature. The glaze surface may have an almost granular texture from a marked degree of pitting, the latter being especially evident over blue and white patterns. Broken pieces show the typical conchoidal fracture and the 'moist and lucid appearance'[1] of all true hard-paste porcelains. The translucency varies from an orange-straw colour to a greenish white.

Cookworthy, the trained chemist, at first followed d'Entrecolles' description meticulously but he soon found that his formulae had to be amended by the inclusion of additional alkalis to make the refractory Cornish materials more fusible. Champion was no chemist but he was able to profit from Cookworthy's experience and he was fortunate in obtaining the skilled services of John Brittan as his manager. The latter, who claimed to have had 'great experience in several China Manufactories', confirmed by his defence of Bristol hard-paste before the Parliamentary Committee in 1775 that he was indeed a master of both theory and practice. He mentioned that at Bristol they could make plates, 'but have had great difficulties; that they have not hitherto much attended to that object, but have applied themselves to perfecting the body as a body, and the glaze as a glaze.' These experiments resulted in the use of additional fluxing substances in the glaze, including 'magnesia, nitre, lime, gypsum, fusible spar, arsenic, lead and tin ashes';[2] and, if Champion's specification is to be believed, they showed that it was possible to vary the proportions of the two body constituents within remarkably wide limits.[3] Champion gives details of two different glazes; the second containing the greater amount of flux may have been used for blue and white. It is likely that by reducing the temperature necessary for the vitrification of the glaze they hoped to avoid over-firing their blue and turning it grey or black which had been a major fault at Plymouth.

Definite improvements followed these experiments and the glaze began to look cleaner 'with the polish so fine as to resist every

[1] The description is by John Brittan, 1737–1804, Champion's experienced manager, Owen, op. cit., p. 117. See J. E. Nightingale, Contributions, 1881, pp. lxxxiv and lxxxv, for particulars of this man, also Owen, op. cit., pp. 14 and 15 and W. J. Pountney, Old Bristol Potteries, 1920, p. 206.

[2] Jewitt, Ceramic Art in Great Britain, vol. 1, p. 376, Champion's specification. Rev. A. W. Oxford, A Catalogue of the Trapnell Collection, Albert Amor, 1912, pp. xvi and xvii, gives a glaze analysis for Plymouth and another for Bristol porcelain showing that the Bristol sample contains the greater amount of silica and alkalis, in proportions that would help to mature the glaze at a lower temperature.

[3] The proportions vary between the limits of one part china stone with a $\frac{1}{4}$ part china clay to one part china stone with 16 parts china clay.

scratch . . .',[1] although even then it was sometimes crazed and misfired. Increasing experience with the materials and the employment of a large number of skilled potters made it possible to produce a variety of shapes with moulded patterns and fanciful handles to disguise the heavy rock-like quality of their hard-paste body. It was eventually discovered how to fire flat wares (I) in greater numbers, although many of these had to have a secondary strengthening foot or bar on the under surface and blue and white examples are very scarce. Cups no longer showed the somewhat ovoid outline of the Plymouth examples and tea bowls and saucers were often made with a double ogee shape.[2] A distinctive handle on tea wares is of the double-scroll type with a small tag continuing the lower part of the major curve inwards towards the body.[3] Cream and sauce-boat handles with their double scrolls appear almost elegant beside their Plymouth counterparts. Moulded wares include a cream boat (2) with an attractive design of fruit and cob nuts that was also used for Derby porcelain as well as for salt-glaze and silver examples.

There were also undoubted improvements in the colour of the blue as proclaimed by an advertisement of 1st February, 1779.[4] 'The blue and white is now brought to the greatest perfection equal to the Nankeen, which with the very great Strength and fine Polish renders it the best for use of any China now in the world.' But in spite of this, comparatively little blue and white appears to have been made, even less it seems than at Plymouth. The painted decoration derived inspiration from the Chinese either directly or second-hand from Worcester, but some of the later wares were sparsely patterned with floral sprays in the Meissen manner (3). A considerable technical innovation was the use of underglaze transfer prints.[5] However, the aesthetic effect was far from satisfactory and very few examples were produced.[6] A fair proportion of the blue and white is marked with a cross in underglaze blue but the sign for tin was probably used while

[1] Owen, *op. cit.*, p. 151, part of an advertisement of a Bath chinaman.
[2] Mackenna, *Cookworthy's Plymouth and Bristol Porcelain*, Fig. 27, illustrates one of the earliest examples of this type marked with the sign for tin. This was probably made at Bristol under Cookworthy. Two examples are in the Schreiber Collection.
[3] Mackenna, *Champion's Bristol Porcelain*, Fig. 8.
[4] *Aris's Birmingham Gazette*, first brought to light by R. J. Charleston.
[5] An extremely difficult procedure as the usual soft-biscuit body of hard-paste wares could not easily withstand the amount of force employed to transfer the design from the paper on to the body.
[6] Mackenna, *op. cit.*, figs. 6, 7 and 8.

(I) *Plate* 95B; (2) *Plate* 94C.
(3) *Plate* 95C.

Cookworthy was still actively connected with the factory at Bristol. A blue and white bowl in the Schreiber Collection bears both marks.

The New Hall factory was the most successful of the three at making the production of hard paste a commercial proposition. This seems to have been achieved by the discovery of a comparatively low temperature glaze and, in the Staffordshire tradition, by increasing the temperature of the initial biscuit firing. These factors enabled the New Hall potters to decorate their wares with underglaze transfer prints and to obtain an improved blue. They almost certainly fired their wares with coal[1] and they seemed to have been able to control the kiln temperatures accurately.

The typical New Hall glaze has a viscid, almost oily surface appearance. It was often applied fairly thickly and small bare areas of paste are commonly found on bases where the glaze has humped round them as if it had a high surface tension. Teapot bases are frequently streaked with glaze as if fingers had been drawn across them to remove the excess after dipping. The New Hall body and the glaze are not as completely fused as in Plymouth and Bristol examples, although some of the earliest New Hall appears to have a higher fired glaze with increased fusion with the body. The New Hall glaze undoubtedly contained greater quantities of fluxing substances and it does not fluoresce under ultra-violet light in the same way as other hard-paste glazes, whether from China, Meissen or Bristol. The body, before about 1810, was however undoubtedly hard paste, and various analyses[2] show the typical aluminium/silica ratio with the absence of other major constituents apart from small amounts of fluxing agents.

New Hall did not produce figures like the Plymouth and Bristol factories; instead it devoted its energies entirely to making simple, practical shapes for domestic use, chiefly tea wares. Saucers are large and deep in the usual Staffordshire manner. Cups and cream jugs may have a typical moulded handle with an interlocked thumb rest (1), or a plain strap-like shape with pointed terminals. Teapots frequently have a straight-sided silver shape (2) with a pierced knob on the cover. Early cream jugs either matched these teapots or were

[1] R. J. Charleston, *Connoisseur*, April 1956, footnote on p. 188 suggests that the Bristol factory also used coal, possibly from the Forest of Dean. This seems unlikely as Cookworthy had originally built his wood-fired kiln to the design used by the brown stoneware manufacturers who had a strong tradition at Bristol. Furthermore, wood was the fuel for hard paste at Meissen and at Sèvres until a late date. Perhaps then the fuel for Champion's kiln came from above and not below the ground in the Forest of Dean.

[2] Eccles and Rackham, *Analysed specimens of English Porcelain*, 1922, pp. 23 and 24. And G. E. Stringer, *New Hall Porcelain*, London, 1949, p. 94.

(1) *Plate* 96A; (2) *Plate* 96B.

made with a helmet shape and a pedestal foot. More rarely they had an upright bulbous form, but the later elongated shapes with a curved lip belong more properly to the nineteenth century. Bread and butter plates (1) in blue and white are comparatively rare, as are tea-poys (2) with a robust barrel-shape. Leaf-shaped pickle trays, asparagus servers and knife handles seem to occur only in blue and white.

Underglaze-blue painting is uncommon, although the Meissen 'onion' or 'immortelle' pattern is occasionally found; and there are pieces decorated with an underglaze-blue ground for superadded gilding such as two fluted tea bowls inscribed 1782 in the Victoria and Albert Museum. On the other hand a number of transfer-printed wares have recently been recognized by Mr. G. Grey, the leading authority on New Hall, and by the author; they are described here for the first time. Many of these pieces are finished with a brown enamelled rim after the Chinese, but some of the earlier wares are embellished with gilding (3). Stringer records an account from the New Hall Company for September 1789 showing that Josiah Wedgwood bought four cups and saucers, blue and white, of four different patterns 3/6d.[1] Ten transfer-printed designs are now known[2], including two previously mentioned by Sprague[3] and excluding a number of small floral sprays on asparagus servers. Among them is an elaborate version of the 'gazebo' pattern (4). There are four variants on the 'willow' pattern theme (5), one of which includes two distinctive flying insects; another has a large house with bamboo fencing looking like rows of trench mortars. Then there are two unusual chinoiserie designs (6) of children playing, possibly derived from Boucher; these chinoiseries are reminiscent of those much finer examples on Swedish faience.[4] Finally there is a distinctive design composed of a willow root, a flowering shrub and two flying doves. Two of the typical printed borders for these designs are formed by inward pointing leaves (7), which call to mind the 'curious border of overlapping petals' described

[1] Stringer, *op. cit.*, p. 78.

[2] Two of the patterns were illustrated and wrongly ascribed to Zachariah Barnes by H. B. Lancaster, *Apollo*, vol. XLVI, no. 269, July 1947, pp. 12 and 13. Earlier collectors such as Arthur Hurst considered them to be of Caughley origin. A number of these wares are in the Bootle Museum, the gift of Ernest Allman, Esq.

[3] Dr. T. A. Sprague, *Hard Paste New Hall Porcelain*, Trans. E.C.C., vol. 3, part 3, 1954, patterns 272 and 274. Stringer illustrates pattern 272, Pl. xxvii, which is an elaborate floral design overpainted with enamels.

[4] R. J. Charleston, 'Transfer Printing on Swedish Faience', *Connoisseur*, October 1960, vol. CXLVI, Fig. 6.

(1) *Plate* 96c; (2) *Plate* 96c; (3) *Plate* 96b; (4) *Plate* 96c; (5) *Plates* 96b, d; (6) *Plate* 96a; (7) *Plate* 96c.

and illustrated by Honey as occurring on Meissen tea wares painted in blue and white.[1] A similar leaf border is found printed on New Hall knife handles together with decorative acanthus scrolls. The colour of the New Hall prints varies in tone from a pale royal blue to an intense indigo. Wreathing is sometimes present on thrown wares such as tea-poys and the translucency by artificial light is usually straw-coloured.

An interesting feature of some examples is that they bear the crowned, rampant lion mark of Frankenthal in underglaze blue (1). At first sight it seems strange that New Hall should choose this some-what unusual mark, but it may be recalled that Nicholas Berthevin, the French arcanist, had successfully decorated a few specimens of Frankenthal hard-paste porcelain by his highly secret method of transfer-printing in underglaze blue about 1770 to 1772. We now find New Hall adopting this Frankenthal mark to commemorate the fact that they were the only other European hard-paste factory to succeed in printing underglaze-blue decorations.

[1] W. B. Honey, *Dresden China*, London, 1934, Pl. XIC.

---

(1) *Plate* 96D.

BIBLIOGRAPHY

References to a number of important papers published in periodicals have been given in the footnotes and are here omitted. Many of the works listed below contain useful illustrations of blue and white, although the attributions are not always correct.

GENERAL WORKS

Llewellyn Jewitt, *The Ceramic Art of Great Britain*, 2 vols., London, 1878.

R. L. Hobson, *Catalogue of The Collection of English Porcelain in the British Museum*, London, 1905.

W. Moore Binns, *The First Century of English Porcelain*, London, 1909.

H. Eccles and B. Rackham, *Analysed Specimens of English Porcelain*, Victoria and Albert Museum, London, 1922.

Bernard Rackham, *Catalogue of the Schreiber Collection of English Porcelain, Earthenware, Enamels, etc.*, vol. 1, *Porcelain* (2nd edition), Victoria and Albert Museum, London, 1928.

Catalogue of the well known collection of fine old English Pottery and Porcelain, the property of Wallace Elliot, Esq. (decd.), Sotheby & Co., London, 24th May, 1938.

Stanley W. Fisher, *English Blue and White Porcelain of the 18th Century*, London, 1947.

W. B. Honey, *Old English Porcelain* (2nd edition), London, 1948.

English Porcelain Circle Transactions, Nos. I to IV, London, 1928–32.

English Ceramic Circle Transactions, vols. I to V, London, 1933 to 1962.

English Ceramic Circle, *English Pottery and Porcelain, Commemorative Catalogue of an Exhibition held at the Victoria and Albert Museum, May 5–June 20, 1948*, London, 1949.

J. P. Cushion, *Pocket Book of English Ceramic Marks*, London, 1959.

TRANSFER-PRINTING

W. Turner, *Transfer Printing on Enamels, Porcelain and Pottery*, London, 1907.

C. Cook, *The Life and Work of Robert Hancock*, London, 1948.

BIBLIOGRAPHY

C. Cook, *Supplement to the Life and Work of Robert Hancock*, London, 1955.

Bow

Frank Hurlbutt, *Bow Porcelain*, London, 1926.

Catalogue of Bow Porcelain, A special exhibition of documentary material, British Museum, London, 1959.

Catalogue of the well-known Collection of Bow Porcelain, the property of John A. Ainslie, Sotheby & Co., London, 7th March, 1961.

Lund's Bristol and Worcester

R. W. Binns, *A Century of Potting in the City of Worcester* (2nd edition), London, 1877.

R. W. Binns, *Catalogue of a Collection of Worcester Porcelain in the Museum at the Royal Porcelain Works*, Worcester, 1884.

R. L. Hobson, *Worcester Porcelain*, London, 1910.

W. J. Pountney, *Old Bristol Potteries*, Bristol, 1920.

F. Severne Mackenna, *Worcester Porcelain*, Leigh-on-Sea, 1950.

F. A. Barrett, *Worcester Porcelain*, London, 1953.

Catalogue of a Selection of Dr. Wall Worcester Porcelain 1751–1783 from the Dyson Perrins Museum at the Royal Porcelain Works Worcester, 1959.

Longton Hall

W. Bemrose, *Longton Hall Porcelain*, London, 1906.

B. M. Watney, *Longton Hall Porcelain*, London, 1957.

Liverpool

H. Boswell Lancaster, *Liverpool and Her Potters*, Liverpool, 1936.

K. Boney, *Liverpool Porcelain*, London, 1957.

Catalogue of the Knowles Boney Collection of Liverpool Porcelain, Williamson Art Gallery and Museum, Birkenhead, 1962.

Derby

F. Brayshaw Gilhespy, *Crown Derby Porcelain*, Leigh-on-Sea, 1951.

F. Brayshaw Gilhespy, *Derby Porcelain*, London, 1960.

Lowestoft

W. W. R. Spelman, *Lowestoft China*, London, 1905.

F. A. Crisp, *Catalogue of Lowestoft China*, privately printed, London, 1907.

A. E. Murton, *Lowestoft China*, Lowestoft, 1932.

M. L. Powell, *Lowestoft China*, Lowestoft, 1934.

ENGLISH BLUE AND WHITE PORCELAIN

Noel H. P. Turner, *Catalogue of The Lowestoft China Bicentenary 1757–1957*, Ipswich, 1957.

Geoffrey A. Godden, *Catalogue of Lowestoft Porcelain: an Exhibition to commemorate the two hundredth anniversary of the founding of the Lowestoft factory*, Worthing Art Gallery, 1957.

Catalogue of a collection of Lowestoft Porcelain, the property of the late D. M. Hunting, Sotheby & Co., London, 31st October, 1961.

CAUGHLEY

F. A. Barrett, *Caughley and Coalport Porcelain*, Leigh-on-Sea, 1951.

PLYMOUTH AND BRISTOL

F. Severne Mackenna, *Cookworthy's Plymouth and Bristol Porcelain*, Leigh-on-Sea, 1946.

F. Severne Mackenna, *Champion's Bristol Porcelain*, Leigh-on-Sea, 1947.

INDEX

1.A. *Beaker cup, raised anchor period Chelsea, about 1750, unmarked, ht. 2⅞ in. Victoria and Albert Museum.*

B. *Octagonal saucer, Chelsea, marked with an anchor in underglaze blue, about 1753. Katz Collection.*

C. *Plate, Chelsea, marked with an anchor in underglaze blue, about 1755, diam. 9 in. Victoria and Albert Museum.*

(See page 2)

2.A. *Ink well inscribed 'Made at New Canton 1750', mark,*
'B' in underglaze blue, Bow, diam. 3¼ in. Colchester Museum.
B. *Leaf-shaped pickle tray, early period, Bow, 1749–1750, width 3¼ in.*
Watney Collection.
C. *Bowl, inscribed 'William and Elizabeth Martin November 20 1750',*
Bow, diam. 8⅛ in. From Ainslie Collection. Now in British Museum.
(*See pages* 18, 20, 21 *and* 23)

3.A. *Mug, mark, incised nick centre of base, Bow, about 1752, ht. 3½ in.*
Toppin Collection.
B. *Mug, marks, 7 on handle and incised nick on base, Bow, about 1752,*
ht. 3½ in. Toppin Collection.
C. *Sauce boat, mark 'G', Bow, about 1752, length 8¾ in.*
From Ainslie Collection.
D. *Ink well inscribed 'Edward Vernon Esqr. July 1752', Bow, diam. 3½ in.*
Brighton Art Gallery and Museum. (See pages 18, 20, 21 and 22)

4.A. *Vase, mark, incised line, one of a garniture, some marked with incised line others with incised 'R', Bow, about 1752, ht. 7 in. From Ainslie Collection.*
B. *Finger bowl stand, mark, incised line, its pair has incised 'R' mark, Bow, about 1752, diam. 6 in. Watney Collection.*
C. *Miniature tea wares. Marks, incised 'R' and incised line, Bow, about 1752, ht. 1½ in. From Ainslie Collection.*
(See page 20)

5.A. *Coffee can, Bow, about 1753, ht.* $2\frac{1}{8}$ *in. Watney Collection.*
B. *Cream jug, Bow, about 1753, ht. 2 in. Victoria and Albert Museum.*
C. *Teapot, Bow, about 1753, ht.* $5\frac{1}{2}$ *in. Victoria and Albert Museum.*
D. *Teapot, Bow, about 1753, ht.* $4\frac{1}{2}$ *in. From Ainslie Collection.*
(*See pages* 21 *and* 23)

6.A. *Bowl, mark in underglaze blue, probably 'I', Bow, about 1753,*
diam. 4⅛ in. Watney Collection.
B. *Cream jug, Bow, about 1753, ht. 2½ in. From Ainslie Collection.*
C. *Cup, Bow, about 1753, ht. 2 9/16 in. Watney Collection.*
D. *Sauce boat, Bow, about 1753, length 5⅞ in. Watney Collection.*
(See pages 19, 21, 22 and 23)

7.A. *Tureen and cover, Bow, about 1753, length* $15\frac{1}{2}$ *in.*
From Ainslie Collection.
B. *Basket, Bow, about 1753, diam.* $5\frac{1}{2}$ *in. Mrs. K. Tilley.*
C. *Butter dish, Bow, about 1753, diam. 5 in. From Ainslie Collection.*
(See page 23)

8.A. *Cream jug, inscribed in underglaze blue 'W. Pether May 10 1754',*
Bow, ht. 3¼ in. Watney Collection.
  B. *Coffee can, Bow, about 1755, ht. 2½ in. From Ainslie Collection.*
  C. *Plate, Bow, about 1754, diam. 8¾ in. From Ainslie Collection.*
(See pages 12, 18 and 22)

9.A. *Centre-piece, mark, an incised nick, Bow, about 1753, ht. 7¼ in.*
From Ainslie Collection.
B. *Vase, Bow, 1754–1775, ht. 10¼ in. Rous Lench Collection.*
C. *Vase, Bow, 1754–1755, ht. 10¼ in. Fitzwilliam Museum, Cambridge.*
(See pages 23 and 25)

10.A. *Pickle trays* (1) *marked '2' in underglaze blue.* (2) *imitation Chinese characters.*
Bow, about 1756, width 4¾ *in.*

B. *Saucer, Bow, about 1760, diam.* 4⁷⁄₁₆ *in.*

C. *Pickle trays* (1) *no mark.* (2) *imitation Chinese characters. Bow, about 1756, width* 3⅝ *in.*

D. *Leaf-shaped pickle trays, Bow, 1756–1765, largest width* 3⅝ *in.*
Watney Collection. (See pages 18, 24, 25, 26 and 28)

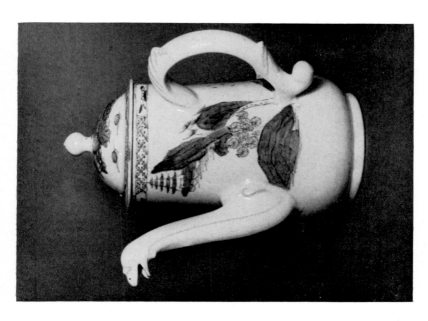

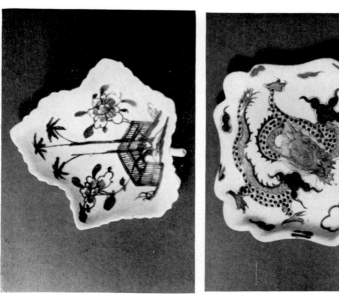

11.A. *Pickle tray, mark '27' on footring, Bow, about 1756, width 4 in. Watney Collection.*
B. *Coffee pot, mark, '20' in underglaze blue, Bow, about 1755, ht. 8¼ in. From Ainslie Collection.*
C. *Teapot stand, mark, '14' in underglaze blue, Bow, about 1756, width 4¼ in. From Ainslie Collection.*
(*See pages 24, 27 and 28*)

12.A. *Bottle, Bow, about 1762, ht. 11¼ in. Victoria and Albert Museum.*
B. *Bowl, inscribed 'John and Ann Bowcock 1759' and 'I.B.', Bow, diam. 8 in.*
British Museum.
C. *Mug, Bow, about 1760, ht. 3¾ in. From Ainslie Collection.*
D. *Covered tankard, Bow, about 1762, ht. 7¼ in. From Ainslie Collection.*
(*See pages 18, 19, 25 and 26*)

13.A. *Egg cup, mark, imitation Chinese characters, Bow, about 1762,*
ht. 2¾ in. From Ainslie (now Mrs. David Watney) Collection.
B. *Cream jug and cover, 'quail' pattern, Bow, about 1763, ht. 5⅜ in.*
Watney Collection.
C. *Egg cup, mark, '23' in underglaze blue, Bow, about 1762, ht. 2⅝ in.*
Victoria and Albert Museum.
D. *Dish, Bow, about 1760, length 10¾ in. Victoria and Albert Museum.*
(See pages 25, 26 and 28)

14. A. and B. *Coronation mug, transfer-printed, Bow, about 1761, ht. 4¾ in. Cheltenham Museum.*
C. *Mug, transfer-printed, Bow, about 1760, ht. 5⅜ in. Watney Collection.*
D. *Mug, painted decoration, inscribed 'Mrs. Ann Ambler 1762', Bow, ht. 3¾ in. The National Museum of Wales, Cardiff.*
(*See pages* 19, 27 *and* 28)

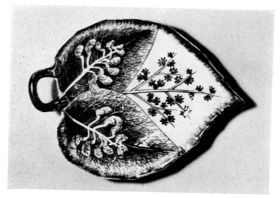

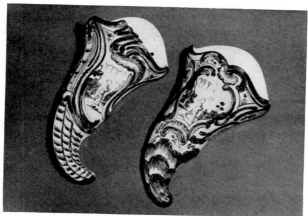

15.A. *Leaf-shaped tray, Bow, about 1763, length 6⅞ in. City Museum,*
Birmingham.
B. *Pair of cornucopiae, Bow, about 1760, length 8½ in.*
Compare with Lowestoft examples, Plate 74B. From Ainslie Collection.
C. *Dish, transfer-printed, Bow, about 1763, length 18½ in.*
Watney Collection. (See page 26)

16.A. *Leaf-shaped cream boat, Bow, about 1763, length 3¾ in.*
From Ainslie Collection.
B. *Cup, inscribed 'I:C 1763', Bow, ht. 2¼ in. From Ainslie Collection.*
C. *Centre-piece, Bow, about 1763, ht. 5¼ in. From Ainslie Collection.*
D. *Dish, Bow, about 1760, length 9½ in. Messrs. Sotheby and Co.*
(See pages 19, 26, 27 and 28)

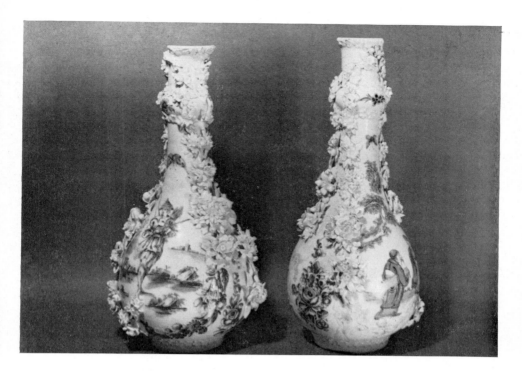

17.A. *Pair of bottles, painted by a hand who also worked in enamels, Bow, about 1760, ht. 11 in. From Ainslie Collection.*
  B. *Mug, Bow, about 1763, ht. 3½ in. From Ainslie Collection.*
  C. Ecuelle *or Caudle cup and stand, Bow, about 1762, ht. 5½ in. From Ainslie Collection.*
(*See pages 25 and 28*)

18.A. *Two cups showing Worcester influence in pattern and shapes,*
Bow, about 1765. Miss L. Russell Collection.
B. *Sauce boat, Bow, about 1760, length 7¾ in. From Ainslie Collection.*
C. *Tureen, cover, stand and ladle, Bow, about 1762, length 8 in.*
From Ainslie Collection. (See pages 25, 29 and 86)

19.A. *Plate, Bow, about 1760, diam. 8 in. F. Barrett Collection.*
B. *Plate, mark in underglaze blue, a circle with a line through it, Bow,*
about 1770, diam. 9¼ in. From Ainslie Collection.
C. *Plate, Bow, about 1765, diam. 7¼ in. From Ainslie Collection.*
(See pages 25, 26, 28 and 30)

20.A. *Sauce boat, no mark, Lund's Bristol factory, about 1750, length* $6\frac{1}{4}$ *in.*
Watney Collection.
B. *Sauce boat, marked 'Bristoll' in relief, Lund's Bristol factory,*
about 1750, length $6\frac{1}{8}$ *in. Victoria and Albert Museum.*
C. *Sauce boat, marked 'Bristol' in relief, Lund's Bristol factory,*
about 1750, length $6\frac{1}{4}$ *in. Victoria and Albert Museum.*
(*See pages* 36 *and* 37)

21.A. *Cream boat, marked 'Bristoll' in relief, Lund's Bristol factory, about 1750, length 4⅜ in. From Dyson Perrins Collection.*
B. *Basket of type sometimes marked with a 'P' and a cross incised, Lund's Bristol factory, about 1750, ht. 2¾ in. Watney Collection.*
C. *Potted meat pan, Lund's Bristol factory, about 1750, diam. 4¼ in. Watney Collection.*
D. *Cream boat, marked 'Bristol' in relief, Lund's Bristol factory, about 1750, length 4½ in. H. E. Marshall Collection.*
(See pages 36, 37, 38 and 43)

22.A. *Mug, no mark, Lund's Bristol factory, about 1750, ht. 6¼ in.*
Watney Collection.
B. *Coffee cans, typical decoration by 'three dot' painter,*
Lund's Bristol factory, about 1750, ht. 2⅜ in. Watney Collection.
C. *Mugs, no mark, Lund's Bristol factory, about 1750, ht. 4¼ in.*
J. W. Jenkins Collection. (See page 37)

23.A. *Cup, no mark, Worcester, about 1752, ht. 2½ in.*
From Dyson Perrins Collection.
B. *Teapot, mark, TF monogram on base and lid, Worcester, about 1754,*
ht. 5 in. J. W. Jenkins Collection.
C. *Bowl, cross incised inside footring, Worcester, about 1752, diam. 8¼ in.*
Watney Collection.
(See pages 41, 42 and 43)

24.A. *Jug with mask moulded lip, marks, cross incised also workman's mark
in underglaze blue, Worcester, about 1754, ht. 9½ in. Watney Collection.*
B. *Bowl, mark, an incised circle in centre of base and workman's mark in
underglaze blue, Worcester, about 1754, diam. 5¼ in. Watney Collection.*
C. *Tureen and cover, workman's mark on cover and base, Worcester,
about 1754, diam. 9 in. J. W. Jenkins Collection.*
(*See pages 43, 44 and 45*)

25. A. *Mustard pot, mark, a cross incised on base and a line on inner side of*
footring, also a cross in blue, and a workman's mark under handle.
Worcester, about 1754, ht. 3⅞ in. Victoria and Albert Museum.

B. *Porringer or bleeding bowl, mark, incised line on inner side of footring,*
also workman's mark in underglaze blue, Worcester, about 1752,
diam. 5¼ in. Victoria and Albert Museum.

C. *Plate, painted on underpart of flange with Chinese 'precious objects' mark,*
imitation Chinese characters in a double ring, Worcester, about 1752,
diam. 9 in. F. Barrett Collection. (See pages 42, 44, 45 and 46)

26.A. *Two mugs and a bowl, 'willow-root' pattern, incised marks and workman's marks in underglaze blue, Worcester, about 1754, bowl diam. $5\frac{3}{4}$ in., mugs ht. $3\frac{3}{4}$ in. Watney Collection.*

B. *Two coffee cups and a mug, marks, incised lines across inside of footrings, a cross in underglaze blue on mug base and under handle of first coffee cup. Worcester, about 1753, mug ht. $3\frac{9}{16}$ in., cups $2\frac{5}{8}$ in. Watney Collection.*

C. *Finger bowl and stand, butter dish, coffee cup and saucer and coffee can, 'cormorant pattern' incised marks and workman's marks in underglaze blue, Worcester, about 1754, finger bowl ht. 3 in., stand diam. $5\frac{3}{4}$ in., butter dish diam. $5\frac{1}{8}$ in. Watney Collection. (See pages 40, 44 and 45)*

27.A. *Vase, mark, cross in underglaze blue and incised line on foot rim,*
Worcester, about 1753, ht. 22½ in. From H. E. Marshall Collection, now
Collection of Anthony Littleton, Esq.
  B. *Bottle, no mark, Worcester, about 1754, ht. 9 in. Watney Collection.*
  C. *Bottle, workman's mark, Worcester, about 1754, ht. 10 in.*
J. W. Jenkins Collection.
(See pages 44, 45 and 46)

28.A. *Sauce boat, no mark, Worcester, about 1754, length 7¾ in.*
Watney Collection.
B. *Octagonal dish, cross in underglaze blue, Worcester, about 1754,*
length approx. 13 in. From H. E. Marshall Collection.
C. *Teapot and bowl, workman's marks and incised strokes, '2' incised on*
teapot lid, Worcester, 1754–1755. From H. E. Marshall Collection.
(See pages 41, 42, 44 and 46)

29.A. *Teapot, 'tambourine' pattern, workman's mark on lid and another under handle, Worcester, about 1755, ht. 4¼ in. J. W. Jenkins Collection.*
B. *Teapot, 'landslide' pattern, no mark, Worcester, about 1756, ht. 4 in. Watney Collection.*
C. *Teapot, two incised marks on base, Worcester, about 1754, ht. 4 in. Watney Collection.*
(See pages 44, 46 and 50)

30.A. *Dish, TF monogram in underglaze blue, Worcester, about 1755, length 18½ in. British Museum.*
B. *Two sauce boats, workman's marks, Worcester, about 1755. Mrs. K. Tilley.*
(*See pages* 41 *and* 42)

31.A. *Tureen and cover, TF monogram in underglaze blue, Worcester,
1754–1755, diam. 10 in. J. W. Jenkins Collection.*
B. *Vase, I h monogram, Worcester, about 1757, ht. 5¼ in.
J. W. Jenkins Collection.*
C. *Jug, workman's mark, Worcester, about 1756, ht. 7¼ in.
J. W. Jenkins Collection.*
(See page 50)

32.A. *Teapot, TF monogram in underglaze blue on base and cover,*
    Worcester, about 1754, ht. 4¾ in. Watney Collection.
B. *Two cream boats, workman's mark under handle of second example,*
    Worcester, 1755–1760, length 4½ in. Watney Collection.
C. *Two vases, no marks, Worcester, about 1755, ht. 5¼ in.*
    Watney Collection. (See pages 42, 49 and 50)

33.A. *Sauce boat, TF monogram, Worcester, about 1754, length 9 in.*
Derby Museum.
B. *Sauce boat, no mark, Worcester, about 1758, length 8¾ in.*
From Watney Collection.
C. *Bowl, no mark, Worcester, about 1756, diam. 6 in. F. Burrell Collection.*
(See pages 41, 50 and 51)

34.A. *Cream boat, mark, crescent in outline, Worcester, about 1760,*
length 3½ in. Watney Collection.

B. *Cream jug, 'gazebo' pattern, workman's mark, Worcester,*
about 1756, ht. 3¾ in. Watney Collection.

C. *Two cream jugs (1) transfer-printed, mark, crescent, ht. 3½ in.*
(2) painted decoration, mark, crescent in outline, ht. 2¾ in.
Worcester, 1760–1765, J. W. Jenkins Collection.

D. *Crocus pot, transfer-printed, 'W' mark, Worcester, about 1765,*
ht. 7¼ in. J. W. Jenkins Collection. (See pages 50, 51 and 52)

35.A. *Bowl, imitation Chinese mark within a double circle, Worcester,
about 1758, diam.* $7\frac{1}{4}$ *in. J. W. Jenkins Collection.*
 B. *Cup and saucer, workman's mark in imitation of Chinese, Worcester,
about 1758, J. W. Jenkins Collection.*
 C. *Cup and saucer, 'quail' pattern, mark, crescent in outline, Worcester,
1765–1770, Albert Amor.*
 D. *Teapot, 'eloping bride' pattern, imitation Chinese mark, Worcester,
about 1758, Albert Amor. (See pages 48, 50 and 51)*

36.A. *Coffee pot, fretted square mark and crescent, Worcester, about 1762,*
ht. 8⅖ in. Truro Museum.

B. *Plate, 'blind earl' pattern, no mark, Worcester, about 1765, diam. 5¾ in.*
Victoria and Albert Museum.

C. *Sauce boat, crescent in underglaze blue, Worcester, 1765–1770,*
length 6¾ in. Victoria and Albert Museum. (See pages 50 and 53)

37.A. *Rice bowl, transfer-printed decoration and painted border, crescent marked, Worcester, about 1770, diam. 5½ in. Rous Lench Collection.*
 B. *Basket, cover and stand, painted decoration, mark, 'To' impressed on footring of basket, crescent mark on basket and stand, Worcester, 1770–1775, length 10 in. F. Burrell Collection.*
 C. *Broth bowl, transfer-printed, crescent marked, Worcester, about 1770, diam. including handles 7¼ in. F. Barrett Collection.*
 D. *Centre-piece, painted decoration, Worcester or possibly Caughley, about 1775, ht. 5¾ in. Victoria and Albert Museum.*
 (See pages 52, 53 and 110)

38.A. *Stand for a leaf-shaped basin, traces of gilding, mark, crossed 'L's, Longton Hall, about 1752, length 9⅞ in., Watney Collection.*
 B. *Leaf dish or stand, mark, crossed 'L's, Longton Hall, about 1752, length 11¼ in. Mrs. K. Tilley.*
C. *Tureen and cover, stand and ladle, no mark, Longton Hall, about 1753, ht. 5¾ in. From the D. MacAlister Collection.*

(See page 57)

39.A. *Vase, powder blue, traces of gilding, no mark, Longton Hall,
about 1754, ht. 7¾ in. Watney Collection.*
B. *Cream jug moulded with 'lily pattern', no mark, Longton Hall,
about 1756, ht. 4⅝ in. Watney Collection.*
C. *Sauce boat, no mark, Longton Hall, about 1753, length 8¾ in.
Victoria and Albert Museum. (See pages 57, 58 and 60)*

40.A. *Tea bowl and saucer, no mark, Longton Hall, about 1755,*
saucer diam. 4½ in. Watney Collection.
B. *Coffee cup and tea cup, mark, '2' in underglaze blue, Longton Hall,*
about 1755, hts. 2⅜ in. and 1¾ in. Watney Collection.
C. *Teapot, no mark, Longton Hall, about 1755, ht. 5 in.*
G. Bradley Collection. (See page 59)

41.A. *Jug, no mark, Longton Hall, about 1755, ht. 8 in.*
Plymouth Museum.
B. *Sauce boat, no mark, Longton Hall, about 1758, length 6 in.*
Watney Collection.
C. *Teapot, no mark, Longton Hall, about 1756, ht. 5½ in.*
Cheltenham Museum. (See pages 59 and 60)

42.A. *Coffee pot, mark, 'e' in underglaze blue, Longton Hall, about 1757,*
ht. 8¾ in. Watney Collection.

    B. *Mug, no mark, Longton Hall, about 1758, ht. 6¼ in.*
Watney Collection.

    C. *Cream jug, pattern associated with 'k' mark, Longton Hall,*
about 1758. L. Pretty Collection.

    D. *Cup, 'prunus-root' pattern, no mark, Longton Hall, about 1756,*
ht. 2½ in. Watney Collection.

    E. *Cream jug, mark, 'B' in underglaze blue, Longton Hall, about 1756,*
ht. 3 in. Watney Collection.

(*See pages 59 and 60*)

43. A. *Pickle tray, no mark, slightly steatitic, William Reid's factory,*
Liverpool, 1755–1761, length 4⅝ in. Watney Collection.
  B. *Dry mustard pot, no mark, William Reid's factory, Liverpool,*
1755–1761, ht. 5 in. Dr. and Mrs. Statham Collection.
  C. *Cup, no mark, non-steatitic type, William Reid's factory, Liverpool,*
ht. 2½ in. G. Godden Collection.
  D. *Tureen and cover, no mark, non-steatitic, William Reid's factory,*
Liverpool, 1755–1761, ht. 7⅜ in. Watney Collection.
(See pages 79, 80 and 81)

44.A. *Sauce boat, no mark, slightly steatitic, William Reid's factory,*
Liverpool, 1755–1761, length 8⅞ in. Watney Collection.
B. *Cream jug and cover, no mark, William Reid's factory, Liverpool,*
1755–1761, ht. 4⅛ in. E. Allman Collection.
C. *Vase, no mark, slightly steatitic, William Reid's factory, Liverpool,*
1755–1761, ht. 8 in. Watney Collection.
(See pages 79 and 80)

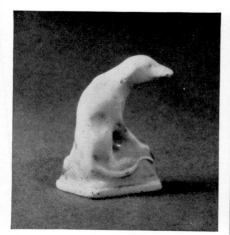

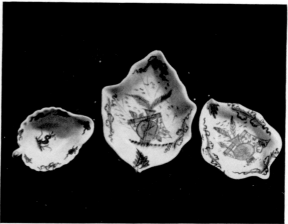

45.A. *Figure of hound, no mark, William Reid's factory, Liverpool,*
about 1756, ht. 1¾ in. By courtesy of Messrs. Sotheby and Co.
B. *Pickle trays, no mark,* (1) *steatitic* (2) *slightly steatitic* (3) *non-steatitic,*
William Reid's factory, Liverpool, about 1755–1761, largest 4⅞ in. in length.
Watney Collection.
C. *Beaker, no mark, William Reid's factory, Liverpool, 1755–1761,*
ht. 4½ in. City Museum, Birmingham.
(See page 80)

46.A. *Teapot, no mark, William Reid's factory, Liverpool,*
about 1755–1761. G. Godden Collection.
B. *Teapot, no mark, William Reid's factory, Liverpool, 1755–1761.*
From L. Godden Collection.
(See pages 79 and 80)

47.A. *Sauce boat, no mark, William Ball's factory, Liverpool,*
1755–1769, length 9⅜ in.
B. *Sauce boat, no mark, William Ball's factory, Liverpool,*
1755–1769, length 7⅜ in.
C. *Sauce boat, no mark, William Ball's factory, Liverpool,*
1755–1769, length 6½ in. Watney Collection. (See page 82)

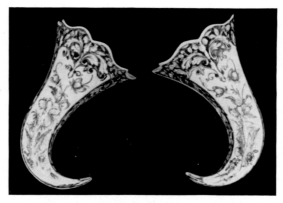

48.A. *Pair of cornucopiae, no mark, William Ball's factory, Liverpool,*
1755–1769, length 4¾ in. J. W. Jenkins Collection.
B. *Plate, no mark, William Ball's factory, Liverpool, 1755–1769,*
diam. 9⅞ in. Watney Collection.
C. *Sauce boat, no mark, William Ball's factory, Liverpool,*
about 1755–1769, length 6½ in. Victoria and Albert Museum.
(*See page 82*)

49.A. *Plate, no mark, William Ball's factory, Liverpool, 1755–1769,*
diam. 8¾ in. F. Barrett Collection.

B. *Tea bowl and saucer, no mark, William Ball's factory, Liverpool,*
1755–1769, saucer diam. 4¾ in. Victoria and Albert Museum.

C. *Teapot, 'M.:.B' in underglaze blue, William Ball's factory, Liverpool,*
1755–1769, ht. 5½ in. Watney Collection.

D. *Cup and coffee can, no mark, William Ball's factory, Liverpool,*
1755–1769, ht. 2½ in. Watney Collection.

(*See page 82*)

50.A. *Chamber candle stick, no mark, William Ball's factory, Liverpool,*
1755–1769, diam. 5¼ in. Victoria and Albert Museum.

B. *Vase, no mark, William Ball's factory, Liverpool, 1755–1769,*
ht. 4⅛ in. Victoria and Albert Museum.

C. *Cream jug inscribed '* $\begin{smallmatrix} C \\ A{:}C \end{smallmatrix}$ *1756', William Ball's factory, Liverpool,*
ht. 3½ in. L. Spillman Collection.

(See page 82)

51.A. *Vase, no mark, William Ball's factory, Liverpool, 1755–1769,
ht. 6½ in. A. J. B. Kiddell Collection.*
B. *Mortar, no mark, William Ball's factory, Liverpool, 1755–1769,
ht. 3¾ in. Watney Collection.*
C. *Plate, mark, a cross in underglaze blue, William Ball's factory,
Liverpool, 1755–1769, diam. 8¾ in. Victoria and Albert Museum.*
(See page 82)

52.A. *Vase and cover, no mark, William Ball's factory, Liverpool,*
1755–1769, ht. 26 in. A. du Boulay Collection.
B. *Plate, no mark, Samuel Gilbody's factory, Liverpool, 1755–1761,*
diam. $9\frac{1}{8}$ in. Watney Collection.
(See pages 77 and 82)

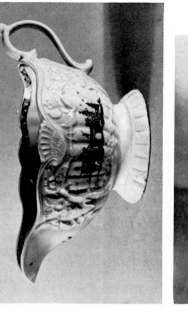

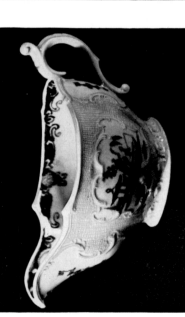

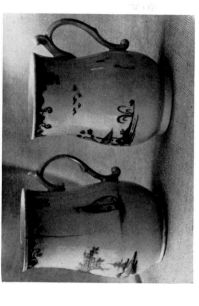

53.A. Cup and coffee can, mark, '4' on cup, in underglaze blue, Chaffers' phosphatic porcelain, Liverpool, about 1755, coffee can, ht. 2⅝ in. Watney Collection.

B. Sauce boat, mark, '4' in underglaze blue, Chaffers' phosphatic porcelain, Liverpool, about 1755, length 8 in. Watney Collection.

C. Sauce boat, no mark, Chaffers' phosphatic porcelain, Liverpool, about 1755, length 8⅜ in. From E. Allman Collection.

D. Two mugs, Chaffers' phosphatic porcelain, Liverpool, about 1755, ht. of smallest 5 in. Hanley Museum.
(See pages 65 and 74)

54.A. *Two sauce boats* (1) *steatitic, no mark,* (2) *phosphatic, with 'I' in underglaze blue inside footring, Chaffers' factory, Liverpool, 1755–1756, length* 5⅛ *in. and* 6 *in.*
B. *Cream jug and cup, steatitic porcelain; tea bowl and saucer and coffee can, phosphatic porcelain, marks, '1', '5' and '6' on inside of footrings, Chaffers' Liverpool, 1755–1756, cream jug ht.* 2¾ *in.*
C. *Mug, phosphatic porcelain, incised rectangular mark and '6' in underglaze blue inside footring, Chaffers' Liverpool, about 1755, ht.* 4⅞ *in.*
D. *Mug, steatitic porcelain, mark, '2' in underglaze blue on base, Chaffers' Liverpool, about 1756, ht.* 4⅝ *in. Watney Collection.*
(*See pages* 65 *and* 66)

55.A. *Basket, steatitic porcelain with small trace of bone ash, no mark, Chaffers' Liverpool, about 1756, ht. $3\frac{1}{2}$ in.*
B. *Two sauce boats, no mark, Chaffers' steatitic porcelain, Liverpool, about 1758, length 5 in. and $5\frac{1}{4}$ in.*
C. *Sauce boat, no mark, Chaffers' steatitic porcelain, Liverpool, about 1758, length $7\frac{5}{8}$ in. Watney Collection.*
(*See pages 67 and 68*)

56.A. *Cups and saucers, 'jumping boy' pattern, imitation Chinese marks, Chaffers' steatitic porcelain, Liverpool, about 1758, diam. of saucers $4\frac{3}{4}$ in. and $4\frac{7}{8}$ in. Watney Collection.*

B. *Mug, painted by the same hand as the documentary John Fell jug, Chaffers' steatitic porcelain, Liverpool, about 1762, ht. $4\frac{5}{8}$ in. Watney Collection.*

C. *Plate, Chaffers' Liverpool, about 1765, diam. $8\frac{1}{4}$ in. Watney Collection.*

D. *Wash basin and jug, painted with Arms of John Hawarden Fazakerley, Chaffers' Liverpool, about 1760, ht. of jug $6\frac{7}{8}$ in., bowl diam. $9\frac{1}{4}$ in. Fitzwilliam Museum, Cambridge. (See pages 67 and 68)*

57.A. *Coffee pot, Chaffers' Liverpool, 1760–1765, ht.* $9\frac{3}{4}$ *in.*
Watney Collection.
B. *Ink well inscribed 'I H 1765', Chaffers' Liverpool.*
Miss Y. Willsmore Collection.
C. *Saucer 'dragon' pattern, 'square' mark in underglaze blue, Chaffers'*
Liverpool, 1760–1765, diam. $5\frac{3}{4}$ *in. L. Pretty Collection.*
D. *Ink well inscribed 'M. S. 1767', Christian's Liverpool, Victoria and*
Albert Museum.
(See pages 67, 68 and 69)

58.A. *Sauce boat, Christian's factory, about 1770, length 6½ in.*
Watney Collection.
B. *Cup and saucer, Christian's steatitic porcelain, about 1775, cup ht. 2½ in.*
Cream jug, Seth Pennington's phosphatic porcelain, about 1776, ht. 3 in.
Watney Collection.
C. *Tureen, Christian's Liverpool factory, about 1770, ht. 8½ in.*
Victoria and Albert Museum.
(See pages 69 and 73)

59.A. *Masked jug, inscribed 'I. H. 1772', Seth Pennington's Liverpool factory, ht. 7¾ in. Williamson Art Gallery, Birkenhead.*

B. *Mug, no mark, Seth Pennington's factory, 1775–1780, ht. 5¾ in. Watney Collection.*

C. *Cream jug and sauce boat, no mark, Seth Pennington's factory, 1775–1780, cream jug ht. 3¾ in., sauce boat length 6½ in. Watney Collection.*

D. *Sauce boat, no mark, Seth Pennington's Liverpool factory, 1775–1780, length 7 in. Victoria and Albert Museum.*

(*See pages 67, 71 and 74*)

60.A and B. *Bowl inscribed 'Success To The Issabella 1779',*
Seth Pennington's factory, diam. 8¼ *in. Liverpool Museum.*
(*See page* 71)

61.A. *Mug, no mark, Seth Pennington's factory, Liverpool, about 1780,*
ht. 5⅛ in. Watney Collection.
B. *Flower pot, inscribed 'W D 1780', Seth Pennington's factory, Liverpool,*
ht. 5⅝ in. Watney Collection.
C. *Bowl, inscribed 'Ralph Farrar 1783', Seth Pennington's factory,*
Liverpool, diam. 8½ in. E. Allman Collection.
D. *Mug, transfer-printed, no mark, Seth Pennington's factory,*
about 1776, ht. 5 in. Watney Collection.
(See pages 72 and 73)

62. A. *Vase and cover, no mark, Seth Pennington's Liverpool factory,*
about 1780, ht. 20 in. E. Allman Collection.
B. *Punch pot and cover, no mark, Seth Pennington's factory, 1780–1785,*
ht. 11 in. E. Allman Collection.
C. *Sauce boat, no mark, Seth Pennington's factory, about 1780,*
length 7½ in. Watney Collection.
D. *Mug, transfer-printed, no mark, Seth Pennington's factory, about 1780,*
ht. 5⅞ in. Watney Collection.
(See pages 73 and 74.)

63.A. *Cream jug, Derby, about 1756, ht.* $3\frac{5}{8}$ *in.*
B. *Chamber candle stick, 'patch' marks, Derby, 1756–1760, length* $5\frac{1}{8}$ *in.*
C. *Trinket stand, 'patch' marks, Derby, 1756–1760, ht.* $2\frac{1}{8}$ *in.*
D. *Dish, 'stilt' marks, Derby, about 1756, length 9 in. Watney Collection.*
(*See pages 85 and 86*)

64.A. *Plate, 'patch' marks, Derby, 1756–1760, diam. 8⅜ in.*
Watney Collection.
B. *Pot pourri bowl, cover and stand, patch marks, Derby, 1756–1760,*
ht. 7½ in. Mrs. F. Smith Collection.
C. *Basket, 'patch' marks, 'Thomas' incised underglaze, Derby,*
1756–1760, length 9¾ in. Watney Collection.
(*See pages 84 and 85*)

65.A. *Kingfisher centre-piece, 'patch' marks, Derby, 1756–1760, ht. 6 in.*
Watney Collection.
B. *Butter dish, 'patch' marks, Derby, 1756–1760, ht. $2\frac{5}{8}$ in.*
Watney Collection.
C. *Cream jug, Derby, about 1770, a late example with early style of*
decoration, ht. $2\frac{3}{4}$ in. Miss L. Russell Collection.
D. *Dish, 'patch' marks, Derby, 1756–1760, length $10\frac{1}{2}$ in.*
Plymouth Museum. (See pages 84, 85 and 86)

66.A. *Sauce boat, 'patch' marks, Derby, 1756–1760, length $6\frac{3}{4}$ in.*
Watney Collection.

B. *Pickle trays and an asparagus butter boat, 'patch' marks, Derby,*
1756–1760, largest $3\frac{1}{4}$ in. length. Watney Collection.

C. *Ecuelle and cover, 'patch' marks, Derby, 1756–1760, ht. 6 in.*
Watney Collection.

D. *Butter or jam dish, cover and stand, 'patch' marks, Derby, 1756–1760,*
diam. $6\frac{3}{10}$ in. British Museum. (See pages 85 and 86)

67.A. *Cup, painted decoration, Derby, 1756–1760, ht. 2⅝ in.*
Watney Collection.
B. *Cup, transfer-printed, Derby, 1764, ht. 2⅝ in.*
A. F. Green Collection.
C. *Spoon tray, transfer-printed, steatitic type, Derby, 1765–1768,*
length 5½ in. Victoria and Albert Museum.
D. *Sauce boat, glassy paste, transfer-printed, Derby, about 1764,*
length 7¾ in. Watney Collection. (See pages 27, 86, 87 and 88)

68. A. *Mug, transfer-printed, mark, a sun and an anchor and the word 'Derby' under handle, Derby, steatitic type, 1764–1765, ht. $3\frac{1}{2}$ in. British Museum.*

B. *Teapot and cover, transfer-printed, Derby, steatitic, about 1765, ht. $5\frac{1}{8}$ in. Watney Collection.*

C. *Plate, transfer-printed, Derby, steatitic type, about 1768. Miss L. Russell Collection.*

D. (1) *Teapoy, painted decoration, 'patch' marks, Derby, steatitic type, about 1765, ht. $5\frac{1}{2}$ in.*

   (2) *Dish, painted decoration, '3 footed stilt' marks, '4' incised, Derby, about 1770, length*

69.A. *Coffee pot, 'patch' marks, Derby, steatitic type, 1765–1770, ht. 8 in.*
City Museum Birmingham.
B. *Mug, 'patch' marks, Derby, 1756–1760, ht. 6½ in. Reading Museum.*
C. *Dish, mark, imitation Chinese symbol, an incense burner, Derby,*
about 1765–1770, length 10½ in. Victoria and Albert Museum.
(See pages 86, 89 and 90)

70.A. *Mug, painted decoration, 'N' incised, Derby, about 1770, ht. 6½ in.*
Bootle Museum.
B. *Sauce boat, painted decoration, Derby, steatitic, about 1770, length 7¼ in.*
Watney Collection.
C. *Two-handled cup, painted decoration, 'Crown over D' mark in underglaze*
blue, 'N' in overglaze blue, glassy paste, Derby, about 1780, ht. 2⅝ in.
Watney Collection.
D. *Teapoy and cover, painted decoration, mark, 'Crown over D' in*
underglaze blue, phosphatic paste, Derby, about 1780, ht. 5⅛ in.
Watney Collection. (See pages 89, 90 and 91)

71. A. *Coffee pot, mark, numeral '1' on base, Lowestoft, 1757–1760, ht. 9¼ in.*
From the D. M. Hunting Collection, now Anthony Lyttleton Collection.
B. *Bowl, mark, '3' on inside of footring, Lowestoft, 1757–1760,*
diam. 9⅜ in. Watney Collection.
(See pages 96, 97 and 98)

72.A. *Coffee cup, mark, '0' on inside of footring, Lowestoft, 1757–1760, ht. 2⅜ in. Watney Collection.*
B. *Spoon tray, no mark, Lowestoft, 1757–1760, length 7¼ in. G. Godden Collection.*
C. *Pickle tray, mark, '3', Lowestoft, 1757–1760, length 5⅝ in. Watney Collection.*
D. *Coffee can, mark, '7' on inside of footring, Lowestoft, 1757–1760,*

73.A. *Sucrier and cover, Lowestoft, about 1760, ht. 5⅜ in.*
Victoria and Albert Museum.
B. *Basket-dish, mark, '3', Lowestoft, about 1760, diam. 6⅜ in.*
Norwich Museum.
C. *Sauce boat, mark, '2', Lowestoft, 1757–1760, length 5½ in.*
Victoria and Albert Museum.
(*See pages* 95, 96 *and* 97)

74.A. *Robert Browne inkwell, inscribed 'R B 1762', and mark, '5' in underglaze blue, Lowestoft, diam. 2½ in. Norwich Museum.*
B. *Two cornucopiae, similar moulds to Bow examples, compare Plate 15B, mark, '3', Lowestoft, 1765–1770, length of smallest 8½ in.*
G. Godden Collection.
C. *Sauce boat, mark, '3', Lowestoft, 1760–1762, length 8 in.*
G. Godden Collection.
(See pages 98, 99 and 101)

75.A. *Sucrier and cover, '5' or '6' on inside of footring, Lowestoft, about 1760, ht. $4\frac{1}{2}$ in. Watney Collection.*
B. *Teapot, embossed with 'I.H.' and '1761', an example of an early mould being used for a 1764 piece, Lowestoft, ht. 5 in. Fitzwilliam Museum.*
C. *Mary and Martha Redgrave birth tablets inscribed '1761' and '1765', Lowestoft, diam. $3\frac{1}{16}$ and $3\frac{1}{8}$ in. Norwich Museum.*
(See pages 93, 96, 98 and 100)

76.A. *Ewer and basin, mark, '3' on footring and 'E A Lowestoft 1764'*
on base, ewer ht. 9½ in., basin diam. 10¾ in. Norwich Museum.
B. *Mug, inscribed 'Ann Hammond Aprill 9th 1764' and 'Rich'd Phillips'*
under handle, mark, '3', ht. 4⅖ in. Lowestoft, at No. 4 South Quay,
Yarmouth.
C. *Mug, inscribed 'John Cooper 1768' and 'R.P.' under handle, mark, '3',*
ht. 4⅕ in. Lowestoft, at No. 4 South Quay, Yarmouth.
(See pages 93 and 98)

77.A. *Teapot, cup and saucer, powder blue decoration, no mark, Lowestoft,*
1763–1770, teapot ht. 4½ in., saucer diam. 4½ in. G. Godden Collection.
B. *Cream jug, Lowestoft, about 1775, ht. 4½ in.*
From D. MacAlister Collection, now British Museum.
C. *Tray, powder blue decoration, Lowestoft, 1763–1770, 4⅝ in. × 4½ in.*
City Museum, Birmingham.
(See pages 100 and 103)

78.A. *Tureen and cover, mark, '5', Lowestoft, 1768–1770, length 12½ in.*
From Mrs. M. M. Paul Collection.
B. *Plate, mark, '7', Lowestoft, 1768–1770, diam. 9 in.*
G. Godden Collection.
C. *Feeding cup, Lowestoft, 1768–1770, ht. 3¼ in. G. Godden Collection.*
(See pages 99, 101 and 102)

79.A. *Flask, Lowestoft, 1780–1784, ht. 5½ in. G. Godden Collection.*
B. *Cream boat, mark probably '11', Lowestoft, about 1770, length 4 in.*
N. H. P. Turner Collection.
C. *Chamber candlestick, mark, '5', Lowestoft, 1770–1773, length 6⅜ in.*
J. H. Nurse Collection.
(*See pages 93, 102 and 104*)

80.A. *Sauce boat, inscribed on one side 'Made at Lowestoft Sept. 6 in the presence of J. S. Browne' and on the other 'Wardrobe Court Doctors Commons London 1770', mark, '5', length 7½ in. Norwich Museum.*
B. *Vase and cover 'Robert Browne' pattern, Lowestoft, about 1770, ht. 4½ in. Norwich Museum.*
C. *Two cups, Meissen 'onion' or 'immortelle' pattern, mark, 'cross swords', Lowestoft, 1775–1780, ht. 2½ in. Watney Collection.*
(*See pages* 101, 103 *and* 105)

81.A. *Oil ewer and vase, unusually broad painted strokes on either side of
handle terminals, Lowestoft, 1775–1780, hts. 6¾ and 6 in.
Victoria and Albert Museum.*
B. *Birth tablet, painted and printed, inscribed 'Eliz. Wyeth Octr ye 10th.
1782', Lowestoft, diam. 5¾ in. Miss Y. Willsmore Collection.*
C. *Pair of salts, Lowestoft, 1770–1775, diam. 2¾ in.
G. Godden Collection.*
(*See pages* 93, 98 *and* 104)

82.A. *Eyebath, painted and printed decoration, Lowestoft, about 1775, ht. 2¼ in. Watney Collection.*
B. *Caddy spoon, Lowestoft, about 1775, length 4¾ in. Watney Collection.*
C. *Two egg cups (1) printed (2) painted, Lowestoft, 1775–1785, hts. 3 in. and 1⅞ in. Watney Collection.*
D. *Pounce pot, Lowestoft, about 1785, ht. 2½ in.*
N. H. P. Turner Collection.
E. *Inkwell, printed decoration in Caughley-Worcester style, Lowestoft, 1775–1780, diam. 2½ in. G. Godden Collection. (See page 104)*

83.A. *Two cream jugs (1) printed with 'Good Cross Chapel' pattern (2)*
painted in Worcester style, Lowestoft, 1772–1780, hts. $3\frac{1}{8}$ and $2\frac{3}{4}$ in.
Victoria and Albert Museum.
  B. *Birth tablet, inscribed on obverse, 'Susan Golder born May 20 1792',*
Lowestoft, diam. $2\frac{7}{8}$ in. N. H. P. Turner Collection.
 C. *Two mustard pots and covers (1) 'prunus-root' with '5' on base, (2) stylized*
peony pattern copied from Worcester, Lowestoft, hts. $3\frac{1}{2}$ in. and 4 in.
Victoria and Albert Museum. (See pages 93, 98, 103 and 104)

84. A. *Tea bowl and saucer, printed decoration, Lowestoft, 1775–1780,
diam. of saucer 4¾ in., in G. Godden Collection.*
B. *Saucer, printed decoration in style of J. Pillement, Lowestoft,
about 1775, whereabouts unknown.*
C. *Tea bowl and saucer printed with 'woman and squirrel' pattern,
Lowestoft, 1775–1780, diam. of saucer 4¾ in. Watney Collection.*
(*See page* 103)

85.A. *Mask jug, Lowestoft, 1775–1780, ht. 8½ in. G. Godden Collection.*
B. *Coffee pot inscribed beneath lip 'S.A.', printed decoration, Lowestoft,*
1772–1780, ht. 7¼ in. From M. M. Paul Collection.
C. *Coffee pot and cover, 'zig-zag fence' pattern, leaf moulded below handle,*
Lowestoft, 1785–1795, ht. 8¾ in. G. Godden Collection.
D. *Jug inscribed 'Willm. Bevein Lowestoft Coachman 1786', ht. 7⅜ in.*
Norwich Museum.
(See pages 102, 103 and 104)

86.A. *Teapot and cover inscribed 'A Trifle from Lowestoft', about 1785–1790,*
ht. 4 in. G. Godden Collection.

B. *Tea bowl and saucer, printed, Lowestoft, 1775–1780, diam. of saucer 4¾ in.*
Watney Collection.

C. *Pair of sauce boats, printed with pattern adapted from Worcester, Lowestoft, 1785–1795,*
length 8½ in. G. Godden Collection.

D. *Teapot and cover, printed 'zig-zag fence' pattern, Lowestoft, about 1775, ht. 4 in.*

87.A. *Jug with mask moulded lip, transfer-printed, mark in blue*
'Gallimore Turner Salopian', about 1775, ht. 5¼ in. Kerr Collection.
B. *Puzzle jug, mark, crescent in outline, inscribed 'Susannah Barber 1778',*
Caughley, ht. 7½ in. Watney Collection.
C. *Jug with mask moulded lip, transfer-printed, mark, a leopard,*
printed on base, inscribed 'Rrd. Wright 1780', Caughley, ht. 7¼ in.
J. Manning Collection.
D. *Jug with mask moulded lip, transfer-printed, inscribed*
'Mr. W^m. Smith 1792', Caughley, ht. 7½ in. E. Allman Collection.
(*See pages* 110 *to* 114)

88.A. *Beaker cup, transfer-printed, Caughley, about 1780, ht. 2¾ in.*
F. Barrett Collection.
B. *Mustard pot, cover and spoon, transfer-printed, mark, 'C', Caughley,*
about 1775, ht. 3¾ in. F. Barrett Collection.
C. *Inkwell and pounce pot, transfer-printed, mark, 'C', about 1780,*
ht. 3⅛ in. Watney Collection.
D. *Custard cup and cover, transfer-printed, Caughley, about 1785,*
ht. 2¾ in. Miss L. Russell Collection.
(See pages 112 and 113)

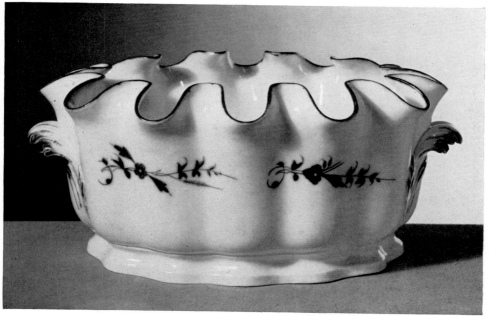

89.A. *Bottle stand, painted decoration, mark, 'S' in underglaze blue and 'H'*
incised, Caughley, about 1780, length 11 in. From L. Spillman Collection.
  B. Verrière *or wine glass cooler, mark, 'S' in underglaze blue and 'H'*
incised, Caughley, about 1780, length 12 in. Victoria and Albert Museum.
(*See pages* 109 *and* 110)

90.A. (*1*) *Bowl, mark, 'S' in underglaze blue*
(*2*) *Saucer, imitation 'hunting horn' mark of Chantilly in underglaze*
blue, Caughley, about 1780, diam. of bowl 4½ in.
B. (*1*) *Bowl, painted decoration mark, 'S'*
(*2*) *Bowl, transfer-printed, mark, hatched crescent, Caughley,*
about 1775, diam. 4⅝ and 6⅛ in.
C. (*1*) *Mug, transfer-printed, mark, hatched crescent*
(*2*) *Trial mug, painted, Caughley, about 1775, hts. 3⅝ and 5⅜ in.*
Watney Collection. (See pages 110, 112 and 114)

91.A. *Coffee can, painted with arms of Plymouth and inscribed*
'Plymouth manufacy.' also 'March 14 1768 C.F.', ht. $2\frac{7}{10}$ in.
British Museum.
B. *Hors-d'œuvre tray and spoon, Plymouth, about 1769, diam. $4\frac{1}{2}$ in.*
Watney Collection.
C. *Mortar, mark, sign for tin, Plymouth, about 1769, diam. $5\frac{2}{5}$ in.*
Plymouth Museum.
(*See pages* 123 *and* 124)

92.A. *Cup and saucer, mark, sign for tin, Plymouth, about 1770, saucer diam. 4⅝ in. From E. Rees Collection, now Truro Museum.*

B. *Sauce boat, mark, sign for tin, Plymouth, about 1770, length 5¼ in. From E. Rees Collection, now Truro Museum.*

C. *Sauce boat, mark, sign for tin, Plymouth, about 1770, length 7½ in. Watney Collection.*

D. *Sauce boat, mark, sign for tin, Plymouth, length 6½ in. From E. Rees Collection, now Truro Museum.*

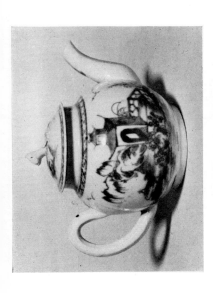

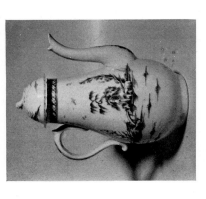

95.A. *Teapot, Plymouth, about 1770, ht. 4¼ in. Plymouth Museum.*
B. *Teapot, mark, sign for tin, Plymouth, about 1770, ht. 5⅞ in. Plymouth Museum.*
C. *Coffee pot, Plymouth, about 1770, ht. 9⅜ in.*
Stephen Simpson Collection, Plymouth Museum.

D. *Teapot, mark, sign for tin, Plymouth, about 1770, ht. 6½ in.*
Stephen Simpson Collection, Plymouth Museum. (See page 125)

94.A. *Sauce boat, Plymouth-Bristol, about 1770, length* 6¼ *in.*
Plymouth Museum.
B. *Shell salt, Plymouth-Bristol, about 1770, length* 6⅛ *in. Plymouth Museum.*
C. *Asparagus butter boat, mark, sign for tin, Plymouth, length* 4¼ *in.*
Cream boat, Bristol hard paste, length 4¼ *in.*
Pickle tray, mark, a cross in underglaze blue, Bristol hard paste, width 3⅝ *in.*
1770–1775, Plymouth Museum. (See pages 123, 124 and 126)

95.A. *Sauce boat, Plymouth-Bristol, 1770–1772, length 8½ in.*
Plymouth Museum.
B. *Plate, Plymouth-Bristol, 1770–1772, diam. 6 in. F. Barrett Collection.*
C. *Cream boat, mark, a cross in underglaze blue, Bristol, about 1775,*
length 4½ in. Watney Collection.
D. *Two mugs, (1) no mark, (2) mark, sign for tin, Plymouth, about 1770,*
ht. 5¼ in. Plymouth Museum. (See pages 123, 124 and 126)

96.A. *Cup and saucer, transfer-printed, New Hall, 1785–1800,
diam. of saucer 5⅛ in. Watney Collection.*
B. *Teapot, transfer-printed, New Hall, 1785–1800, ht. 6¼ in.
Watney Collection.*
C. *Teapoy, ht. 4⅜ in., plate diam. 8½ in., transfer-printed, New Hall,
1785–1800, Watney Collection.*
D. *Cream jug and cover, transfer-printed, mark, imitation Frankenthal
rampant lion with crown, about 1785–1800, ht. 4⁹⁄₁₀ in. From E. Rees
Collection, Truro Museum.*
(See pages 127, 128 and 129)